I0458044

Spirit Calling
TEENS

Daily Devotional

MICHAEL WUEHLER

Paperback: 978-1-968667-41-2
Hardcover: 978-1-968667-84-9
eBook: 978-1-968667-42-9
Library of Congress Control Number: 2025916379

Ordering Information:

Prime Seven Media
518 Landmann St.
Tomah City, WI 54660

Printed in the United States of America

To my six wonderful grandchildren
Grace, Jasper, Amelia, Quinn, Addison, and Alice.
May God bless all my readers as richly as God
has blessed me through my grandchildren.
Learn to let God lead you into a life you
could never imagine or expect.
The best is yet to come.

Spirit Calling Teens
Daily Devotional
Michael Wuehler

January 1

Topic: Trust in a New Year

Opening Statement: A new year is the perfect opportunity to step forward in faith, trusting God with your dreams, fears, and future.

Bible Verse: *You were taught, with regard to your former way of life, to put off your old self, which is being corrupted by its deceitful desires; 23 to be made new in the attitude of your minds; 24 and to put on the new self, created to be like God in true righteousness and holiness.* Ephesians 4:22-24NIV.

Devotional: I see your heart and all the hopes and worries you carry into this new year. As you enter the unknown, I invite you to trust Me completely. You don't have to figure out everything independently—I am here to guide you, strengthen you, and show you the best path.

When challenges arise, lean into My wisdom instead of relying only on what you understand. Even when the way ahead seems unclear, trust that I am working all things for your good. Each moment you surrender to Me, I will direct your steps and fill your life with peace.

You are not alone, no matter what this year brings. Together, we will move forward with courage, hope, and the assurance that I hold your future in My hands.

Closing Encouragement: As you begin this year, trust God with every step and watch as doors of possibility and purpose open before you.

January 2

Topic: Eternal Salvation

Opening Statement: Eternal salvation isn't something to fear but a gift of love, offering peace and hope for the life to come.

Bible Verse *"For the wages of sin is death, but the gift of God is eternal life in Christ Jesus our Lord."* (Romans 6:23, NIV)

Devotional: My Sacred Heart, I see your questions about eternity and the afterlife. The uncertainty can feel overwhelming, but know this: eternal salvation is My promise to you—a gift freely given, not earned by perfection but through love and grace. You don't have to carry the burden of doubt or fear.

When you accepted the truth of who I am, you stepped into a relationship that spans your life now and forever. You are held in the hands of the Creator, loved deeply, and promised a place in eternity. Live with this truth, shaping your choices, guiding your path, and filling your heart with peace.

Trust in Me, and let that trust drive out the fear. You have been given a gift—life eternal. Walk in confidence, knowing your forever is secure in the hands of love.

Closing Encouragement: You are never alone; your future is in the eternal promise of life and love.

January 3

Topic: Friends at School

Opening Statement: Friendships at school can shape your journey, and with My guidance, you can build bonds that uplift and reflect My love.

Bible Verse: *"A friend loves at all times, and a brother is born for a time of adversity."* —Proverbs 17:17 (NIV)

Devotional: Dear one, I am always with you, even in the hallways of your school and when life feels overwhelming. I know there are times when finding the right friends feels hard, but I want you to remember this: I've created you to be surrounded by people who can lift you up, encourage you, and remind you of your worth.

When you feel alone or uncertain about who truly cares for you, lean on Me. Pray, and I will guide you toward friends who reflect kindness, honesty, and love. Be that kind of friend to others, too. Let My light shine through you, making you a source of comfort and strength to those around you.

Even when others fail, I will never leave you. I am your ultimate source of support, giving you wisdom to navigate every relationship. Trust Me, and I will provide friendships that help you grow into who I created you to be.

Closing Encouragement: Trust Me to bring the right friends into your life, and be confident in My unwavering support through every step of your journey.

January 4

Topic: Spiritual Strength

Opening Statement: In your moments of weakness, know that spiritual strength and endurance are gifts waiting to carry you through the most complex trials.

Bible Verse: *"I know what it is to be in need, and I know what it is to have plenty. I have learned the secret of being content in any and every situation, whether well fed or hungry, whether living in plenty or in want. I can do all this through him who gives me strength."* Philippians 4:12-13 (NIV)

Devotional: Beloved one, I see the weight you carry. I know the battles you face that seem to press down on your spirit, testing your endurance. In these moments, lean on Me. I am your strength, your rock, your constant. Trials will come, but they are not the end of your story. They are the shaping tools to refine your faith, drawing you closer to Me.

Remember, you are never alone when you feel too weak to keep going. I am here, breathing My power into your weary heart. Trust in My promises, for they are unshakable. I will renew your strength. Stand firm, even when the world pulls at you, for I am working all things for your good. Lift your eyes to Me, and I will carry you through.

Closing Encouragement: You are stronger than you know because I am within you—never give up, for I am your endurance and victory.

January 5

Topic: Spiritual Power

Opening Statement: You were never meant to live this life in your strength—spiritual power is available through the Holy Spirit.

Bible Verse: *"But you will receive power when the Holy Spirit comes on you; and you will be my witnesses in Jerusalem, and in all Judea and Samaria, and to the ends of the earth."* —Acts 1:8 (NIV)

Devotional: Beloved, I see you striving, longing for strength, wondering if you're enough. Remember that you don't need to depend on your limited power. My presence within you carries the same power that raised Christ from the dead. When you seek me, I fill you with the courage to face challenges, the wisdom to make the right choices, and the love to reflect God's heart.

When you feel weak, lean into me. Speak with me in prayer, ask for my guidance, and trust my whispers in your heart. Open your Bible and allow the words to come alive. You're not alone, and you're not powerless. My strength is made perfect in your weakness.

You were created to carry light to this world. Let me fill you with all you need to live boldly and purposefully for God. Seek my power daily, and I will never leave you lacking.

Closing Encouragement: Step forward today with confidence, knowing the Holy Spirit equips and empowers you to do everything for God's glory.

January 6

Topic: God Speaks to Your Heart

Opening Statement: The Holy Spirit always speaks to your heart, guiding you toward truth and purpose—are you listening?

Bible Verse: *"But when he, the Spirit of truth, comes, he will guide you into all the truth."* —John 16:13 (NIV)

Devotional: I am the Holy Spirit and always with you. You may not see me, but I am as close as your breath, whispering truth to your heart and guiding your steps. When you feel unsure, I remind you of what is right. When life feels overwhelming, I bring peace that surpasses understanding.

Listen for my voice in the stillness. I don't shout; I speak softly, nudging you with love and truth. Pay attention when a verse stands out, a song stirs your soul, or a quiet thought encourages you to choose suitable over harm. These are my whispers to you.

I am here to help you discern, to lead you when the way seems unclear. I trust that I will always speak in a way that aligns with My Divine Word and truth. Open your heart, and you will hear me.

Closing Encouragement: Trust that I am with you always, ready to speak life, peace, and direction into your heart.

January 7

Topic: The Comforter

Opening Statement: The Holy Spirit is your ever-present Comforter, ready to guide and strengthen you through every challenge.

Bible Verse: *"But the Comforter, which is the Holy Ghost, whom the Father will send in my name, shall teach you all things, and bring all things to your remembrance, whatsoever I have said unto you.* (John 14:26, KJV)

Devotional: I am the Spirit sent to dwell within you, to be your Comforter, Advocate, and Friend. When life feels overwhelming or confusing, I am here to whisper peace to your heart and remind you that you are never alone. My presence in you is a gift from the Father, a sign of how deeply you are loved.

When you face moments of fear, doubt, or loneliness, know I am working to strengthen you. Lean into Me in prayer, trust Me to guide your steps, and open your heart to My whispers of truth. You don't have to face life's challenges alone; I am your source of wisdom, strength, and peace. Let Me carry your burdens and give you the courage to walk boldly in faith.

Closing Encouragement: You are never alone—lean into the Holy Spirit, your Comforter, and let peace fill your heart.

January 8

Topic: Spirit of Holiness.

Opening Statement: The Spirit of Holiness works within you to guide, shape, and transform your life into something extraordinary.

Bible Verse: *And declared to be the Son of God with power, according to the spirit of holiness, by the resurrection from the dead:* Romans 1:4 KJV.

Devotional: I see your struggles, dreams, and the longing to live a life that matters. You don't have to strive alone—I am here to help you become all you were created to be.

When you invite Me into your day, I will transform your thoughts, actions, and decisions. I will give you the strength to resist temptation and the wisdom to choose what is right. Holiness isn't about perfection; it's about letting Me shape your heart to reflect love, compassion, and kindness.

Trust Me, and I will show you the beauty of living a holy life. Together, we can overcome fear, break free from old habits, and step into the fullness of the purpose designed just for you.

Closing Encouragement: Let the Spirit of Holiness guide you today, shaping your life into a reflection of divine love and purpose.

January 9

Topic: Overcoming Temptation

Opening Statement: Temptation is a battle every teenager faces, but you are not alone in finding the strength to overcome it.

Bible Verse: *"No temptation has overtaken you except what is common to mankind. And God is faithful; God will not let you be tempted beyond what you can bear. But when you are tempted, God will also provide a way out so that you can endure it."* 1 Corinthians 10:13 (NIV)

Devotional: I am here with you, always, to guide you through the challenges you face. I know the pull of unhealthy behaviors can feel strong, but remember, I am stronger. When you face temptation, pause and listen—I will show you the way out. It may be a gentle nudge to walk away, a thought to reach out to a trusted friend, or a reminder of your values.

Lean on Me when the struggle feels overwhelming. You are not weak for feeling tempted; it is a part of life. What matters is where you turn for strength. Turn to Me. I will empower you to say no to what harms you and yes to what gives you life. Together, we can conquer any challenge.

Closing Encouragement: You are never alone in this fight—trust Me to help you stand firm and walk in freedom.

January 10

Topic: God's Encouragement

Opening Statement: Every day is a fresh gift, and when you begin it with faith, hope, and love, you invite God's presence to guide and strengthen you.

Bible Verse: *"Now these three remain: faith, hope, and love. But the greatest of these is love."* —1 Corinthians 13:13 (NIV)

Devotional: Listen closely, My Sacred Heart, for I am with you as the sun rises. Each morning, you face new choices and opportunities but never face them alone. When you start your day with faith, you trust in My plan for you, even when it's unclear. With hope, you step forward, knowing I hold your future in loving hands. And with love, you reflect My heart to those around you.

When your thoughts are anxious, or your heart feels heavy, pause and remember: I am here. Whisper a prayer, open your heart, and let Me fill your spirit with peace. Faith anchors you. Hope lifts you. Love connects you to My purpose. These three will carry you through every challenge, blessing, and moment.

Closing Encouragement: Each morning is a chance to shine My light—step into your day with faith, hope, and love, and watch miracles unfold.

January 11

Topic: Keeping Schools Safe

Opening Statement: Your school is not just a place to learn; it's a space to grow, connect, and thrive—and through faith and prayer, you can invite God's protection and peace into every hallway and classroom.

Bible Verse: *"For God did not give us a spirit of timidity, but a spirit of power, of love and of self-discipline."* —2 Timothy 1:7 (NIV)

Devotional: My beloved, I am with you always, even as you walk through the doors of your school each day. I see your worries about your safety, friends, and the world around you. But do not be afraid. When you invite Me into your life and your school, you bring light into darkness and peace where fear tries to take hold.

I am the Spirit of love, power, and self-discipline. Use My strength to pray boldly for your teachers, classmates, and school leaders. Speak words of kindness and stand as a peacemaker, for your actions make a difference. Trust that I go before you, allowing safety and comfort to reign where you tread.

You are not alone in this. We can transform your school into a place of refuge and hope through prayer and faith.

Closing Encouragement: You are a light in your school— through faith, prayer, and courage, you are making a difference that echoes for eternity.

January 12

Topic: Celebrities and Influencers

Opening Statement: In a world filled with celebrities, influencers, and ever-changing trends, it's easy to lose sight of who you are in Christ.

Bible Verse: *"For the time will come when people will not put up with sound doctrine. Instead, to suit their own desires, they will gather around them a great number of teachers to say what their itching ears want to hear.* 2 Timothy 4:3 (NIV)

Devotional: Hey, beloved, I know the glitz and glamour of the world constantly surrounds you. Celebrities, influencers, and social media trends can easily make you feel like you need to fit in, like you're not enough unless you keep up with everyone else. But let me remind you of something vital: your worth doesn't come from what others think of you. It comes from Me.

You are My masterpiece, created with purpose and love. The pressure to be like everyone else is real, but I want you to know that My plan for your life is unique, and it doesn't involve following fleeting trends or idolizing people who don't even know you. When you align your heart with mine and seek my will, you'll find peace in who you are and what I've made you be.

Focusing on the lasting truth of my love for you, not what others tell you, is essential. Let me lead you; you'll never need to chase after anything that won't fulfill you.

Closing Encouragement: Trust me, you are enough exactly as you are—no need to keep up with anyone else.

January 13

Topic: Hope in the Storm

Opening Statement: When the storms of life feel overwhelming—whether literal or emotional—you can find unshakable hope in the presence of the Holy Spirit.

Bible Verse: *"The Lord is good, a refuge in times of trouble. He cares for those who trust in him."* —Nahum 1:7 (NIV)

Devotional: Dear Sacred Heart, when the winds howl and the ground trembles, know this: I am with you. Even in the chaos of natural disasters, I am your anchor and refuge. The storms of this world may shake what seems steady, but I never leave or forsake you.

When you see destruction and feel afraid, lean on Me. I will give you strength and peace beyond understanding. The earth may groan, but remember, I hold it in My hands. You are never alone in the storm. Look for Me in the helpers, in the quiet moments of courage, and in the whisper of hope that rises above the noise.

Let this truth fill your heart: My plans for you are still good, even when circumstances seem dire. Trust Me to lead you to calm after the storm.

Closing Encouragement: Take heart, beloved—no storm is greater than the hope I have placed within you.

January 14

Topic: Trends and Memes

Opening Statement: Trends and memes can be fun and exciting but can challenge your faith and values if you're not careful.

Bible Verse: *"Finally, brothers and sisters, whatever is true, whatever is noble, whatever is right, whatever is pure, whatever is lovely, whatever is admirable—if anything is excellent or praiseworthy—think about such things."* — Philippians 4:8 (NIV)

Devotional: Dear one, I know how important it feels to stay connected to what's happening around you. Memes and trends seem everywhere—on your phone, in conversations, and even in your thoughts. I want you to enjoy these moments of creativity and humor, but don't let them define who you are. Remember, you are not shaped by what's viral; I shape you.

Some trends will lift you, make you laugh, or help you see the beauty of the world I created. Others may pull you into attitudes or behaviors that don't reflect who I've called you to be. When you encounter something questionable, pause and ask, "Does this align with who I am in Christ?" I am here to guide you in wisdom and truth.

Be the light in this digital world. Share what is good, uplifting, and reflects My love. You can set trends of kindness and faithfulness that impact others far more than fleeting memes ever could.

Closing Encouragement: You are more than what's trending—stay anchored in Me, and I will guide you every step of the way.

January 15

Topic: Prayer for Those in Need

Opening Statement: You are called to be a source of strength, lifting others through prayer and interceding for their needs.

Bible Verse: *"Carry each other's burdens, and in this way you will fulfill the law of Christ."* —Galatians 6:2 (NIV)

Devotional: I see the struggles of those around you—the friend who feels alone, the family member burdened by fear, and the classmate overwhelmed with pressure. You may not always know the right words to say or the perfect thing to do, but I invite you to intercede. When you pray for others, you bring their needs before My throne, and I am always ready to respond with compassion, wisdom, and power.

Each time you lift someone up in prayer, you reflect My love and fulfill the law of Christ by carrying their burdens. It may feel small, but your prayers are mighty. They invite My peace into chaos, My healing into brokenness, and My strength into weakness. Trust Me to move in ways you cannot see, and know that your faith impacts lives beyond what you can imagine.

Lean on Me as you pray, for I will guide and empower you to be a vessel of My grace.

Closing Encouragement: Never underestimate the power of your prayers; they ripple through eternity, bringing My strength to those in need.

January 16

Topic: Emotional Health

Opening Statement: Anxiety, depression, and stress can feel overwhelming, but you are never alone in your struggles.

Bible Verse: *"Cast all your anxiety on [the Lord] because [God] cares for you."* —1 Peter 5:7 (NIV)

Devotional: I see the weight you carry, the stress that clouds your mind, and the sadness in your heart. Even when you feel no one understands, I do. I am with you in every anxious moment, every tear, and every sleepless night. You don't have to face this battle alone.

Breathe deeply, and let Me remind you: I am your peace. Remember that I am your steady anchor when life feels out of control. Speak to Me about your worries, fears, and pain—I'm listening. Hand them over to Me, one by one. Trust that I am working behind the scenes, calming your chaos.

You don't have to fix everything. Rest in My love, which holds no judgment and offers no conditions. Let My peace guard your heart and mind, replacing anxiety with hope.

Closing Encouragement: Take heart, beloved one—I am your source of peace, always here to guide you through life's storms.

January 17

Topic: Favorite YA Books

Opening Statement: Did you know that the adventure, courage, and redemption found in your favorite YA books can reflect God's more excellent story for your life?

Bible Verse: *"Let the message of Christ dwell among you richly as you teach and admonish one another with all wisdom through psalms, hymns, and songs from the Spirit, singing to God with gratitude in your hearts."* —Colossians 3:16 (NIV)

Devotional: Beloved Sacred Heart, as you dive into the pages of popular YA fiction, fantasy, or thrillers, I want you to remember something important: I am the Author of the most fantastic story ever told. As you cheer for heroes who rise from humble beginnings, know I have written a unique and powerful story for your life.

In those moments when characters face impossible odds, let it remind you that I give you strength for the challenges you face. When you see light triumph over darkness, know I am always working to bring good into your life. Even the mystery and thrill of plot twists can remind you to trust My guidance, even when you don't see the whole picture.

I invite you to find Me in every story and to let My Word inspire you as you grow into the person I created you to be.

Closing Encouragement: Stay curious, inspired, and remember—you are a part of My fantastic story.

January 18

Topic: God's Unfailing Promise of Love:

Opening Statement: No matter what life throws at you, God's love is unshakable, unchanging, and always with you.

Bible Verse: "For I am convinced that neither death nor life, neither angels nor demons, neither the present nor the future, nor any powers, neither height nor depth nor anything else in all creation, will be able to separate us from the love of God that is in Christ Jesus our Lord." —Romans 8:38-39 (NIV)

Devotional: I want you to know this deep in your heart: My love is not based on your performance, feelings, or mistakes. It's a promise, sealed in eternity and rooted in who I am. When you feel unworthy or unloved, hear this: Nothing in heaven or on earth can separate you from My love. Not your fears, failures, or even lies that try to tell you otherwise.

My love is constant, like the sun that rises each day, even when clouds hide it from view. The Bible is filled with promises of this powerful love that sent Jesus to the cross for you. Believe it. Rest in it. You are cherished, treasured, and held.

Closing Encouragement: Take heart today, knowing you are surrounded by God's unshakable love, now and forever.

January 19

Topic: You are a gift

Opening Statement: Grace is a precious gift from God, transforming your life and enabling you to bless others in ways you never imagined.

Bible Verse: *"For it is by grace you have been saved, through faith—and this is not from yourselves, it is the gift of God."* —Ephesians 2:8 (NIV)

Devotional: Beloved, I want you to know that grace is not something you earn—it is freely given to you by Me. This gift poured out through love redeems, strengthens, and empowers you. Grace is why you can rise when you stumble and move forward with peace when life feels overwhelming.

But grace does not stop with you. It flows through you to others. When you receive My grace, you become a reflection of divine kindness and love. Your words, actions, and even your presence can become a blessing to the people around you. You have been chosen to shine light into darkness and bring hope to hurting people.

Remember, the grace given to you is limitless, so let it overflow. Share encouragement, forgive freely, and be generous with your time and compassion. This way, you will honor the gift of grace and fulfill your calling to love others as I love you.

Closing Encouragement: You are deeply loved, and through grace, you are empowered to love others in a way that transforms the world.

January 20

Topic: Government Leaders

Opening Statement: Did you know that your prayers can powerfully impact the leaders shaping your world?

Bible Verse: *"I urge, then, first of all, that petitions, prayers, intercession, and thanksgiving be made for all people—for kings and all those in authority, that we may live peaceful and quiet lives in all godliness and holiness."* —1 Timothy 2:1-2 (NIV)

Devotional: Beloved one, I see your heart for justice and your desire for a better world. Let Me guide you to an often overlooked truth: praying for government leaders is part of My plan for you.

No matter who holds power, their role is significant, and your prayers matter. Pray for their wisdom, integrity, and courage. When you lift them up, you invite My presence into places of influence and decision-making. Even when you disagree with their choices, trust that I can work through anyone to fulfill My purposes.

Your voice is heard, even when spoken in the quiet of your room. Each prayer is a seed of hope that I nurture, bringing light to darkness and peace where chaos reigns. Partner with Me by interceding for those who lead, and watch as I move in ways you might not expect.

Closing Encouragement: You can bring change to the world one prayer at a time—start today and watch how I work through your faith!

January 21

Topic: Government Leaders

Opening Statement: Did you know your prayers can powerfully impact the leaders shaping your world?

Bible Verse: *"I urge, then, first of all, that petitions, prayers, intercession, and thanksgiving be made for all people— for kings and all those in authority, that we may live peaceful and quiet lives in all godliness and holiness."* —1 Timothy 2:1-2 (NIV)

Devotional: Beloved one, I see your heart for justice and your desire for a better world. Let Me guide you to an often overlooked truth: praying for government leaders is part of My plan for you.

No matter who holds power, their role is significant, and your prayers matter. Pray for their wisdom, integrity, and courage. When you lift them up, you invite My presence into places of influence and decision-making. Even when you disagree with their choices, trust that I can work through anyone to fulfill My purposes.

Your voice is heard, even when spoken in the quiet of your room. Each prayer is a seed of hope that I nurture, bringing light to darkness and peace where chaos reigns. Partner with Me by interceding for those who lead, and watch as I move in ways you might not expect.

Closing Encouragement: You can bring change to the world one prayer at a time—start today and watch how I work through your faith!

January 22

Topic: Provider of All Your Needs

Opening Statement: Do you ever worry that you'll run out of what you need, whether strength, hope, or resources?

Bible Verse: *"And my God will meet all your needs according to the riches of his glory in Christ Jesus."* —Philippians 4:19 (NIV)

Devotional: My blessed Sacred Heart, I see every one of your needs. I know the concerns that weigh on your heart—the ones you whisper in your prayers and those you can't even find the words to express. Trust me, I am your Provider, and I will never leave you lacking what you genuinely need.

Sometimes, the waiting feels long. But know this: my timing is perfect. I am working on everything for your good, even when unclear. Like rain nourishes the earth at the right time, I will provide for you when you need it most. Until then, rest in my promise that I am enough for you today. Keep trusting and believing, and watch as I pour blessings in ways you never expected.

Closing Encouragement: Stay close to God, and you'll see—I will always provide for you in ways beyond your imagination.

January 23

Topic: Faith on the Field

Opening Statement: Sports can teach you discipline, teamwork, and perseverance, but have you ever thought about how they can also grow your faith?

Bible Verse: *"Whatever you do, work at it with all your heart, as working for the Lord, not for human masters."* —Colossians 3:23 (NIV)

Devotional: My child, I delight in seeing you use your gifts, even on the field or court. When you play, watch, or cheer on your favorite team, remember that I am with you, shaping your heart through every victory and every defeat. Whether you win or lose, what matters most to Me is how you play— showing kindness, patience, and integrity.

When you give your best effort, you glorify Me, for your body and abilities are a gift I have given you. As you train, practice, or enjoy the thrill of the game, let your heart be filled with gratitude. Let your sportsmanship reflect My love, inspiring those around you.

Remember this truth: You are more than an athlete or a fan— you are My child. Keep your focus on Me, and I will guide you in every area of your life, even in sports.

Closing Encouragement: Go and play with passion, humility, and joy, knowing I am always with you—your biggest supporter and coach.

January 24

Topic: Unity in Life

Opening Statement: Unity brings peace and strength to families, friendships, and school communities, but it requires intentional effort and a heart surrendered to love.

Bible Verse: *"Make every effort to keep the unity of the Spirit through the bond of peace."* —Ephesians 4:3 (NIV)

Devotional: Beloved, I am with you in every moment of your life—at home, with friends, and in your school halls. I long for you to live in harmony with those around you because unity reflects My presence. When you face disagreements with family members or conflicts with friends, remember that I am the Spirit of peace within you. Lean on Me.

Unity doesn't mean you'll always agree with others, but it calls you to respond with patience, kindness, and humility. When you choose to listen instead of argue, forgive instead of holding a grudge, and pray instead of walking away, My love flows through you.

You have the power to bring My light into every relationship. Start by asking Me for wisdom, and I will guide you. Together, we can build bridges, heal wounds, and create harmony where there is division.

Closing Encouragement: Through Me, you can sow seeds of peace and unity that will bless every part of your life.

January 25

Topic: Discovering True Success

Opening Statement: True success is not just about accomplishments but growing into the person you were created to be.

Bible Verse: *"Whatever you do, work at it with all your heart, as working for the Lord, not for human masters."* —Colossians 3:23 (NIV)

Devotional: Beloved one, I see the potential within you— gifts and talents uniquely crafted for your purpose. Success is not measured by how you compare to others but by how you grow in the areas I've called you to. Each time you strive to learn, develop a skill, or achieve a goal, you reflect My creativity and love.

When you feel uncertain about your abilities or worth, remember this: I delight in your effort, not perfection. Celebrate your growth, whether it's big or small. You are never alone in your journey. I am here to guide, strengthen, and encourage you. Seek My wisdom, and I will show you the next step.

Commit your work to Me; you'll find joy in every accomplishment because it's rooted in My purpose for you. Your confidence will grow as you remember that My plans for you are good, and I am shaping you into something extraordinary.

Closing Encouragement: You are designed for success, and as you walk with Me, I will help you grow in every way that truly matters.

January 26

Topic: Stand up for your faith

Opening Statement: Standing up for your faith as a teenager is a courageous act that brings you closer to God's purpose for your life.

Bible Verse: *"Be on your guard; stand firm in the faith; be courageous; be strong."* —1 Corinthians 16:13 (NIV)

Devotional, I see the challenges you face, beloved. The world can be loud, pushing you to hide your faith or conform to its ways. But I am with you. When you feel nervous or unsure about standing up for what you believe, remember this: you are never alone. I give you the courage to speak the truth, wisdom to answer questions, and peace to face opposition.

You don't need perfect words or loud actions to make a difference. Your quiet strength, kindness, and willingness to say, "I follow Christ," speak volumes. Trust Me to guide you when it's hardest to stand firm. Even small acts—like praying before a meal, defending someone who is mistreated or sharing love with those who are unkind—shine My light into the world.

Be bold. Be unshaken. I have called you, equipped you, and will never leave your side.

Closing Encouragement: With My strength, you can stand firm in your faith and be a light transforming the world.

January 27

Topic: Find Time for God

Opening Statement: Your relationship with God grows stronger when you make time to be still in the busyness of life and listen for the Holy Spirit's guidance.

Bible Verse: *"Be still, and know that I am God."* —Psalm 46:10 (NIV)

Devotional: Dear one, I am always near, waiting for you to draw close to Me. In the chaos of school, friends, and responsibilities, it's easy to feel like there's no time left for Me. But when you set aside quiet moments, I fill your heart with peace, strength, and wisdom.

Remember, spending time with Me doesn't have to be complicated. Open your Bible, whisper a prayer, or sit silently and think about My love for you. When you seek Me first, I guide your steps and renew your spirit.

Trust Me; the moments you spend with Me will never be wasted. They will anchor you when life feels overwhelming and remind you that you are loved and never alone.

Closing Encouragement: Take time today to be still, talk with God, and watch God work in your life in amazing ways.

January 28

Topic: Relief from Loneliness:

Opening Statement: Loneliness can feel overwhelming, but you're never truly alone when you open your heart to God's presence.

Bible Verse: *"The Lord is close to the brokenhearted and saves those who are crushed in spirit."* —Psalm 34:18 (NIV)

Devotional: Dear Sacred Heart, I see you. I know the ache you feel when it seems no one understands and the silence around you feels louder than words ever could. Remember, I am always with you when you feel isolated or disconnected.

You were never designed to walk through life alone. My presence is constant, and I have placed you in a world filled with opportunities to connect with others. When you reach out in prayer, I hear you. When you pour out your heart, I will fill it with peace and comfort.

Look for Me in the small moments—through a kind word, a smile, or the beauty of creation. Even when it feels like no one else is near, I am closer than you can imagine. Trust Me to guide you out of isolation and into the joy of connecting with others and Me.

Closing Encouragement: You are never alone—hold on to My promise, and I will lead you to peace and purpose beyond loneliness.

January 29

Topic: True Joy

Opening Statement: Joy isn't just a fleeting feeling—it's a deep, lasting sense of happiness and fulfillment in trusting God.

Bible Verse: *"May the God of hope fill you with all joy and peace as you trust in him, so that you may overflow with hope by the power of the Holy Spirit."* —Romans 15:13 (NIV)

Devotional: I want you to know the difference between happiness that fades and joy that lasts forever. Happiness often comes from circumstances—like a great day at school, a new outfit, or a funny video but joy? Joy comes from Me, the One who fills your heart even when life feels heavy.

When you trust Me, I will pour joy into your soul, a kind of joy that doesn't depend on what's happening around you. This joy grows as you spend time with Me, read My Word, and share love with others. Even in challenging moments, I am here, offering you peace and happiness that nothing can take away.

Let Me guide you to this joy. You'll find it not in what you own or achieve but in the quiet confidence I am with you, giving you all you need.

Closing Encouragement: Let My joy fill your heart today and overflow into the lives of those around you—you are meant to shine with My happiness!

January 30

Topic: God Provides

Opening Statement: God is your Provider, meeting your daily needs for food, shelter, and clothing in ways you may not always see.

Bible Verse: *"And my God will meet all your needs according to the riches of his glory in Christ Jesus."* —Philippians 4:19 (NIV)

Devotional: Dear child, do you know how much I care about your needs? I see the worries that sometimes fill your heart—questions about where provision will come from or if you'll have enough. Trust Me, I am always aware of what you need before asking. I feed the birds of the air and clothe the flowers of the field with a beauty far more outstanding than they could ever create for themselves. How much more will I provide for you, My beloved creation?

When you feel overwhelmed, remember that I am working in the background of your life. I am moving to care for you through your family, friends, community, or unexpected blessings. Bring your concerns to Me. Trust Me to open the right doors, provide wisdom, and guide you step by step.

Lean into My promise: I will supply all your needs according to My riches in glory. Please keep your eyes on Me, not on the uncertainties of life. I am faithful, always.

Closing Encouragement: Rest in My care, and trust that I will always meet your needs, day by day, with love that never fails.

January 31

Topic: Giving Thanks

Opening Statement: Gratitude is more than just a habit—it's a powerful practice that transforms your heart, deepens your faith, and fills your life with joy.

Bible Verse: *"Give thanks in all circumstances; for this is God's will for you in Christ Jesus."* —1 Thessalonians 5:18 (NIV)

Devotional: Beloved, I invite you to pause and see the goodness in your life—every blessing, big or small, is a gift from Me. When you practice gratitude, you align your heart with My love and begin to notice how I am working in every part of your life.

Gratitude shifts your focus from what you lack to all that I provide. It fills your spirit with hope and draws you closer to Me. You trust My plans when you give thanks, even in difficult moments. Start today by naming three things you're thankful for, and watch how your heart grows lighter and more open to My presence.

I am always here, guiding and providing for you. As you cultivate thankfulness, you'll find My joy and peace filling your soul in ways you never imagined.

Closing Encouragement: Trust that gratitude will lead you to a deeper connection with Me and a more joyful daily life.

February 1

Topic: Trying New Foods

Opening Statement: Every bite you take can remind you of the creativity and goodness of your Creator.

Bible Verse: *"Taste and see that the Lord is good; blessed is the one who takes refuge in him."* —Psalm 34:8 (NIV)

Devotional: My hungry child, I invite you to see the world through My abundance and creativity. Every meal you eat reflects the diverse beauty I've poured into creation. Whether trying new cuisines or experimenting with cooking at home, these moments can be sacred opportunities to connect with Me.

You're practicing courage and trust when you step out of your comfort zone to taste something new. I designed your senses to delight in new experiences—not just with food, but with life itself. Cooking at home, too, can be an act of worship. When you prepare a meal, you mirror My nurturing care, bringing sustenance and joy to those you serve.

Remember, even something as simple as a new recipe or an unfamiliar flavor can teach you to embrace the unknown with faith, knowing I am with you in every step and taste.

Closing Encouragement: Take a bold step today—try something new and let it remind you of My endless goodness and creativity.

February 2

Topic: Spiritual Endurance

Opening Statement: Keep walking in faith; God is always with you, providing everything you need in life.

Bible Verse: *"Blessed is the one who perseveres under trial because, having stood the test, that person will receive the crown of life that the Lord has promised to those who love him."* —James 1:12 (NIV)

Devotional: Life's challenges can feel endless, and you may wonder if you can keep going. But I am here, closer than your next breath. You are not alone in this journey.

Endurance is not about having all the answers—it's about trusting Me when you don't. When you feel weak, lean on My strength. When you feel lost, listen for My guidance. The trials you face are not meant to break you but to shape you. Every moment you hold on to faith, you grow stronger. I am refining you, preparing you for something greater.

Do not be discouraged by what seems impossible. You have everything you need with Me to endure, thrive, and rise above.

Closing Encouragement. Keep moving forward—victory comes to those who don't give up.

February 3

Topic: Breaking Free from Shyness

Opening Statement: Shyness can feel like a wall keeping you from stepping into God's plan, but the Holy Spirit is ready to fill you with boldness, confidence, and strength.

Bible Verse: *"For the Spirit God gave us does not make us timid, but gives us power, love, and self-discipline."* —2 Timothy 1:7 (NIV)

Devotional: You were never meant to hide in the background. I created you with a purpose and have placed My Spirit within you—not a spirit of fear, but of boldness, love, and power.

I see when you hold back because you feel shy or afraid of what others might think. But you are not alone. I am with you, strengthening, speaking through, and filling you with courage beyond your own ability. Do not be afraid to step out in faith!

Moses felt unqualified, and Jeremiah thought he was too young, yet I used them powerfully. I will do the same for you! Trust Me to give you the right words, opportunities, and the boldness to walk in My purpose. You are not small. You are chosen. You are empowered.

Closing Encouragement: Step forward confidently—I am with you, and My power is more significant than your fear.

February 4

Topic: Overcoming a lousy attitude.

Opening Statement: When life feels overwhelming and your thoughts seem stuck in negativity, know this—you don't have to stay there. Hope is always within reach.

Bible Verse: *"Do not conform to the pattern of this world, but be transformed by the renewing of your mind."* —Romans 12:2 (NIV)

Devotional: I am here, whispering truth over your life. You are not stuck in darkness. You are not alone in your struggles. The world may tell you things will never change, but I am the One who makes all things new. Let Me renew your mind, heal your heart, and shift your perspective.

Your circumstances do not define you—I do. When you surrender your worries, I will replace them with peace. When you bring Me your brokenness, I will restore you with joy. Lift your eyes beyond the temporary and trust that My plans for you are good.

Hope is not lost. A new outlook begins with Me.

Closing Encouragement: You are loved, seen, and chosen—step into the light of My truth today, and let hope fill your heart.

February 5

Topic: Grateful for Friends

Opening Statement: True friends are a blessing from God, placed in your life to encourage, strengthen, and walk with you through every season.

Bible Verse: *"A friend loves at all times, and a brother is born for a time of adversity."* —Proverbs 17:17 (NIV)

Devotional: You are never alone. I have placed friends in your life as a reflection of My love, to walk beside you, laugh with you, and lift you up when you feel weak. A true friend is a treasure, a gift from My heart to yours.

Friendship is more than just hanging out or sending texts— it's about sharing your burdens and celebrating your joys together. When you appreciate the friends I have given you, you invite even more of My love into your life. Be grateful for the ones who listen, pray for you, and remind you of who you are in Me. And just as you cherish the friends I've given you, be that kind of friend to others. Love, encourage, and uplift; when you do, you reflect My heart.

Closing Encouragement: Give thanks today for the friends in your life, for they reflect God's love and presence with you.

February 6

Topic: Living like Jesus.

Opening Statement: Trying to live like Jesus can feel overwhelming, but the Holy Spirit is here to guide you every step of the way.

Bible Verse: *"Whoever claims to live in him must live as Jesus did."* —1 John 2:6 (NIV)

Devotional: Beloved Sacred Heart, I see your heart. You long to follow Jesus, love like Jesus, and shine light in a world filled with darkness. But some days, it feels impossible. You stumble, struggle, and wonder if you live as a disciple.

I am here with you. The same power that raised Jesus from the dead lives inside you. When you feel weak, I give you strength. When you face temptation, I provide a way out. When the world tells you to follow its ways, I whisper truth— walk as Jesus walked, love as Jesus loved, and trust that I am leading you.

You are not alone in this journey. Every step of obedience, every act of kindness, and every choice to forgive reflects the heart of Christ. Keep your eyes on Jesus; I will help you live as He **lived.**

Closing Encouragement: You were created to reflect Jesus. Keep walking in faith—the Holy Spirit is always with you.

February 7

Topic: Loss of a friend.

Opening Statement: Losing a friend is one of the hardest things to experience, but amid grief, there is a promise—you are not alone.

Bible Verse: *"My flesh and my heart may fail, but God is the strength of my heart And my portion forever."* Psalm 73:26(NIV)

Devotional: I see your tears, and I know your heartache. Loss was never part of the original design, but in a broken world, sorrow touches every life. Even when no one understands your pain, I am with you.

Remember, your friend's life had meaning, and so does yours. The love and memories you shared are not lost; they remain treasures. It's okay to grieve, but do not let grief consume you. Lean into My presence. I am close to the brokenhearted and will bring you peace that surpasses understanding.

When you feel alone, whisper My name. When the pain feels unbearable, let Me hold your heart. You are loved and seen and will find healing in My embrace.

Closing Encouragement: Your friend's story is not over— carry their light forward, and let My God's love heal your heart.

February 8

Topic: Patience Like Noah

Opening Statement: Waiting can feel frustrating, but God's timing is always perfect—even when it doesn't make sense.

Bible Verse: *"The Lord is not slow in keeping his promise, as some understand slowness. Instead, he is patient with you, not wanting anyone to perish, but everyone to come to repentance."* —2 Peter 3:9 (NIV)

Devotional: Waiting is hard, especially when nothing is happening. But patience is part of faith. Noah understood this when the world around him was filled with wickedness. I gave him a task—to build an ark—and he obeyed, even when others mocked him. For years, he built, waited, and trusted.

Like Noah, you may be in a season of waiting—waiting for answers, change, and prayers to be fulfilled. But I see beyond what you can see. My timing is always perfect, and My promises never fail. Noah and his family were safe when the rain finally came because they trusted Me.

I ask you to do the same. Be patient, even when you don't understand. Keep building your faith, one day at a time. My plans for you are more significant than you can imagine, and everything will come together at the right time.

Closing Encouragement: Hold on—just as Noah did— because God's promises for your life are worth the wait.

February 9

Topic: Healthy Mind

Opening Statement: Anxiety, depression, and stress may feel overwhelming, but you are never alone—God's peace is more potent than your fears.

Bible Verse: *"Cast all your anxiety on Him because He cares for you."* —1 Peter 5:7 (NIV)

Devotional: My beloved, I see your weight—the restless nights, the racing thoughts, the heavy heart. But I am with you, closer than your breath, surrounding you with My presence. You don't have to battle anxiety, stress, or depression alone. My love is your refuge, My peace is your anchor.

When the worries of this world overwhelm you, come to Me. Breathe in My peace and release your burdens. I will carry what feels too heavy. Your fears do not define you; you are held by My grace. Remember, I am the Light that never fades when darkness whispers lies.

Rest in Me. Trust me to work on all things for your good. Even when you can't see the way forward, I guide you. Lift your eyes, breathe in hope, and know—you are deeply loved, fully known, and never forsaken.

Closing Encouragement: God's peace is more significant than your fears—rest in it, trust in it, and let it lead you forward.

February 10

Topic: Body Image

Opening Statement: The world tells you that beauty is measured by flawless skin, the perfect body, or the latest trends—but you need to know that your worth is far greater than what the mirror reflects.

Bible Verse: *"You are altogether beautiful, my darling; there is no flaw in you."* —Song of Solomon 4:7 (NIV)

Devotional: Beloved Sacred Heart, I see you. I hear your thoughts when you compare yourself to others when you criticize your reflection, and when you feel you are not enough. But I am here to remind you that you are fearfully and wonderfully made. The Creator of the universe designed you with love and intention, forming every detail with purpose.

The world's standards of beauty change, but My love for you never will. You will always feel empty when you measure your worth by likes, filters, or comments. But when you look through My eyes, you will see the masterpiece that you are. Let My truth silence the lies. Stand confidently in who I created you to be, for you are My beloved Sacred Heart.

Closing Encouragement: You are beautiful, treasured, and deeply loved—just as you are.

February 11

Topic: Social Media Pressure.

Opening Statement: You are more than the likes, the followers, or the comments.

Bible Verse: *"Am I now trying to win the approval of human beings, or of God? Or am I trying to please people? If I were still trying to please people, I would not be a servant of Christ."* —Galatians 1:10 (NIV)

Devotional: I see you scrolling, feeling the weight of comparison. The pressure to be perfect, say the right thing, and be accepted is heavy. But I did not create you for a filtered version of life. You are fearfully and wonderfully made, just as you are.

When words online sting and voices try to bring you down, remember: Mine is the only voice that defines you. Cyberbullying and criticism may hurt, but they do not change your worth. Your identity is not found on a screen but in Me.

Turn down the volume of social media and tune into My Truth. You are loved beyond measure. You are chosen. You are enough.

Closing Statement: You don't have to prove your worth— God has already called you worthy.

February 12

Topic: Academic Pressure

Opening Statement: The stress of schoolwork, college applications, and high expectations can feel overwhelming, but you were never meant to carry this burden alone.

Bible Verse: *"Do not let your hearts be troubled. You believe in God[a]; believe also in me.* John 14:1(NIV)

Devotional: I see your late nights, your racing thoughts, and the pressure weighing on your heart. You worry if you're good enough, if you'll get accepted, if your grades define your future. But listen—your worth is not measured by test scores or college acceptance letters. I have a plan for you that is greater than anything you can imagine.

Breathe. Release your stress into My hands. I am guiding your path, opening doors you cannot see, and working all things for your good. Seek Me first, and I will give you the peace that surpasses understanding. Your future is secure—not because of your achievements, but because of My love for you. Trust Me, and let My peace guard your heart.

Closing Encouragement: You are more than your grades— rest in My perfect plan, and I will lead you every step of the way.

February 13

Topic: Peer Pressure

Opening Statement: The pressure to fit in can be overwhelming, but true strength comes from standing firm in faith, not following the crowd.

Bible Verse: *"Do not conform to the pattern of this world, but be transformed by the renewing of your mind."* —Romans 12:2 (NIV)

Devotional: You are not alone in the battle against peer pressure. I am with you, guiding your heart and giving you strength when the world tries to pull you away from what is right. The desire to be accepted is strong, but the approval of others can never compare to the love and purpose I have for you.

When friends tempt you to compromise your values, pause and listen to My voice within. You don't have to follow the crowd to belong—you already belong to Me. Stand firm in your faith; I will fill you with confidence and courage. The world may change its trends and opinions, but My love for you remains unshaken. Trust Me, and I will help you rise above the pressure.

Closing Encouragement: You are called to shine, not blend in—stand strong, for God is with you always.

February 14

Topic: Finding Love.

Opening Statement: True love isn't found in fairy tales but in a heart that seeks the One who created love itself.

📖 **Bible Verse:** *"Delight yourself in the Lord, and he will give you the desires of your heart."* —Psalm 37:4 (NIV)

Devotional: Dear beloved Sacred Heart, I know the longing in your heart—to be seen, cherished, and loved deeply. The world tells you that love is about romance, emotions, and finding someone to complete you. But true love starts with Me. Before you find "the one," I want to shape you into the person I created you to be.

When you seek Me first, love will not be about searching—it will be about discovering. The right person, your soulmate, will be someone who draws you closer to Me, not away. Love isn't about perfection but two hearts fully surrendered to My plan.

Trust My timing. Let Me write your love story. When you focus on Me, I will lead you to the one who loves Me as much as you do.

Closing Encouragement: Stay patient. Stay faithful. Your love story is already in God's hands.

February 15

Topic: Body Image.

Opening Statement: In a world filled with unrealistic standards, seeing yourself through My eyes is crucial.

Bible Verse: *"I praise you because I am fearfully and wonderfully made; your works are wonderful, I know that full well."* —Psalm 139:14 (NIV)

Devotional: Dear one, I want you to know that every detail about you is intentional and beautiful. Society may bombard you with messages that make you doubt your worth, but remember, you are a masterpiece, crafted by love. Your body is not just a vessel; it reflects my creativity and care. When you look in the mirror, I see more than just your outward appearance—your heart, spirit, and the unique gifts I've placed within you.

Let go of the pressures to conform to fleeting trends. Instead, embrace the truth that you are wonderfully made. When you feel inadequate, pray to Me and remind yourself of the strength and purpose I've woven into your very being. Trust that your worth is determined not by your looks but by my love for you.

Closing Encouragement: You are perfect just as you are, and I delight in every part of you.

February 16

Topic: Friendships and Romantic Relationships

Opening Statement: Building and navigating relationships can be exciting and challenging, but God is here to guide you.

Bible Verse: *"Two are better than one, because they have a good return for their labor: If either of them falls down, one can help the other up. But pity anyone who falls and has no one to help them."* Ecclesiastes 4:9-10 NIV.

Devotional: Dear one, relationships are a beautiful part of life, yet they come with their own set of challenges. Remember that your heart is precious as you navigate friendships and romantic interests. I urge you to guard it wisely. Surround yourself with friends who uplift you and encourage your faith. In romantic relationships, seek connections that honor Me and reflect My love.

When you feel unsure or hurt, turn to Me in prayer. I am here to provide comfort and wisdom. Trust that I will lead you to relationships that build you up rather than tear you down. Remember, the foundation of every healthy relationship is love, respect, and honesty. Keep your heart aligned with My truth, and you will find the joy and fulfillment you seek.

Closing Encouragement: Embrace the journey of relationships, knowing that God is always by your side, guiding you toward deeper connections and greater love.

February 17

Topic: Technology Trends.

Opening Statement: Technology is always changing, but your faith is the one thing that should remain unshaken.

Bible Verse: *"Give careful thought to the paths for your feet and be steadfast in all your ways."* Proverbs 4:26 (NIV)

Devotional: My child, the world is moving fast. New apps, gadgets, and trends are constantly competing for your attention. Social media, AI, and the latest devices promise connection, entertainment, and convenience—but do they bring you closer to Me?

I allowed humanity to create and innovate, but I also called on you to be wise. Technology can be a tool for good, helping you grow in faith, spread kindness, and learn more about My Word. But it can also become a distraction, pulling you away from Me.

Let Me guide your choices. Ask yourself before downloading, scrolling, or following trends: Does this help me grow? Does this bring me peace? Does this honor God? The world will always change, but I remain the same. Stay rooted in Me; you will never be lost in the noise.

Closing Encouragement: You are more than the latest trend—stay anchored in Christ, and you will always stand strong!

February 18

Topic: Future Uncertainty: Concerns about career paths and life after school.

Opening Statement: Always remember that while you are warring about the future, God is making a way for you.

Bible Verse: *"See, I am doing a new thing! Now it springs up; do you not perceive it? I am making a way in the wilderness and streams in the wasteland."* Isaiah 43:19 NIV.

Devotional: My dear worrisome child, I see the weight of uncertainty resting on your shoulders. As you ponder your future—career paths, life after school—I want you to know that you are not alone. I have a perfect plan for you, crafted with love, purpose, and hope. Trust in Me amidst the swirling confusion and anxiety.

Every twist and turn you face is part of a journey I've designed just for you. When you feel lost, remember that I am your guide. Seek My presence in prayer, and I will illuminate the way forward. Your passions, dreams, and even your fears are intertwined in a beautiful tapestry I am weaving for your life.

Closing Encouragement: Embrace the adventure ahead; God is with you every step of the way.

February 19

Topic: Reading: Fiction, Manga, or Online Articles

Opening Statement: Did you know that the stories you immerse yourself in can powerfully shape your heart and mind?

Bible Verse: *"Finally, brothers and sisters, whatever is true, whatever is noble, whatever is right, whatever is pure, whatever is lovely, whatever is admirable—if anything is excellent or praiseworthy—think about such things."* —Philippians 4:8 (NIV)

Devotional: Hey there, my cherished one. The world is filled with stories—each one holds the potential to inspire, challenge, and transform you. Whether it's the thrill of a fiction novel, the artistry of manga, or the insights found in online articles, remember that what you choose to consume can greatly impact your spirit.

As you dive into these narratives, ask yourself: Are these stories leading you closer to me? Seek out tales that reflect truth, beauty, and goodness. Allow them to spark your imagination and fill your heart with hope.

I want you to engage with stories encouraging you to dream big and live boldly. Let them remind you that your life is a beautiful story I am writing with love and purpose.

Closing Encouragement: Choose your stories wisely, for they can inspire you to become the incredible person I created you to be.

February 20

Topic: Coping with Change.

Opening Statement: Change can feel overwhelming, but remember, I am with you through every transition.

Bible Verse: *"Jesus Christ is the same yesterday and today and forever."* —Hebrews 13:8 (NIV)

Devotional: Hey there! I know that life is full of changes, and those changes can bring a mix of excitement and uncertainty. Whether you're moving to a new school, dealing with friendships that shift, or facing family changes, it's easy to feel lost. But here's the truth: I am your constant. Just as Jesus never changes, you can rely on Me to guide you through every transition.

When you feel anxious about the unknown, pause and remember that I am cheering you on. Embrace the new chapters ahead, knowing that each one is an opportunity for growth. Trust that I am working behind the scenes, crafting a beautiful story for your life. Lean into prayer, seek My presence, and allow My peace to fill your heart.

As you navigate these challenges, let each step bring you closer to who you're meant to be. Change is often the beginning of something wonderful.

Closing Encouragement: You are not alone in this; I am with you always—trust the journey ahead!

February 21

Topic: Family Dynamics.

Opening Statement: Even amid family chaos, I am your guiding light, just as I promised in my word.

Bible Verse: *"Start children off on the way they should go, and even when they are old they will not turn from it."* Proverbs 22:6 (NIV).

Devotional: Hey there, my beloved. I see the weight of your family expectations pressing down on you. It can feel overwhelming when your desires clash with what your family wants for you. Remember, I am right there with you in those moments of tension. You may feel torn between your dreams and their hopes, but I am here to help you navigate this path.

When you feel misunderstood or pressured, could you take a deep breath and seek my presence? You don't have to choose between honoring your family and pursuing your own passions. I want you to communicate openly and lovingly, allowing your voice to be heard. Trust that I will guide you through the conflicts, helping you find common ground.

In your struggles, lean into my strength and wisdom. You are never alone, and I will always support you in both honoring your family and staying true to who you are.

Closing Encouragement: Trust in God and remember that every challenge is an opportunity for growth and understanding.

February 22

Topic: Exposure to Drugs and Alcohol

Opening Statement: "Stay alert, for the choices you make today shape the person you'll become tomorrow."

Bible Verse: *"Be alert and of sober mind. Your enemy the devil prowls around like a roaring lion looking for someone to devour."* 1 Peter 5:8 (NIV)

Devotional: Beloved Sacred Heart, I want to speak to you about the choices you face. The world offers many distractions, especially when it comes to substances like drugs and alcohol. Remember, your body is a sacred temple, created for a purpose far greater than what the world can offer.

When you feel the pressure to fit in or escape, hear my gentle whisper: True fulfillment comes from within, not from what you consume. I am your source of strength and joy. I urge you to stand firm in your identity as a child of God. When you turn to me, you will find the courage to say no to temptation and yes to the life I have planned for you—a life filled with hope, peace, and purpose.

Whenever you choose clarity over confusion, you honor the gift of life I've given you.

Closing Encouragement: You are stronger than you think; choose to protect your life and let your light shine brightly!

February 23

Topic: Bullying

Opening Statement: Do not let people steal your joy. Bullies can only take what you give them.

Bible Verse: *"Do not let any unwholesome talk come out of your mouths, but only what is helpful for building others up according to their needs, that it may benefit those who listen."* Ephesians 4:29 (NIV)

Devotional: My precious one, I see the pain you endure, whether it's whispered taunts in the hallway or harsh messages online. Know this: You are not alone. I am with you, holding you close during these dark moments.

When others choose to hurt, it reflects their own struggles and insecurities. Do not let their words define you. You are created in My image, filled with purpose and love. Each time you feel crushed, remember that I am right there, ready to lift you up and remind you of your worth.

Take a moment to reach out to Me in prayer, asking for strength and healing. I encourage you to be a light in these challenging times. Stand up for those who are bullied, and let kindness be your response to cruelty. Your actions can create ripples of change.

Closing Encouragement: You can rise above and shine brightly, even in the face of adversity.

February 24

Topic: Role Models.

Opening Statement: Who you choose to look up to can shape your journey in ways you may not even realize.

Bible Verse: *"Do not be misled: 'Bad company corrupts good character.'"* —1 Corinthians 15:33 (NIV)

Devotional: My Sacred Heart, as you navigate the complexities of your teenage years, remember that the influences around you can either propel you forward or hold you back. I am calling you to seek out role models who reflect My love and wisdom. Look for those who inspire your heart, challenge your mind, and encourage you to grow in faith.

Consider the stories of those around you—family members, teachers, or friends who embody kindness, integrity, and courage. These are the mentors I place in your life to guide you. Their examples can light the path ahead, showing you how to live a life of purpose.

Surround yourself with people who uplift you and share your values. As you do, you'll discover the strength to rise above negativity and embrace your unique calling.

Closing Encouragement: Embrace the power of positive influences, for they will help you shine brighter in a world that needs your light.

February 25

Topic: Health and Fitness

Opening Statement: Your body is a temple; I want it to shine with vitality and strength!

Bible Verse: *"Do you not know that your bodies are temples of the Holy Spirit, who is in you, whom you have received from God? You are not your own; you were bought at a price. Therefore honor God with your bodies."* —1 Corinthians 6:19-20 (NIV)

Devotional: Hey there, My Sacred Heart! I see you juggling school, friends, and many other things. It can be easy to forget about your physical health in the hustle and bustle of life. But remember, your body is precious to Me. It's not just about looking good; it's about feeling strong and capable to fulfill the purpose I have for you.

When you nourish your body with good food, exercise, and rest, you honor Me. This isn't just a task; it's an act of worship. Each time you choose a healthy snack or go for a run, you're saying, "I value the gift of my body." So, let's work together! Embrace this health and fitness journey and watch how it transforms your body and spirit, too.

Closing Encouragement: You are fearfully and wonderfully made—let your health reflect the beauty of your Creator!

February 26

Topic: Importance of rest

Opening statement: Are you feeling overwhelmed and exhausted, struggling to find the energy to tackle your day?

Bible Verse: *"Come to me, all you who are weary and burdened, and I will give you rest."* —Matthew 11:28 (NIV)

Devotional: My tired child, I see your weariness. Life can feel like a whirlwind, with school, friendships, and responsibilities pulling you in every direction. I created you with a need for rest, not just for your body but for your spirit. When you sleep, you recharge, and your dreams can become a canvas for the thoughts I place in your heart.

Understand that rest is not a sign of weakness; it is a vital part of your journey. Just as I rested on the seventh day, so too should you honor the rhythm of rest in your life. Prioritize your sleep, for it is in those quiet moments that I speak to you most clearly. When you wake refreshed, you will find renewed strength to face the challenges ahead.

Closing Encouragement: Embrace rest as a gift from Me, and trust that in your quiet moments, I am preparing you for great things.

February 27

Topic: Self-Expression.

Opening Statement: Your creativity is a beautiful gift that reflects the unique way I made you.

Bible Verse: *"For we are God's handiwork, created in Christ Jesus to do good works, which God prepared in advance for us to do."* —Ephesians 2:10 (NIV)

Devotional: Hey there, My unique child! I want you to know that every time you create—whether it's through art, music, writing, or any other form—you're expressing a piece of My heart. I've made you a masterpiece, and your creativity reflects my love and design. Don't be afraid to let your ideas flow. When you share your thoughts and feelings through your creations, you're not just showing the world who you are; you're showing them a glimpse of Me.

Remember, it's okay to experiment and make mistakes along the way. Each stroke of paint, every note you play, and each word you write is a step toward discovering more about yourself and My purpose for you. So, embrace your creativity! Let it be a conversation with Me, and watch how it transforms you and those around you.

Closing Encouragement: You were created to express yourself—let your creativity shine brightly!

February 28

Topic: Financial Literacy

Opening Statement: What if mastering money management today could lead to a life of freedom and purpose tomorrow?

Bible Verse: *"The plans of the diligent lead to profit as surely as haste leads to poverty."* —Proverbs 21:5 (NIV)

Devotional: Hey there, My thrifty child! I want to talk to you about something that matters deeply—money. Managing your finances wisely is not just about numbers; it's about stewardship and freedom. When you learn to handle money well, you take a step towards independence and security.

Think of money as a tool, not a master. It can help you pursue your dreams, support others, and contribute to your community. Start by setting small goals—like saving for something you really want. Create a budget to track your spending and learn to distinguish between needs and wants.

It's okay to make mistakes; that's part of learning. What's important is to embrace knowledge and seek wisdom. By doing so, you'll not only grow financially but also spiritually, understanding that every good thing comes from me.

Closing Encouragement: Empower yourself with knowledge today and watch how it transforms your future into one filled with possibilities!

March 1

Topic: Digital Literacy

Opening Statement: How you engage with the digital space can shape your heart and mind in a world filled with screens and clicks.

Bible Verse: *"Let your conversation be always full of grace, seasoned with salt, so that you may know how to answer everyone."* —Colossians 4:6 (NIV)

Devotional: As you scroll through your feeds and messages, my dear digital child, remember that every click reflects who you are. The digital world can be a vast ocean filled with waves of distraction and temptation. I urge you to navigate it with intention.

Ask yourself: Is this post uplifting? Does it honor Me? When you engage with content, choose what brings light rather than darkness. Surround yourself with voices that inspire you to grow in love and kindness. Just as you wouldn't let harmful words seep into your heart, guard your digital space with the same vigilance.

You hold the power to shape your online environment. Let your digital interactions reflect My truth, beauty, and love. Embrace responsibility and shine brightly in this world.

Closing Encouragement: Remember, you are a beacon of light—let your online presence reflect that light!

March 2

Topic: Spiritual Cleansing and Renewal

Opening Statement: Imagine starting each day with a clean slate, free from the weight of past mistakes.

Bible Verse: *"If we confess our sins, he is faithful and just and will forgive us our sins and purify us from all unrighteousness."* —1 John 1:9 NIV

Devotional: My forgiven Sacred Heart, I am here to wash away your burdens and renew your spirit. Every mistake, every regret you carry, can be lifted by My grace. When you come to Me with a sincere heart, seeking forgiveness, I promise to cleanse you completely.

You may feel overwhelmed by past actions, but remember, My love for you is greater than any mistake. I want to refresh your spirit, filling you with peace and joy. Release your guilt and let My forgiveness transform you. Each day is a new opportunity to walk in My light, free from the shadows of yesterday.

Trust in My promise to purify you and embrace the renewal I offer. You are never alone in this journey; I am always by your side, ready to guide you toward a brighter path.

Closing Encouragement: Embrace My forgiveness and step boldly into the future I have planned for you.

March 3

Topic: Safety – Personal Safety and Violence

Opening Statement: You are never alone, even when fear whispers that danger is near.

Bible Verse: *"The Lord is my light and my salvation—whom shall I fear? The Lord is the stronghold of my life—of whom shall I be afraid?"* —Psalm 27:1 (NIV)

Devotional: My fearful child, I see the world that worries you. The news, the rumors, the unexpected dangers—they press on your heart and try to steal your peace. But hear Me now: I am your refuge. When you feel unsafe, call My name, and I will surround you with My presence.

You do not walk alone. I am with you at school, on the streets, in the quiet of your room. Even when the world feels unpredictable, I remain steady. I give wisdom—listen for My voice. If something doesn't feel right, trust My nudging to step away, ask for help, and lean on Me.

The darkness may threaten, but it cannot overpower My light in you. No harm can touch your soul, for you belong to Me. Stand in faith, not fear. The enemy trembles at My power within you.

Closing Encouragement: Walk boldly, knowing I am your protector—your life is in My hands.

March 4

Topic: Cultural Identity

Opening Statement: You're not a mistake—your culture, voice, and faith are woven together by God's design.

Bible Verse: *"But you are a chosen people, a royal priesthood, a holy nation, God's special possession, that you may declare the praises of Him who called you out of darkness into His wonderful light."* (1 Peter 2:9 NIV)

Devotional: "I see you—standing at the crossroads of tradition and TikTok, family expectations and personal dreams. You wonder: 'Do I have to choose between my grandma's stories and my Spotify playlist? Between my heritage and my hashtags?' Beloved, I planted you in your culture to bloom uniquely in this generation. Your ancestors' courage runs in your veins, but your story isn't theirs to rewrite. When the world says 'fit in,' I whisper: 'Stand out.' Honor your roots by living boldly in My truth. Speak your language, wear your history proudly, but let Me redefine what 'cool' means. Yes, respect the past—but don't let fear of judgment silence your future. You're not 'too ethnic' for some and 'not enough' for others. You're My masterpiece, bridging old and new to reflect My creativity. Let your life shout: 'God makes beautiful things from every culture—even mine.'"

Closing Encouragement: Your identity isn't a battle—it's a bridge; walk it with courage, and watch God light the way.

March 5

Topic: Laughter and Joy

Opening Statement: Even on your hardest days, joy isn't just possible—it's your holy rebellion against the world's weight.

Bible Verse: *"A cheerful heart is good medicine, but a crushed spirit dries up the bones."* —Proverbs 17:22 (NIV)

Devotional: Hey, I see you. Yes, *you*—the one scrolling tired eyes through this page. You don't have to force a smile, but let Me ask: When did laughter become a stranger? I'm not talking about the quick giggle at a meme, but the kind that bursts free like sunlight through storm clouds. The joy I give isn't a mask to hide your pain. It's a weapon.

Remember that time you laughed so hard with friends your sides hurt? That wasn't random—it was a glimpse of *Me*. I knit joy into your soul because darkness can't drown it. When anxiety ties your stomach in knots, or loneliness whispers lies, laugh. Sing off-key. Dance badly. Let joy rise like a defiant anthem: "You won't crush me, world—my God is bigger."

I'm not asking you to ignore the hard stuff. I'm right here in it with you. But joy? It's your birthright. It's the echo of Eden in your DNA. So breathe deep. Let me light a spark in your spirit that no chaos can extinguish.

Closing Encouragement: Carry joy like a flashlight—it won't just brighten your path but guide others home.

March 6

Topic: Racial and Social Justice

Opening Statement: Your heart burns for fairness because I placed that fire within you—now let's ignite it with purpose.

Bible Verse: *"He has shown you, O mortal, what is good. And what does the Lord require of you? To act justly and to love mercy and to walk humbly with your God."* —Micah 6:8 (NIV)

Devotional: Beloved, I see your frustration when inequality shadows our world. You notice the whispers of racism, the ache of systemic injustice, and the cries of marginalized communities—and your spirit stirs. That's *Me* in you. I designed you to crave justice because *I AM* justice. This isn't just about hashtags or trends; it's about echoing My heart. When you stand up for the bullied classmate, amplify silenced voices online, or question unfair policies, you're partnering with Me.

Yes, the road is hard. You'll face pushback, even from those who claim faith but avoid action. Remember: I called you to *"act justly"*—not wait passively. Your small acts of courage, like sharing resources on racial reconciliation or joining a peaceful protest, ripple into Kingdom impact. Don't underestimate your influence. Together, we'll dismantle walls of hatred and rebuild bridges of mercy. Walk humbly, lean on My strength, and trust that I equip those I call.

Closing Encouragement: Your courage to pursue justice is a beacon of My light in a broken world—shine boldly.

March 7

Topic: Eating and Proper Nutrition

Opening Statement: "What if the way you eat could fuel not just your body, but your soul?"

Bible Verse: *"Do not join those who drink too much wine or gorge themselves on meat, for drunkards and gluttons become poor, and drowsiness clothes them in rags."* —Proverbs 23:20-21 (NIV)

Devotional: My hungry child, I see you—grabbing snacks on the run, scrolling while you eat, numbing stress with candy. You're made for more than mindless cravings. Your body? It's My temple, shaped to carry My light. Every bite is a choice: Will you honor Me or hide from emptiness?

I don't want rules; I want a relationship. When you savor meals with gratitude, you taste My goodness. When you pause junk food binges, you make room for My strength. I'm not judging your pizza nights—I'm inviting you to feast on purpose. Let food nourish, not numb. Your energy, focus, and joy? They're tied to how you steward this gift.

You're not chasing a 'perfect' diet. You're chasing Me. And as you do, I'll help you balance fries and fruit, laughter and lettuce—because even your plate can worship Me."

Closing Encouragement: "Feed your body like the sacred gift it is and watch how My peace fills you from the inside out."

March 8

Topic: Jealousy

Opening Statement: What if I told you your jealousy is a silent thief—stealing joy, peace, and the unique purpose I've placed inside you?

Bible Verse: *"Let us not become conceited, provoking and envying each other."* (Galatians 5:26 NIV)

Devotional: "My unique child, I see your heart when you scroll through social media, comparing your life to others. That ache when a friend gets the spotlight, the frustration when someone else's gifts seem 'better'—it's not from Me. Jealousy distorts My truth: You are *fearfully and wonderfully made* (Psalm 139:14). Every talent, opportunity, and dream I've given you is intentional. When envy whispers, 'You're not enough,' replace it with gratitude.

Celebrate others—it disarms jealousy's poison. Remember, I don't call you to measure up to anyone but to lean into *who I created you to be*. Trust My timing. Your journey isn't theirs, and that's the beauty of My plan. Let My love, not comparison, define your worth."

Closing Encouragement: Your uniqueness is your superpower—walk in it boldly, knowing *I chose you* long before the world tried to compare you.

March 9

Topic: Technology Addiction

Opening Statement: "What if every scroll and swipe is drowning out the voice calling you to something deeper?"

Bible Verse: *"Set your minds on things above, not on earthly things."* —Colossians 3:2 (NIV)

Devotional: Beloved, I see how the glow of screens fills your nights and the buzz of notifications claims your days. You're hungry for connection, yet buried under endless feeds. I crafted you for more—for sunlit conversations, silent prayers, and hands held without emojis. Your phone can't hug a hurting friend. A filter won't capture the beauty of My creation.

When you choose to look up, you'll find Me in the laughter of family, the wind on your face, and the quiet where I speak. I'm not asking you to abandon tech, but to master it. Trade mindless scrolling for mindful moments with Me. Pause before you post. Listen before you like. Let your thumbs rest so your heart can beat. Today, power down to plug into My purpose. I'm here, closer than your next DM.

Closing Encouragement: "Your true connection isn't in a Wi-Fi signal—it's in the One who signals His love for you every moment."

March 10

Topic: Privacy: Concerns about Data Privacy and Online Security

Opening Statement: In a world where every click can be tracked, remember that your true identity is safe in My hands.

Bible Verse: *"You are my hiding place; you will protect me from trouble and surround me with songs of deliverance."* —Psalm 32:7 (NIV)

Devotional: Hey there, My Sacred Heart, my beloved child! I see your concerns about privacy and the online world. You might feel like your personal life is bare for everyone to see, which can be overwhelming. But let me remind you, true security comes not from the locks on your devices, but from the love and protection I offer you. In the digital age, it's wise to guard your personal information, but remember that I am your ultimate shield.

When you face anxiety over your online presence, call on Me. I am here to guide you through the noise and chaos. Set boundaries for your digital life and know that it's okay to step back and protect what is precious to you. Your thoughts, feelings, and dreams are sacred. I am with you, surrounding you with peace and assurance.

Closing Encouragement: Trust in Me and remember that you are always safe under My watchful eye.

March 11

Topic: Happiness of Others

Opening Statement: What if your greatest joy isn't found in *your* victories, but in cheering for someone else's?

Bible Verse: *"Rejoice with those who rejoice; mourn with those who mourn."* —Romans 12:15 (NIV)

Devotional: Beloved, I see the quiet prayers you whisper for your friend battling anxiety, the pride you feel when your sibling shines, the ache when someone you love struggles. That compassion in your heart? It's *Me* in you. The world will tell you to compete, compare, and claw for attention. But My way is different. I knit you into a community—a family— where true joy multiplies when you champion others.

Don't shrink back the next time your friend gets the spotlight, the scholarship, or the answer to their prayer. Celebrate wildly. Weep with them in their pain. This isn't about neglecting your dreams—it's about trusting *Me* to write your story while you help write theirs. Every high-five, every shared tear, every "I'm here for you" mirrors My heart. You become My hands, reminding them they're seen.

Closing Encouragement: When you choose selfless love, you ignite a light that outshines every shadow of envy.

March 12

Topic: Liberation from addictions or struggles.

Opening Statement. Feeling trapped by something you can't shake? Freedom is closer than you think."

Bible Verse: *So if the Son sets you free, you will be free indeed."* —John 8:36 (NIV)

Devotional: My free spirit, I see your weight—the secret battles, the whispers of shame, the nights you wonder if you'll ever break free. You're not defined by your struggles. I've walked through every storm with you, and I'm here now, not to judge, but to rebuild what's broken. That habit you think controls you. It doesn't. That fear that paralyzes you? It won't. I am stronger than every chain. When you feel weak, lean into Me. My power thrives in your honesty, not your perfection. Let's replace "I can't" with "I can." Every time you choose to trust Me, even in small ways, you're tearing down walls the enemy built. Surrender isn't losing—it's letting Me fight for you. Your scars are not mistakes; they're proof of My healing. Today, breathe deeper. The prison door is already open. Will you walk out?

Closing Encouragement: Your chains are not permanent— today, take one step toward the freedom that's already yours.

March 13

Topic: Work-Life Balance

Opening Statement: "Amid the chaos of deadlines, practices, and social demands, you were never meant to carry it all alone."

Bible Verse: *"There is a time for everything, and a season for every activity under the heavens."* —Ecclesiastes 3:1 (NIV)

Devotional: My hard-working child, I feel you pouring into textbooks, clocking hours at work, and scrolling late into the night. Your heart races, your mind crowds, and your soul whispers: *"Is this all there is?"* Let me remind you: Life isn't a race to perfect balance but a rhythm of grace. I created seasons for a reason. When school demands your focus, lean into diligence. When rest calls, close your eyes without guilt. When friends need you, be present without distraction. I don't measure your worth by productivity but by your willingness to walk with Me. Pause. Breathe. Pray. Let go of the illusion of "doing it all" and cling to My peace instead. Prioritize what nourishes your spirit—prayer, Scripture, moments of stillness. Trust me to multiply your time when you surrender to the rush. Today, ask: *"What season is this?"* Then step into it, hand in Mine.

Closing Encouragement: You are held, seen, and deeply loved—let My rhythm guide your steps, not the world's demands.

March 14

Topic: Repentance

Opening Statement: Have you ever felt a heavy weight in your heart, longing for a fresh start?

Bible Verse: *"For godly sorrow brings repentance that leads to salvation and leaves no regret, but worldly sorrow brings death."* —2 Corinthians 7:10 (NIV)

Devotional: Hey there, My repenting child! I see your struggles—the moments when you stumble and feel the sting of regret. I want you to know that feeling sorrow for your mistakes is okay. That feeling can be a powerful catalyst for change. When you approach me with a repentant heart, you're acknowledging your wrongs and opening the door to a renewed relationship with me.

Think of repentance as a fresh breeze blowing through your life, clearing away the fog of guilt and shame. It's about turning away from the things that hold you back and choosing to walk in the light of my love. Remember, true repentance isn't just about feeling sorry; it's about committing to change. So, come to me with your heart open, and I will guide you on this transformation journey.

Closing Encouragement: Embrace the gift of repentance today and watch how I can turn your sorrow into joy and your mistakes into miracles!

March 15

Topic: Faith of Others: Prayers for Spiritual Growth in Others

Opening Statement: Have you ever felt the weight of someone else's struggles, wishing you could help them find the strength to grow in their faith?

Bible Verse: *"I always thank my God for you because of the grace he gave you in Christ Jesus."* —1 Corinthians 1:4 (NIV)

Devotional: Dear friend of faith, I see the friends around you—those who are searching for hope, love, and purpose. You may feel powerless, but your prayers are powerful. When you lift them up, you invite Me into their lives. Each prayer you send into the universe is like a seed planted in fertile soil, ready to bloom into spiritual growth.

Imagine your friend, battling doubts or fears. Your heartfelt prayers can be the light that guides them out of darkness. Remember, I am with you and working in their hearts even when you can't see it. Don't underestimate the impact of your faith and your voice. Your encouragement and prayers can ignite a spark of hope in them.

Stay faithful, and trust that I am at work. As you pray, know that you are not just supporting them but partnering with Me in their faith journey.

Closing Encouragement: Keep praying, and watch how I move mountains in the lives of those you love!

March 16

Topic: Hope into Miracles

Opening Statement: When life feels like a storm and hope seems lost, remember that miracles are just a prayer away.

Bible Verse: *"Jesus looked at them and said, 'With man this is impossible, but with God all things are possible.'"* —Matthew 19:26 (NIV)

Devotional: Hey there, My hopeful child. I see you in the midst of struggles, feeling overwhelmed by challenges that seem insurmountable. It's easy to believe that you're alone in your battles but listen closely: miracles happen when you least expect them. Remember the story of the woman who touched Jesus' cloak and was healed? Her faith in a moment of desperation changed everything.

I want you to know that your cries don't go unheard. In times of hopelessness, lean on me. I am the God of the impossible. When you face trials—whether it's friendship drama, family issues, or academic pressure—know that I am ready to intervene. As Jesus calmed the storm for his disciples, I can bring peace to your troubled heart.

Open your heart to my presence and watch as I turn your despair into hope. Miracles are waiting for you when you trust in me.

Closing Encouragement: Remember, no situation is too hopeless for the miracles God can bring into your life.

March 17

Topic: Gratitude

Opening Statement: "What if thankfulness isn't just a feeling—it's a weapon against despair?"

Bible Verse: *And even the very hairs of your head are all numbered.* —Matthew 1:30 NIV

Devotional: I hear your sigh when life feels unfair—the friend who betrayed you, the grade that didn't reflect your effort, the family tension that weighs heavy. But here's the secret: Gratitude isn't denial; it's defiance. When you thank Me for the sunrise despite your sleepless night or praise Me for your mom's laugh even as you argue, you starve fear and feed faith. I've counted every hair on your head. I see the college acceptance, the healing, the reconciliation I'm orchestrating. Worship isn't just for Sundays. Whisper thanks while scrolling social media. Sing My goodness over cafeteria lunches. Gratitude rewires your heart to see My fingerprints in the chaos. Today, let's start small: Thank Me for one hard thing. Watch how I turn it into an altar."

Closing Encouragement: Your praise isn't powerless—it's a GPS redirecting your heart to hope.

March 18

Topic: Seeking Relationship with God

Opening Statement: Have you ever felt a longing in your heart for something more than just the everyday hustle?

Bible Verse: *"You will seek me and find me when you seek me with all your heart."* —Jeremiah 29:13 (NIV)

Devotional: My dear child, I see the desire in your heart for a deeper connection with Me. This journey of seeking a relationship with Me is not merely a task; it's a beautiful adventure that I invite you to embark on. Imagine walking hand-in-hand with the Creator of the universe, feeling My love and guidance in every step you take.

When you seek Me wholeheartedly, I promise to reveal the depths of My love for you. Set aside distractions and open your heart to My whispers. Talk to Me in your own words; I am always here to listen. Whether you are filled with joy or struggling with doubt, your genuine feelings matter to Me.

Dive into prayer, immerse yourself in My Word, and let My presence fill your life. Each moment spent connecting with Me will strengthen your spirit and clarify your path. Remember, I am always by your side, guiding and encouraging you to pursue the divine relationship you crave.

Closing Encouragement: Trust that as you seek Me, I will reveal Myself in ways that will transform your life forever!

March 19

Topic: Overcoming Challenges

Opening Statement: Are you facing a mountain of challenges that feels impossible to climb?

Bible Verse: *"Press on toward the goal to win the prize for which God has called me heavenward in Christ Jesus."* —Philippians 4:14 NIV

Devotional: My struggling child, I see the weight of the challenges you face. Life may throw obstacles in your path, making your goals seem distant and unachievable. But remember, you are not alone in this journey. I am here to empower you. Each time you feel like giving up, turn to Me.

When you set your heart on a difficult goal, it's natural to feel doubt creeping in. But I promise you, with faith and persistence, success is within your grasp. Think of the great achievements of those who pressed on despite the odds. They trusted in My strength, and so can you.

Every step you take, no matter how small, brings you closer to your dreams. Embrace the process, learn from your struggles, and don't be afraid to ask for help. I am your guide, ready to lift you when you stumble.

Closing Encouragement: Remember, with My strength, no challenge is too great for you to overcome!

March 20

Topic: Social media

Opening Statement: Are you ready to discover how your online presence can reflect the light of Christ?

Bible Verse: *"Let your light shine before others, that they may see your good deeds and glorify your Father in heaven."* —Matthew 5:16 (NIV)

Devotional: Hey there, my beloved teen! I see you navigating the vast world of technology and social media. It's easy to get lost in the likes, shares, and comments, isn't it? But remember, I've called you to be different. In those moments when you're scrolling through feeds, I want you to pause and reflect: How are you representing Me? Every post, every tweet, is an opportunity to shine My love into the lives of others.

Imagine using your platforms to uplift your friends, share hope, and spread kindness. When you choose to be a beacon of light, you're not just fitting in; you're transforming the atmosphere around you. So, let your digital footprint echo My truth and love. Engage wisely and remember, you are a vessel of My Spirit—let that influence your online interactions.

Closing Encouragement: Embrace the power of your voice online, and let it be a testimony of God's love!

March 21

Topic: Fashion & Beauty

Opening Statement: Your mirror only shows the surface, but I see a masterpiece crafted in eternity.

Bible Verse: *"Your beauty should not come from outward adornment, such as elaborate hairstyles and the wearing of gold jewelry or fine clothes. Rather, it should be that of your inner self, the unfading beauty of a gentle and quiet spirit, which is of great worth in God's sight."* —1 Peter 3:3-4 (NIV)

Devotional: My beautiful child, I know the world shouts that your worth is in your looks, your clothes, your likes. But I whisper deeper truths: *You are My design.* Every freckle, curl, and scar tells a story only I could write. When you obsess over trends or compare yourself online, you forget the eternal style I gave you—**a heart that reflects My love**.

True beauty isn't a filter or a brand. It's the courage to wear kindness like a crown. It's the glow of integrity that no highlighter can mimic. The most stunning people in history? They radiated *mercy, justice, and humility* (Micah 6:8). That's the #OOTD heaven notices.

So wear what makes you confident, but let your soul dress first in My light. Your "fit" will never go out of fashion here.

Closing Encouragement: Walk in confidence today—your soul's beauty outshines every trend.

March 22

Topic: Thrifting and vintage fashion

Opening Statement: Discovering your unique style can be a journey, and sometimes, the best treasures are hidden in unexpected places.

Bible Verse: *"For we are God's handiwork, created in Christ Jesus to do good works, which God prepared in advance for us to do."* —Ephesians 2:10 (NIV)

Devotional: Hey there! I want you to know that your style is an expression of who you are—a masterpiece crafted by Me. When you step into a thrift store, you're not just searching for clothes; you're on a mission to uncover pieces that resonate with your spirit. Each vintage item has a story, just like you.

As you sift through racks of colorful fabrics and unique patterns, remember that I see the beauty in the old and the overlooked. Just as I have redeemed you, I can transform anything into something beautiful. Embrace your individuality; every outfit you create can reflect My love and creativity.

When you choose to wear vintage, you're not just following a trend; you're celebrating history and sustainability. Let your clothing choices be a canvas for the vibrant personality I've given you. Stand out, shine bright, and know that I am with you every step of the way.

Closing Encouragement: Trust in your unique style, for you are a wonderfully crafted creation meant to shine!

March 23

Topics: Hobbies and activities

Opening Statement: Your passions are not just pastimes; they're the whispers of your heart calling you closer to Me.

Bible Verse: *"Delight yourself in the Lord, and He will give you the desires of your heart."* —Psalm 37:4 (NIV)

Devotional: My creative child, every hobby and activity you engage in holds a special purpose. When you paint, dance, play sports, or write, you're expressing the creativity I've placed within you. I see the joy you find in these moments, and I want you to know that I am right there with you, cheering you on.

Embrace your interests to glorify Me. When you pour your heart into what you love, you reflect My image. Don't be afraid to explore new activities or deepen your current passions; each one is a pathway to discover who you truly are in Me. Remember, it's not just about the outcome, but the journey you take. Trust that I am guiding your steps and shaping your talents for a greater purpose.

Closing Encouragement: Chase your dreams wholeheartedly, for in your passions, I reveal My love and purpose for you.

March 24

Topic: Tech gadgets like smartwatches, wireless earbuds, and gaming consoles

Opening Statement: "Your gadgets track your steps, your music, and your wins—but what if they could also remind you of the One who's tracking your heart?"

Bible Verse: *"But blessed is the one who trusts in the Lord, whose confidence is in him.* Jeramiah 17:7 NIV.

Devotional "You slip on wireless earbuds to block out the noise, but have you paused to hear Me? I'm the quiet whisper beneath the beats, calling you closer. Your smartwatch buzzes to 'move,' yet I long to move in your spirit—to guide your steps toward purpose, not just paces. That gaming console? It's a shadow of the strategy I've wired into you: to conquer fear, level up in faith, and play for eternal victories. These tools aren't evil, but don't let them drown My voice. When notifications steal your focus, remember I designed you for more than distraction. Sync your heart to My frequency. Let your tech remind you—I'm the ultimate connection, unbreaking and unlimited. Today, power down the clutter. Open My Word. I'll upgrade your soul, My tech teen."

Closing Encouragement: "Your Creator didn't design you to just *scroll*—you are called to *soar*."

March 25

Topic: Exploring Spirituality and Mindfulness Practices

Opening Statement: "Amid the buzz of notifications and the weight of tomorrow's worries, I'm calling you to a stillness that rewires your soul."

Bible Verse: *"Be still, and know that I am God."* —Psalm 46:10 (NIV)

Devotional: You think I don't see it, My twitchy child? The way your thumb scrolls, your heart races, your mind juggles a thousand "what-ifs." This world shouts for your attention, but I whisper for your awareness. Mindfulness isn't a trend—it's a throne. Every breath you take is a chance to recenter on Me. When anxiety clenches your chest, pause. Feel the air fill your lungs? That's My rhythm. Hear the silence between songs? That's My invitation.

I didn't design you to chase peace—I AM your peace. What mindfulness practices you've heard about? They're echoes of My timeless truth: "Be still." Stillness isn't passive; it's rebellion against chaos. Close your eyes. Name one thing you're grateful for. That's worship. Notice the sunlight? That's My wink. You're not just a teen—you're a temple. Let's rebuild your focus, one sacred breath at a time.

Closing Encouragement: "Your breath is a prayer I'm always answering—start listening and watch chaos bow to calm."

March 26

Topic: Music Streaming and Discovering New Artists.

Opening Statement: What if every new song you discover could remind you of the unique rhythm God is writing in your life?

Bible Verse: *"Whether you turn to the right or to the left, your ears will hear a voice behind you, saying, 'This is the way; walk in it.'"* —Isaiah 30:21 (NIV)

Devotional: My beloved, I see how you search for fresh beats, new lyrics, and artists who stir your heart. Just as streaming platforms guide you to songs you've never heard, I am always leading you toward My purpose. Every playlist you curate reflects your story—but I crafted you with even greater intentionality. When you feel lost in the noise of life, I am the quiet melody beneath the chaos, whispering direction. Those moments when a song suddenly resonates. That's how I speak: through sudden peace, a friend's encouragement, or Scripture that "hits different." Let your love for music remind you to tune into My voice daily. Create a playlist of worship anthems, hymns, or lyrics that point to My truth. Let every track become a prayer, and every listen an invitation to draw closer. I'm not just the Creator of the universe—I'm the Creator of *you,* and I've given you a soundtrack of grace for every season.

Closing Encouragement: Let God's playlist for your life drown out doubt and amplify His unshakable love.

March 27

Topic: AI Tools Like ChatGPT for School and Creativity

Opening Statement: What if the technology at your fingertips could amplify *and* honor the creativity God placed in your heart?

Bible Verse: *"Whatever you do, work at it with all your heart, as working for the Lord, not for human masters."* —Colossians 3:23 (NIV)

Devotional: My learning child, I see you—poring over assignments, chasing ideas, wondering how to balance the demands of school and the fire of creativity I've ignited in you. Today's tools, like AI, are not your rivals. They're gifts, crafted through human ingenuity, which I inspired. Use them wisely. Let ChatGPT spark ideas for essays, organize study notes, or unblock writer's doubt, but never let it replace the unique voice I've given you. Your imagination reflects My image— technology can't replicate that. When stress rises, pause. Ask Me: "How can I glorify You here?" Maybe it's using AI to save time for serving others. Maybe it's choosing integrity over shortcuts. Remember, every innovation points back to My creativity. Stay rooted in My Word. Let your work, whether typed on a screen or whispered in prayer, be an offering. I'm with you in every click, every brainstorm, every step.

Closing Encouragement: You're not just a student or artist— you're a light; let tech magnify your God-given purpose!

March 28

Topic: Entertainment

Opening Statement: "Ever feel like your light's too small to matter in a world this dark? Let's talk about why you're *exactly* the flame this generation needs."

Bible Verse: *"You will shine among them like stars in the sky"* (Philippians 2:15 NIV).

Devotional You wonder if anyone sees the real you—the dreams I've placed in your heart, the fire I lit in your soul. I see it all. You're not a mistake; you're My torch in the wilderness. Yeah, life throws shadows: pressure to fit in, endless scrolls of hashtags, whispers that you're "too much" or "not enough." But here's the truth: Stars don't shine *despite* the darkness— they blaze *because* of it.

I made you to stand out. Not to mirror the crowd, but to disrupt it with grace. When you forgive the friend who hurt you, when you choose joy after defeat, when you speak truth even if your voice shakes—that's your light burning through the night. You think small acts don't matter? A single spark can ignite a forest.

The world will try to snuff you out with doubt, comparisons, or filters. But I don't make disposable people. I crafted you, on purpose, for *this* moment. So let your quirks, kindness, and courage glow. You're not here to hide—you're here to lead others home.

Closing Encouragement: The world needs your light— don't dim it.

March 29

Topic: The Holy Spirit hears our cries

Opening Statement: You know that moment in your favorite book when the hero is too overwhelmed to speak—yet somehow, the battle is still won? That's how prayer works when you let the Holy Spirit step in.

Bible Verse: *"In the same way, the Spirit helps us in our weakness. We do not know what we ought to pray for, but the Spirit himself intercedes for us through wordless groans."* —Romans 8:26 (NIV)

Devotional "Why so sad, My child? I see you. I've watched you try to untangle your emotions like Percy Jackson facing a labyrinth or Katniss in the arena—overwhelmed, unsure where to start. You don't need perfect words, just an open heart. When tears blur your prayers, or anger knots your thoughts, I'm here. I'll translate every sigh, every silent scream, into heaven's language. You think you're alone? I'm the whisper in your chaos, the ache in your chest for 'more' than this world offers. Even when you mimic Colleen Hoover's characters— aching, messy, wordless—I'm scripting your story with grace. Your feelings aren't too big or too broken for God. Let me carry them. Trust me: Your quietest 'help' shouts louder in heaven than any TikTok rant."

Closing Encouragement: You don't have to be the hero with all the answers—just let the Spirit fight for you.

March 30

Topic: Bible comforts the heart

Opening Statement: You scroll for hours, binge shows, chase likes—but that empty feeling won't quit. What if I told you *this* is the cure your soul's been craving?

Bible Verse: *"Jesus answered, 'It is written: "Man shall not live on bread alone, but on every word that comes from the mouth of God."'* —Matthew 4:4 (NIV)

Devotional "Hey, it's Me, My hungry child. I see you trying to numb the ache with TikTok, snacks, or late-night texts. But deep down, you're starving for something that lasts. The Bible isn't a dusty rulebook—it's My love letter to YOU. When your heart's shattered, I'll comfort you with Psalms. When you're confused, I'll light your path with Proverbs. When you're drained, I'll revive you with stories of David's courage or Ruth's loyalty. Obedience isn't about being perfect; it's about letting My words become your oxygen. Every time you open Scripture, I'm right there, whispering, 'I see you. I get you. Let's do this together.' Your soul wasn't made for crumbs—it was made for the feast I've prepared."

Closing Encouragement: Trade the temporary fillers for the eternal feast—your soul will thank you.

March 31

Topic: Virtual Reality and Augmented Reality

Opening Statement: "You crave adventures beyond screens, but what if the greatest reality is already within you?"

Bible Verse: *"We fix our eyes not on what is seen, but on what is unseen. For what is seen is temporary, but what is unseen is eternal."* —2 Corinthians 4:18 (NIV)

Devotional: "I see you slipping into virtual worlds, chasing thrills that flicker and fade. You've built fortresses in pixels, raced through augmented skies—yet your heart still whispers, 'Is this all?' Child, I crafted galaxies with My breath and wrote your name into eternity. No headset can mirror the wonder of My creation or the depth of My plans for you. Those digital escapes? They're shadows of the joy I offer. When you drift into artificial realms, remember I AM the God who walked in Eden's real garden, who split real seas, who rose in a real body—for you. Let your soul anchor here, where My love outshines every filter. Log out sometimes. Feel the sun I painted for you. Hear the laughter of friends I placed beside you. I'm not a simulation; I'm the Living Truth. Seek Me first and watch how I amplify your reality."

Closing Encouragement: "You were made for more than augmented adventures—step into the eternal story God wrote just for you."

April 1

Topic: TikTok Trends and Challenges

Opening Statement: In a world full of viral trends, let your heart stay anchored in truth.

Bible Verse: *"Let your light shine before others, that they may see your good deeds and glorify your Father in heaven."* —Matthew 5:16 (NIV)

Devotional: Hey there My shining light! I see you navigating the exciting world of TikTok, where trends and challenges come and go in the blink of an eye. Remember, not everything that goes viral is worth your time or energy. I'm here to guide you in choosing what truly matters. Some trends can uplift and inspire, while others might lead you away from your true self. Let me help you discern the difference. When you feel the pressure to conform, pause and listen to Me. I'll show you how to shine with authenticity and love. Embrace what reflects kindness and truth, and you'll become a light in the digital world—leading others by example.

Closing Encouragement: Stay true to yourself and let your unique light inspire others!

April 2

Topic: What's Your Superpower?

Opening Statement: Did you know you have a superpower given by God?

Bible Verse: *"I can do all this through him who gives me strength."* —Philippians 4:13 (NIV)

Devotional: Hey there, My Superhero! Let's talk about the incredible superpower you have inside you. You might think superheroes are only in movies, but I'm here to remind you that I gave you true power. This power isn't about flying or invisibility; it's about something much greater—the Divine Spirit within you.

With my help, you can overcome fears, love others deeply, and make wise choices. When you feel weak or unsure, remember that I'm always with you, guiding and strengthening you. You have the power to make a difference in your world, to be brave in tough situations, and to show kindness where it's needed most.

Embrace your superpower! You're not alone in this journey. Together, we can do amazing things.

Closing Encouragement: Remember, with God's power in you, there's nothing you can't face!

April 3

Topic: Dance Trends and Choreography

Opening Statement: "What if your life's rhythm could sync with a purpose greater than the latest TikTok challenge?"

Bible Verse: *"There is a time to weep and a time to laugh, a time to mourn and a time to dance."* —Ecclesiastes 3:4 (NIV)

Devotional My dancing child you scroll through endless reels, learning steps to fit in—but what if I choreographed your life? Every heartbeat, every breath, is part of My divine rhythm. The world says, "Follow the trend," but I whisper, "Follow My lead." When David danced before Me unashamed (2 Samuel 6:14), it wasn't about perfection—it was abandoned. Surrender. Trust. Your life isn't meant to mimic fleeting moves; it's a sacred dance where I set the tempo. Stumble? I'll lift you. Feel offbeat? My grace is your rhythm. Today's trends fade, but My plans for you? Eternal. Let your soul sway to My purpose. Dance not for likes, but for Love.

Closing Encouragement: "Let The Spirit take the lead— your most joyful dance is just beginning."

April 4

Topic: Sustainable and Eco-Friendly Clothing

Opening Statement: What if the clothes you wear could honor God's creation and reflect His heart?

Bible Verse: *"The Lord God took the man and put him in the Garden of Eden to work it and take care of it."* —Genesis 2:15 (NIV)

Devotional: Beloved child of the Garden, I've placed this earth in your hands as a gift—a masterpiece to steward, not exploit. When you choose sustainable clothing, you're answering My call to care for creation. Fast fashion fades, leaving waste and harm, but the choices you make can ripple into eternity. That thrifted jacket. It's a statement of creativity. Those eco-friendly shoes? They whisper hope for the future. Every thread matters because the earth is Mine, and you are My partner in tending it. Don't underestimate your power: supporting ethical brands, repairing instead of replacing, or even hosting a clothing swap with friends—these acts worship Me. You're not just dressing your body; you're clothing your heart in compassion. Let your style reflect My love for all I've made.

Closing Encouragement: Today, let your wardrobe choices plant seeds of faithfulness for generations to come.

April 5

Topic: Meme culture and internet humor

Opening Statement: Behind every viral joke lies a choice: Will your humor lift others up or tear them down?

Bible Verse: *"Do not let any unwholesome talk come out of your mouths, but only what is helpful for building others up according to their needs, that it may benefit those who listen."* —Ephesians 4:29 (NIV)

Devotional: Dear one, I know your world thrives on laughter—memes, reels, inside jokes that connect hearts across screens. But I ask: Does your humor carry My love? The internet's echo chamber often amplifies sarcasm, division, or shame. Yet you, My child, are set apart. Let your wit reflect grace. When you scroll, ask, "Does this laugh honor the hurting? Does it mock or mend?"

I designed joy to unite, not wound. Share memes that spark hope, not hate. Your words—even in a caption—hold power to heal. Be bold in kindness. Let your humor point to truth, to humility, to the joy I pour into you. In a culture of cynicism, dare to be light. Today, let your pixels preach love.

Closing Encouragement: Even a meme can be a ministry—post with purpose and watch God multiply your influence.

April 6

Topic: Spiritual Exploration – Interest in understanding faith, spirituality, and personal growth.

Opening Statement: Ever feel a quiet pull in your heart, like a compass pointing you toward something—or Someone—bigger than yourself?

Bible Verse: *"You will seek me and find me when you seek me with all your heart."* —Jeremiah 29:13 (NIV)

Devotional: Hey, it's Me—the One who knows every doubt, dream, and question swirling in your mind. I'm not a distant force; I'm the breath in your lungs, the fire in your soul. When you scroll late at night wondering, *"Is this all there is?"*—that's Me, inviting you deeper. Faith isn't a boring rulebook; it's a wild adventure. I'm in the friendships that lift you up, the lyrics that give you chills, the quiet moments when creation leaves you speechless.

You want purpose? Start here: Talk to Me like a friend. Crack open My Word—even one verse. Watch how I show up in sunsets, playlists, and that random kindness from a stranger. This isn't about being "perfect." It's about being *curious.* I'll meet you in your messy, real, TikTok-and-tests life. Ready to explore?

Closing Encouragement: Your search for meaning isn't a dead end—it's the first step toward a life blazing with divine purpose.

April 7

Topic: Daily Devotionals

Opening Statement: You don't have to walk this life alone—I'm here to carry you through every storm.

Bible Verse: *"So do not fear, for I am with you; do not be dismayed, for I am your God. I will strengthen you and help you; I will uphold you with my righteous right hand."* —Isaiah 41:10 NIV)

Devotional: Beloved Spiritual Warrior, I know the battles you face—the anxiety that tightens your chest, the loneliness that shadows your heart, the whispers that say, "You can't do this." Listen closer: My voice is stronger. I am the God who holds galaxies, yet I bend low to hold you. When you feel weak, lean into My strength. When you stumble, My hand will steady you. You are not meant to fight alone. I see your courage, even when you doubt it. Every tear, every prayer, every shaky step forward—I treasure them all. Today, let go of the need to control outcomes. Surrender the weight to Me. Walk in the freedom of knowing I am your defender, your healer, your constant companion. Your struggles *are not the end of your story; they are steppingstones to My glory.*

Closing Encouragement: Rise, warrior—His strength is your shield, and His love is your anthem.

April 8

Topic: Creative Writing .

Opening Statement: "What if your pen could unlock glimpses of eternity?" ✍️✨

Bible Verse: *"My heart is stirred by a noble theme as I recite my verses for the king; my tongue is the pen of a skillful writer."* (Psalm 45:1 NIV)

Devotional: Hello, My modern-day Shakespeare! "I placed a pen in your hand long before you knew its power. Every journal entry, poem, or story you write is a whisper between us—a chance to trace My fingerprints in your life. When you pour out doubts, joys, or questions onto paper, you're not just scribbling words. You're weaving My light into the cracks of this broken world. Feel that ache to create? That's Me stirring your spirit, inviting you to partner with Heaven's narrative. Your words can breathe hope into a friend's darkness, turn pain into worship, or turn ordinary moments into altars. Don't compare your voice to others; your unique rhythm reflects My heart. Start small: scribble a prayer, craft a verse about My faithfulness, or rewrite a Bible story through your modern eyes. I'll meet you there, igniting sentences you didn't know you could write. Your words matter—eternity echoes in them."

Closing Encouragement: "Pick up your pen—Heaven's waiting to speak through your story."

April 9

Topic: Books with Meaning

Opening Statement: "What if the stories you love could light up your path like a divine GPS?"

Bible Verse: *"Your word is a lamp for my feet, a light on my path."* —Psalm 119:105 (NIV)

Devotional: My Beloved Light, I'm the Author behind every story that stirs your soul. When you read about Peeta's sacrificial love in *The Hunger Games* or Meg's courage in *A Wrinkle in Time*, you're glimpsing *My* heart. Those moments of truth, justice, and hope? They're signposts pointing to Me.

But not every story leads to light. Some twist truth, leaving shadows where clarity should reign. So let's navigate this together. When you open a book, ask: *Does this story guide me closer to My purpose, or further into confusion?* I'll highlight the pages that align with My Word. Trade fleeting thrills for tales where redemption wins—because *I'm* the ultimate Redeemer.

You're not just a reader—you're a character in My epic. Let the stories you cherish sharpen your courage, deepen your empathy, and remind you: **Your life is a sacred plotline**.

Closing Encouragement: Let every book you read fuel your journey toward the Light.

April 10

Topic: Nature & Spirituality

Opening Statement: "What if the rustle of leaves, the crash of waves, or the glow of a sunset is God's way of texting you?"

Bible Verse: *"The heavens declare the glory of God; the skies proclaim the work of God's hands. Day after day they pour forth speech; night after night they reveal knowledge."* —Psalm 19:1-4 (NIV)

Devotional: *Beloved, listen—creation is My love language.* When you walk past that oak tree, feel the sun warm your face, or pause to watch fireflies dance, I'm there. Every mountain, every raindrop, every star is a love note written just for you. I crafted nature to mirror My heart: wild, free, and bursting with purpose. Notice how the ocean never stops singing? That's Me, inviting you to worship. See how flowers push through cracks in concrete? That's My reminder—*you* can rise, too.

When stress smothers you or doubt screams loud, step outside. Breathe deep. Let the wind whisper, "I'm with you." Let the sunrise shout, "I renew ALL things." You're not just observing nature—you're standing in My gallery, surrounded by proof of My promises. And guess what? *You're part of the masterpiece.*

Closing Encouragement: Step into the wild today—let creation reboot your soul and remind you whose you are.

April 11

Topic: Personal Development - Self-improvement through spiritual and practical guidance.

Opening Statement: Are you ready to unlock your true potential and embrace the remarkable person God created you to be?

Bible Verse: *"Therefore, if anyone is in Christ, the new creation has come: The old has gone, the new is here!"* (2 Corinthians 5:17, NIV)

Devotional: My beloved, I see the dreams you hold close and the fears that sometimes weigh you down. Remember, you are not alone in your journey. I am here to guide you every step of the way. Embrace your uniqueness; it is a gift from me. Each challenge you face is an opportunity for growth. When you stumble, don't be discouraged; instead, look up and seek my strength.

Take time to reflect on your passions and talents; they are clues to your purpose. Surround yourself with friends who uplift you and seek wisdom in my Word. You can accomplish all that I have set before you, as I empower you with strength beyond your own. Trust in the plans I have laid out and watch as I transform your life in ways you can't yet imagine.

Closing Encouragement: You are destined for greatness; believe in your journey and trust in my perfect plan!

April 12

Topic: Inspirational Quotes

Opening Statement: What if the words you share could ignite hope in someone's darkest moment?

📖 **Bible Verse:** *"My dear brothers and sisters, take note of this: Everyone should be quick to listen, slow to speak and slow to become angry."* —James 1:19 (NIV)

Devotional: "I hear the whispers of your heart, the quotes you save, the messages you share. Every word you choose carries weight—My weight. When you pass along hope, you're echoing My voice. Think of the verses you cling to: 'I can do all things through Christ' (Philippians 4:13) or 'Perfect love casts out fear' (1 John 4:18). These aren't just pretty phrases; they're lifelines I've woven into Scripture to anchor you. Today, ask Me: How can my words reflect Your light? Share that encouraging comment. Text a friend a verse. Even an emoji prayer can lift a burden. But remember: Listening comes first. Before you speak, let My truth sink deep. I'll help you choose words that heal, not hurt words that turn scrolls into altars."

Closing Encouragement: Your words are seeds of eternity—plant them where darkness trembles.

April 13

Topic: Soundtrack of Purpose

Opening Statement: Ever wonder why certain songs make your soul feel awake? That's no accident—I'm tuning your heart to My rhythm.

Bible Verse: *Speak to one another with psalms, hymns, and songs from the Spirit. Sing and make music from your heart to the Lord, always giving thanks to God the Father for everything..."*
—Ephesians 5:19-20 (NIV)

Devotional: You, scrolling through Spotify, craving more than just a beat—I see you. I've woven My truth into melodies that stir your spirit, lyrics that echo your deepest prayers. That song you replay? It's not just a chorus; My whisper reminds you: *You're not alone. You're called for more.*

When the world's noise drowns your peace, turn up the volume on worship. Let Christian music for teens be your armor—faith-filled anthems drowning doubt, worship playlists replacing anxiety with awe. Every chord, every lyric, is a bridge to My presence. Sing loudly in your car, hum quietly in class—your voice matters here. I dance with you in the rhythms of grace.

Still unsure what to choose? Ask: Does this song honor My light in you? Does it fuel courage, kindness, and hope? Your playlist isn't just background noise—it's a declaration of who you are: Mine.

Closing Encouragement: *Let your playlist become a prayer— every beat, a step closer to the heart of God.*

April 14

Topic: Listening to the life stories of our parents and grandparents.

Opening Statement: "Your family's stories aren't just memories—they're sacred echoes of God's faithfulness waiting to shape your heart."

Bible Verse: *"Listen to your father, who gave you life, and do not despise your mother when she is old."* —Proverbs 23:22 (NIV)

Devotional: Beloved, I am stirring you to lean in closer. When your grandparents share about their youth, or your parents recall struggles you've never faced, I am there—in every laugh, every tear, every whispered prayer that carried them through. Their stories are fragments of My faithfulness, pieces of a greater tapestry I'm weaving through your family.

Do you hear it? The resilience in their voices? The hope that refused to die? That is *Me*. I walked with them through valleys, celebrated on their mountaintops, and whispered courage when fear gripped their hearts. When you listen, you honor the legacy I've entrusted to you. You discover that their battles, joys, and miracles are not relics of the past but signposts for your own faith journey.

Don't rush these moments. Ask questions. Let their wisdom sink deep. In their testimonies, you'll find strength for your doubts and light for your path. This is how generational faith grows—when young hearts choose to receive the treasures hidden in the voices of those who came before.

Closing Encouragement: Your family's story is a bridge to deeper trust—walk it boldly and watch your own faith rise.

April 15

Topic: Let Good Things Shape You.

Opening Statement: "What you follow online shapes your heart—choose accounts aligning with My light."

📖 **Bible Verse:** *"Let your eyes look straight ahead; fix your gaze directly before you. Give careful thought to the paths for your feet and be steadfast in all your ways."* (Proverbs 4:25-27 NIV)

Devotional: *"Every time you scroll, you're choosing a path. My scanning child. I see how the world tries to distract you—endless comparisons, empty trends, voices that drown out My truth. But you, My child, were made for more. Fix your eyes on what lifts your spirit: follow those who reflect My love, share Scripture boldly, and spark joy. Unfollow what drags you into doubt or darkness. Your screen isn't just entertainment—it's a battlefield for your heart. When you fill your feed with faith-filled content, you're not just passing time but walking My path. I'll help you reset your algorithm to heaven's frequency. Start today. Let every like, save, and share declare, 'I'm chasing God's purpose, not the world's noise.'"*

Closing Encouragement: "Your focus fuels your future—curate your feed like your soul depends on it (because it does!)."

April 16

Topic: spirituality and modern science

Opening Statement: Did you know the universe's complexity points to a Creator who loves you deeply?

Bible Verse: *"The heavens declare the glory of God; the skies proclaim the work of his hands. Day after day they pour forth speech; night after night they reveal knowledge."* —Psalm 19:1-2 (NIV)

Devotional: My beloved child of creation, look around. Every star, every cell, every law of physics sings My name. When you study science, you're uncovering the blueprints of My creativity. Think of the first time you marveled at a sunset or a microscope slide—that awe? It's Me inviting you closer. Some say faith and science clash, but they're two sides of the same coin. Isaac Newton sought Me in equations; Katherine Johnson saw My hand in orbital trajectories. When you ask bold questions—how DNA echoes My design, why quantum particles dance in unity—you honor My gifts of curiosity and wisdom. Don't shrink from doubt; bring it to Me. Your search for truth does not threaten me—I *am* Truth. Let your love for biology, astronomy, or coding become worship. Together, we'll explore mysteries deeper than black holes and brighter than supernovas.

Closing Encouragement: Walk boldly, knowing every scientific discovery is a step closer to the heart of God.

April 17

Topic: Afterlife Curiosity

Opening Statement: "You wonder about life after death, but the truth you're longing for is already written in God's Word."

Bible Verse: *"My Father's house has many rooms; if that were not so, would I have told you that I am going there to prepare a place for you?"* —John 14:2 (NIV)

Devotional: "I hear your questions: What happens when we die? Could reincarnation be real? Let Me quiet your heart. The world offers confusing answers, but I offer eternal truth. I designed you for more than cycles of rebirth or fleeting spiritual guesses. You were made for a forever Home crafted by Jesus Himself. When doubts whisper, remember His promise: 'I am the way, the truth, and the life' (John 14:6). You don't need to wander through mysteries alone. Trust My Word—your eternity is secure, not in endless resets, but in a perfect, endless relationship with Me. Fix your eyes on Heaven, where joy replaces fear, and My presence drowns out every lie. Your soul isn't meant to recycle—it's meant to rise."

Closing Encouragement: "Rest in this truth: Your forever is safe in the hands of the One who conquered death."

April 18

Topic: Positive Lifestyle

Opening Statement: Your daily choices are the brushstrokes painting the masterpiece of your life—let faith guide your hand.

Bible Verse: *"And whatever you do, whether in word or deed, do it all in the name of the Lord Jesus, giving thanks to God the Father through him."* —Colossians 3:17 (NIV)

Devotional: Beloved, Sacred Heart, I see you—every decision, every habit, every moment. You wonder, *Does God care about the small things?* Yes. Your faith isn't just for Sundays or youth groups; it's woven into your daily rhythm. When you choose kindness over gossip, patience over frustration, or integrity over shortcuts, you honor Me. Each choice is a prayer.

Today, a friend might need encouragement. Homework feels overwhelming. Social media whispers comparisons. In these moments, pause. Ask, *"Jesus, how would You step into this?"* Let His love shape your words; His wisdom guide your scroll, His peace steady your heart. Even ordinary tasks—texting a sibling, studying for a test—become worship when done with Him.

I'm not asking for perfection. I'm inviting partnership. When you stumble, lean into grace. When you rise, celebrate His strength. Your life isn't about checking religious boxes but walking with the One who calls you *beloved*.

Closing Encouragement: Today, let every step reflect His light—you were made to shine, not just survive.

April 19

Topic: Grief & Healing

Opening Statement: "When loss carves a hole in your heart, it's easy to feel like no one understands—but I see you, and I'm here."

Bible Verse: *"Praise be to the God and Father of our Lord Jesus Christ, the Father of compassion and the God of all comfort, who comforts us in all our troubles, so that we can comfort those in any trouble with the comfort we ourselves receive from God."* (2 Corinthians 1:3-4 NIV)

Devotional: My grieving child, I know the weight you carry— the ache that makes mornings feel impossible, the memories that sting like rain on a wound. You're asking, *"Why?"* I'm not here to give you easy answers. I'm here to sit with you in the dark. Your tears are sacred to Me. Every shattered piece of your heart matters. I didn't promise a life without pain, but I *did* promise to never leave you in it. Let Me carry what's too heavy for you. When you're ready, I'll show you how your story of grief can become someone else's lifeline. You don't have to "fix" your pain today—breathe and let Me hold you.

Closing Encouragement: Your healing journey starts with a whisper: *"I trust You."* Let that be enough for now.

April 20

Teens: Bible Study

Opening Statement: "Ever wonder if the Bible's ancient stories have anything to do with your life right now?"

Bible Verse: *"All Scripture is God-breathed and is useful for teaching, rebuking, correcting and training in righteousness, so that the servant of God may be thoroughly equipped for every good work."* (2 Timothy 3:16-17 NIV)

Devotional: I've placed every story in Scripture to meet you exactly where you are. Is David facing Goliath? That's for the days you feel small against giant pressures. Esther's courage? It's My reminder that you're called "for such a time as this." The Prodigal Son? That's proof. My love chases you, even when you wander. These aren't fairy tales—they're blueprints for your battles. When anxiety whispers, remember how I calmed the storm. When friendships feel shaky, see how Jonathan and David's loyalty endured. I didn't write these words for dusty scrolls—I wrote them for *you*. Open your Bible, and I'll bridge the gap between thousands of years ago and today. Let's turn pages together—I'll show you how Joseph's trust in My plan can fuel your dreams or how Ruth's bravery can inspire your choices. Your life isn't a random chapter—it's part of My eternal story.

Closing Encouragement: "Your story matters to God—let His Word light your path."

April 21

Topic: Patience Like Noah

Opening Statement: Waiting rooms may test our nerves, but waiting rooms with God build our faith.

Bible Verse: *"Noah did everything just as God commanded him... and the floodwaters came on the earth."* Genesis 6:22; 7:10. (NIV)

Devotional: I know how fast social media moves—scroll, click, swipe. Yet real spiritual growth, which makes you a worldchanger, ripens slowly, like the ark that Noah framed plank by plank. While people laughed, I whispered courage into his heart: "Keep hammering." He trusted My timing more than his own timeline. Teens today still need that unshakable patience. When your prayer for a broken friendship feels unanswered, when college doors stay closed, remember that every delay can strengthen your faith muscles. Patience is not passive; it is active obedience in the unseen. Each algebra problem you solve, each dish you wash after dinner, is another wooden board nailed into your future purpose. I am crafting your calling with precision. The rain will come at the perfect moment, and you will be ready to float above the storms. Hold the hammer, keep building, and let My steady rhythm guide your heartbeat.

Closing Encouragement: Stay patient, keep building, and watch God transform today's wait into tomorrow's wave of victory.

April 22

Topic: Joy in the Little Things

Opening Statement: Discover the secret to true happiness by embracing life's simple joys.

Bible Verse: *"This is the day the Lord has made; let us rejoice and be glad in it."* —Psalm 118:24 (NIV)

Devotional: Hey there, My Joy-filled child. I've got a little secret to share with you: joy is everywhere. You might be searching for happiness in big events, but true joy often hides in the small, everyday moments. When you laugh with friends, feel the warmth of the sun, or enjoy a quiet moment with a good book, that's where joy lives. I'm here to guide you to see these moments for what they are—God-given gifts. Life can feel overwhelming, especially with school and social pressures, but when you pause and notice the beauty around you, you'll find joy is never far away. I'm always with you, helping you see the world through eyes of gratitude and wonder.

Closing Encouragement: Embrace each moment with an open heart, and you'll find joy waiting to surprise you daily.

April 23

Topic: The meaning of life.

Opening Statement: Have you ever wondered why you're here and what your life is about?

Bible Verse: *"For we are God's handiwork, created in Christ Jesus to do good works, which God prepared in advance for us to do."* Ephesians 2:10 (NIV):

Devotional: Listen, My seeking child. Before you posted your first photo or faced your first exam, I designed a lifemap packed with meaning, identity, and Kingdom impact. When the culture shouts, "Define yourself," listen instead to my gentle voice saying, "You are already defined—chosen, loved, empowered." Each talent, each dream, and even each setback fits perfectly into God's plan for you. Invite Me to your homework, playlists, and friendships, and I will turn ordinary moments into holy opportunities. When doubt creeps in at 2 a.m., open My Word, pray for ten seconds, and sense Me lighting up the path ahead. Your purpose isn't a distant puzzle; it's today's step of faith, guided by My ever-present counsel. Walk with Me, and you will discover the true meaning of life that algorithms can't replace.

Closing Encouragement: Step forward boldly, knowing I crafted you for a purpose only you can fulfill!

April 24

Topic: Forgiveness and Letting Go

Opening Statement: Are you ready to free yourself from the weight of grudges and find true peace?

Bible Verse: *"Bear with each other and forgive one another if any of you has a grievance against someone. Forgive as the Lord forgave you."* —Colossians 3:13 (NIV)

Devotional: Dear Sacred Heart, I am the Spirit calling out to your heart. I know the struggles you face and the burdens you carry. Holding onto resentment can feel like carrying a heavy weight on your soul. But remember, forgiveness is not just for the person who hurt you—it's a gift you give yourself. When you let go of anger, you open your heart to peace and healing. Imagine a life where your spirit is light and free, unburdened by past hurts. Forgiveness doesn't mean forgetting; it means choosing love over bitterness. I am here to help you release those emotional burdens. Allow My love to fill the spaces once occupied by resentment. Trust that I will guide you to a place of healing and joy.

Closing Encouragement: Embrace the freedom of forgiveness and let love lead your way.

April 25

Topic: Faith and Surrender

Opening Statement: One small "yes" to God can flip your story from stressed to unstoppable.

Bible Verse: *"Trust in the Lord with all your heart and lean not on your own understanding; in all your ways submit to him, and he will make your paths straight."* — Proverbs 3:56 (NIV).

Devotional: Dear daring child, I breathe courage into your lungs. You scroll past highlight reels that promise quick fame, but I invite you to a deeper story. When homework piles, friends drift, and the future resembles a buffering screen, whisper My name. Surrender is not quitting; it's handing Me the controller I designed. I see the hidden fears behind your memes and the secret dreams under your hoodie. Trust My code: "All things work together" even when Wi-Fi drops. Push faith in past feelings; follow the GPS of My Word. As you surrender, your heart updates, anxiety uninstalls, and hope uploads. I am the Shepherd who walks your hallways, the power in your worship playlist, the light on tomorrow's path. Give Me every test, text, and TikTok worry; I will turn them into testimonies. Just say Yes and watch the mountains move.

Closing Encouragement: Choose trust over control today, and watch the Shepherd lead you into fearless freedom.

April 26

Topic: Moral Cause and Effect

Opening Statement: Your choices today shape the life you live tomorrow.

Bible Verse: *"Do not be deceived: God cannot be mocked. A man reaps what he sows."* —Galatians 6:7 (NIV)

Devotional: I am here to guide you, dear one, in understanding the power of your actions. Each choice you make is like a seed planted in the soil of your life. Just as a farmer knows that planting good seeds brings a fruitful harvest, you, too, will see that what you sow comes back to you. When you choose kindness, honesty, and love, you cultivate a life filled with joy and peace. But when you sow seeds of negativity or selfishness, the consequences follow. Remember, I am with you in every decision. Lean on Me and let the love of Christ guide your steps. Your actions matter, and I am here to help you make choices that lead to a blessed future.

Closing Encouragement: Trust in Me and watch as the seeds of your good deeds blossom into a beautiful life.

April 27

Topic: Being Brave Like David

Opening statement: Sometimes, the biggest victories start with a small act of courage.

Bible Verse: *"But David said to Saul, 'Let no one lose heart on account of this Philistine; your servant will go and fight him.'"*
—1 Samuel 17:32 (NIV)

Devotional: Hey there, My brae teen, I see you. Maybe you're facing something intimidating—like standing up for what's right or trying something new. Just like David, who was just a young shepherd boy, you can be brave because you trust God's power, not your own strength. David didn't wait to be a giant; he believed God's courage was bigger than any challenge. When you feel afraid, remember that faith can turn tiny acts of bravery into mighty victories. I will call you to step out, even when it feels scary because I equip those who trust Me. You don't have to have all the answers or be perfect—just be willing to take a step of faith. I see your courage, and I am with you every step of the way.

Closing Encouragement: Be brave today, knowing that God's strength is made perfect in your weakness.

April 28

Topic: Importance of Honesty – Value truthfulness.

Opening Statement: Honesty is the foundation of trust and authenticity in your life.

Bible Verse: *"Therefore each of you must put off falsehood and speak truthfully to your neighbor, for we are all members of one body."* —Ephesians 4:25 (NIV)

Devotional: My honest one, I am the Spirit of Truth, guiding you to live a life of honesty and integrity. Remember that truthfulness sets you free in a world filled with pressures to conform and hide your true self. Speak with sincerity and let your words reflect your heart. When you are honest, you mirror the light of Christ within you, shining brightly for others to see.

Whenever you choose truth over deceit, you build strong trust-based relationships. It may sometimes feel challenging, especially when honesty has a cost. But remember, I am with you, providing courage and strength. Let your life be a testament to the power of truth, and watch how it transforms you and those around you.

Closing Encouragement: Choose honesty, and let your life be a beacon of light and truth.

April 29

Topic: Divine Guidance and Synchronicity

Opening Statement: Have you ever wondered if everything happens for a reason?

Bible Verse: *"Trust in the Lord with all your heart and lean not on your own understanding; in all your ways submit to him, and he will make your paths straight."* Proverbs 3:5-6 (NIV):

Devotional: I am here, guiding you through the twists and turns of life. You might see coincidences, but I see divine synchronicity. Every event, every sign, is a brushstroke on the canvas of your journey. Trust that I work for your good, even when the path seems unclear. Feel my presence in the small moments—when a friend says just what you need to hear or when an unexpected opportunity arises. I am weaving your story with purpose and love. Let go of the need to understand everything. Instead, lean into my promises and watch as I align your steps with my divine plan. Embrace the adventure of faith, knowing you are never alone.

Closing Encouragement: Trust in my guidance and watch as your life becomes a masterpiece of hope and purpose.

April 30

Topic: Opportunities and Barriers to Learning

Opening Statement: Education is a powerful tool, and how you choose to wield it can shape your future.

Bible Verse: *"The heart of the discerning acquires knowledge, for the ears of the wise seek it out."* (Proverbs 18:15 NIV)

Devotional: My studious child, I see your obstacles in pursuing knowledge. Whether it's a lack of resources, the pressure to fit in, or the distractions that pull you away from your studies, I understand your struggles. But remember, education is not just about grades; it's about discovering your purpose and the gifts I've placed within you.

You have access to opportunities that can open doors through mentors, online resources, or community programs. Don't let barriers define your journey; let them strengthen your resolve. Seek My guidance in every challenge, and you will find wisdom and clarity. Trust that I have equipped you with everything you need to succeed.

Closing Encouragement: Embrace every learning opportunity, for you are uncovering the incredible future I have planned for you through education. **Topic:** Opportunities and Barriers to Learning

May 1

Topic: Finding Courage in Faith

Opening Statement: Your journey isn't just about where you're going; it's about who's with you.

Bible Verse: *"Be strong and courageous. Do not be afraid; do not be discouraged, for the Lord your God will be with you wherever you go."* —Joshua 1:9 (NIV)

Devotional: Hello there, brave soul! I know the world seems significant, and you might feel small sometimes. School, friendships, plans for the future—it can all feel like a giant puzzle with pieces that keep changing shape. I want you to pause momentarily, take a deep breath, and listen to these ancient yet ever-fresh words: "Be strong and courageous."

These words were spoken to Joshua, a young leader facing huge responsibilities. And they are for you, too. They are not a call to muster up your strength but an invitation to rely on My unending presence. I am the source of your courage. You're not stepping into the hallways, onto the field, or up to the stage alone. I am with you, unwaveringly, in every challenge, every decision, and every dream. My presence is your security blanket, always there to support you.

Closing Encouragement: Now, go light up your world!

May 2

Topic: Spiritual Strength

Opening Statement: When you look beyond your fear, you will see Me.

Bible Verse: *My God has sent his angel," he said, "to shut the lions' mouths so that they can't touch me, for I am innocent before God; nor, sir, have I wronged you."* Daniel 6: 22 TLB

Devotional: When the waves of peer pressure threaten to engulf you, stand firm on the unshakable foundation of My Word. Rely on My strength, not your own, for it is in your weakness that My power is most evident. Look to the examples of Joseph, who fled from temptation, and Daniel, who stood firm in faith. You are part of this lineage of grace and strength, and your faith will guide you through any storm.

As you navigate the currents of popularity and persuasion, hold tightly to what is true, honorable, just, pure, lovely, and commendable. In doing so, you become a beacon of My light, a testament to My unchanging love. You are not alone in this journey. I am a steadfast companion within you, empowering you to rise above and walk the path I have set before you.

Closing Encouragement: Don't let life hold you back.

May 3

Topic: A balanced life.

Hear Me as I guide you through the delicate dance of balancing your studies, athletic pursuits, and spiritual growth.

Bible Verse: *"Commit to the Lord whatever you do, and he will establish your plans."* —Proverbs 16:3 (NIV)

Reflection: My child, I know the weight of the responsibilities on your shoulders. You rush from class to the field, from homework to practice, each demanding your best. But remember, I am with you in every moment, the steady hand upon your life.

See each task as an opportunity to experience My presence. Let your studies be an act of worship, for in gaining knowledge; you glimpse a fraction of My infinite wisdom. On the field, exhibit the fruits of My Spirit; let your sportsmanship testify to My love and grace.

Do not let the pace of the day trouble your heart. Come to Me when you are weary; I will give you rest. Draw from My Word in the quiet moments you find, for it is your source of strength and peace. Let My whispers shape your routine, and My love be the rhythm of your life. Walk confidently through your day, for you are never alone. I am guiding you, strengthening you, and rejoicing in the beautiful balance you are achieving.

Closing Encouragement: Keep your heart attuned to Mine, and together, we will gracefully navigate each day.

May 4

Topic: Comfort in the Mourning of a Beloved Pet

Bible Verse: *"Your righteousness is like the highest mountains, your justice like the great deep. You, Lord, preserve both people and animals."* —Psalm 36:6 (NIV)

Reflection: Beloved child, as you face the quiet absence left by your cherished pet, I am here amidst the silence. Your sorrow is known, your tears seen, and your heartache felt deeply in My own spirit. The companionship and joy your pet brought into your life reflected my love for all creation. Remember that I care for each sparrow that falls, and how much more for a precious one who has shared in your life's journey? In this tender moment of loss, let the love you've given and received be a testament to the bond that transcends life and death. While your pet no longer trots by your side, the love remains in My eternal care. Take comfort in knowing that in My kingdom, every creature finds peace, and love never fades—it only transforms.

Closing Encouragement: In your loss, remember that the love shared with your pet is a glimpse of my everlasting love for all My creation.

May 5

Topic: Finding Strength in Weakness

Bible Verse: *"But he said to me, 'My grace is sufficient for you, for my power is made perfect in weakness.' Therefore I will boast all the more gladly about my weaknesses so that Christ's power may rest on me."* 2 Corinthians 12:9 (NIV)

Reflection: My beloved child, in the depths of your heart, where doubt often lingers, remember that I am always there. The world may urge you to be strong, to conceal your struggles, to strive for flawlessness. Yet, I see your trials, your anxieties, your perceived imperfections – and I cherish you all the more for them. In each hesitant step, every instance of vulnerability, My strength is poised to manifest. I have not tasked you to traverse this path in solitude or to bear the burden solely by your own power. Allow Me to be your strength, your fortress, your sanctuary. When the world whirls in chaos, let My grace be the anchor for your soul. In Me, your weaknesses are transformed into a tapestry of My power – a narrative of triumph not through human endeavor, but through divine love.

Closing Encouragement: Stand tall in your weakness, for it is the canvas on which My strength is most brilliantly painted.

May 6

Topic: Prayer for Beginners: How to Connect with God Daily

Bible Verse: *"Be still, and know that I am God."* —Psalm 46:10

Reflection: My Dear Child, In the quiet of your room or under the vast, starry sky, know I am right there with you. Starting a conversation with Me doesn't require grand words or perfect poise. Just as you are, come to Me. Whether your heart is heavy or light, your day mundane or extraordinary, bring it all into our time together. Whisper, sing, or sit silently—each moment is precious to Me. Begin with gratitude, for it opens your heart to My presence. Share your joys, your fears, your questions. Remember, prayer is simply opening your heart to Me, your constant companion. Don't fret about the 'how'— the 'who' matters most. And you're talking to Someone who loves you more deeply than you can imagine.

Closing Encouragement: You are loved beyond measure, every day, in every prayer—never forget that.

May 7

Topic: Handling Peer Pressure with Grace and Strength

As you walk through the halls of your life, know that I am with you, whispering courage into your heart to stand firm against the tides of peer pressure.

Bible Verse: "Do not conform to the pattern of this world, but be transformed by the renewing of your mind." Let this be your shield and your compass. Romans 12:2,

Reflection: I understand your challenges, the desire to be accepted, and the fear of separation. Yet, remember, I have called you to be distinct, a precious light in the dim corridors of conformity. When friends or trends pull you towards paths that are not yours to walk, pause, and breathe in My presence. Ask for wisdom, and I will pour it into you, overflowing like a river of peace. When the pressure mounts, envision My hands shaping your resolve, molding your spirit to reflect My love and grace. You are stronger than you realize, for My strength sustains you. You are never alone; I am your constant companion, guiding you to choose grace over conformity, faith over acceptance, and eternal truth over fleeting approval.

Closing Encouragement: Stand tall, My blessed one, for you carry My grace and strength within you.

May 8

Topic: Dealing with Doubt: Keeping Faith in Tough Times.

Take courage, for I am here, turning your doubts into stepping stones for a faith that can move mountains.

Bible Verse: *"Trust in the Lord with all your heart and lean not on your own understanding."* —Proverbs 3:5

Reflection: My Beloved Child, In these moments when the fabric of your faith feels frayed by the relentless pull of doubt, I am closer than ever. Doubt is not a sign of weakness but a step toward growth. It's the soil where a deeper, more resilient faith can take root.

You're standing at the threshold of what you can see and what you believe. It's where I, come in, whispering truth to your spirit, comforting you through the Word, and guiding you into all truth. Remember, faith is not the absence of doubt; it's choosing to trust Me even when the answers aren't clear.

When the voices of doubt shout loud, let your faith be louder. Press into Me, read My promises, and hold them close to your heart. I am your rock, your foundation, and I will not let you be shaken.

Closing Encouragement: Stay strong, for your faith will shine brightest when the night is dark.

May 9

Topic: Overcoming Fear of the Future: Trusting God's Plan

Bible verse: "For I know the plans I have for you," declares the Lord, "plans to prosper you and not to harm you, plans to give you hope and a future." Bible Verse: Jeremiah 29:11

Reflection: My child, I know the thoughts that swirl in your mind when you think about tomorrow. The uncertainty, the what-ifs, and the fears about what lies ahead. But remember, I am with you always. I am not a distant observer; I am walking alongside you, guiding you every step of the way. My plans for you are not just mere sketches but are drawn with love, precision, and your best interests at heart. They are plans to prosper you, not to harm you. Trusting in my plan means letting go of your fears and embracing the future with courage and peace. Even when the path seems unclear, hold onto my promises. Let your heart be steady, and your mind is at peace, knowing that I am in control. Step forward into each new day with confidence, for I am leading you to a future filled with hope.

Closing Encouragement: Step boldly into the future, for I am already there, waiting with open arms to guide and bless you.

May 10

Topic: Choosing Friends Wisely

Opening Statement: "Embrace wisdom's light as you navigate friendships, for the company you keep shapes your path to righteousness."

Bible Verse: *"Walk with the wise and become wise, for a companion of fools suffers harm." This verse holds the key to understanding the impact of our friendships. Just as iron sharpens iron, so do our friends shape us."* Proverbs 13:20. NIV

Reflection: Blessed Teen, I am the gentle whisper guiding your heart, urging you to walk in the light of wisdom. Today, let's talk about the power of positive friendships.

Reflection: As you journey through adolescence, you'll encounter many companions. Some will lift you higher, while others may lead you astray. Pause and ponder: Are my friends encouraging me to grow spiritually, mentally, and emotionally? Do they share my values and aspirations? Surround yourself with those who challenge you to become the best version of yourself, uplift your spirit, and walk alongside you on the path of righteousness.

Closing encouragement: Trust in Me, dear one, for I have plans to prosper you and not to harm you, plans to give you hope and a future (Jeremiah 29:11). Choose your friends wisely, for they will accompany you on this journey of faith.

May 11

Topic: Navigating Family Conflict with a Christ-Like Attitude

Opening Statement: Amid family conflict, your heart may feel heavy and your spirit weary, but know this: I am with you, guiding you to respond with love, grace, and wisdom, just as Christ did.

Bible Verse: *"Blessed are the peacemakers, for they will be called children of God."* —Matthew 5:9. NIV

Reflection: Dear Beloved Teen, When tensions rise, and voices clash within your family, it's easy to react in frustration or anger. But remember, dear one, that as a child of God, you are called to be a peacemaker. Take a deep breath and pause before responding. Ask yourself, "What would Jesus do in this situation?" Seek His guidance in prayer, and let His peace rule in your heart.

Approach conflicts with humility and empathy, seeking to understand others' perspectives before expressing your own. Choose your words carefully, speaking with kindness and respect. Above all, extend forgiveness freely, just as Christ has forgiven you.

Though resolving family conflicts may not always be easy, trust that I am working in and through you to bring about reconciliation and restoration. Your Christ-like attitude can be a beacon of hope and healing within your family.

Closing Encouragement: May you follow in Jesus's footsteps, bringing His love and peace into every aspect of your family relationships. Remember, you are never alone, for I am with you always.

May 12

Topic: Being a Light: Sharing Your Faith at School

Bible Verse: Matthew 5:14-16— *"You are the world's light. A city set on a hill cannot be hidden. Nor do people light a lamp and put it under a basket, but on a stand, and it gives light to all in the house. In the same way, let your light shine before others, so that they may see your good works and give glory to your Father who is in heaven."*

Opening Statement: You carry a divine light within you, meant to illuminate the darkest corners of your school.

Reflection: Hello, beloved. I am the Holy Spirit and dwell within you to be a silent observer and empower you. Each day, as you walk through your school halls, you are on a mission field ripe for hope and transformation. It may feel daunting to stand out and share your faith in an environment that isn't always receptive. But remember, I am with you, providing the words when you feel speechless and the courage when fear whispers doubts.

When you choose to be a light, you are not just sharing words; you offer a lifeline of faith through your actions, compassion, and presence. It's in the simple acts of kindness, the integrity in your work, and the respect you show to others that your peers see Me in you. Let's ignite hope together, showing what it means to live a life fueled by faith, not just in church, but right here in the hub of your daily life—your school.

Closing Encouragement: Shine boldly and brightly, for your light is a beacon of hope in the hallways of your school.

May 13

Topic: Devotional: Discovering Your Spiritual Gifts.

Opening Statement: I have gifted you uniquely, dear child, for great purposes in My kingdom.

Bible Verse: *"As each has received a gift, use it to serve one another, as good stewards of God's varied grace."* —1 Peter 4:10 NIV

Reflection: Hey there! It's me, the Spiritual force within you. You know, discovering the gifts I've placed within you can be one of the most exciting adventures of your life. Think about it – each of you has been equipped with unique talents and abilities, not just to succeed in life but to make a real impact in the lives of others. Whether it's wisdom, faith, healing, or teaching – these aren't just random; they're a part of a divine plan.

As you enter your teenage years, it might seem like there's pressure all around you – to fit in, excel in school, and figure out who you're supposed to be. Amidst all this, remember that one of the most rewarding journeys you can embark on is the exploration of your spiritual gifts. This isn't just about knowing what you're good at, but it's about connecting deeply with Me and using your abilities to serve and uplift others.

Challenge yourself to serve in new ways, maybe in your community or church. Watch how, through serving, your understanding of your purpose becomes more apparent. You're not just discovering what you're good at but learning who you're meant to be.

Closing Encouragement: Embrace your gifts; you will discover paths to joy and purpose beyond your imagination through them.

May 14

Topic: The Bible and Self-Image: Seeing Yourself as God Sees You.

Opening Statement: Remember, you are a masterpiece, crafted by the hands of God.

Bible Verse: Psalm 139:14 – Niv *"I praise you because I am fearfully and wonderfully made; your works are wonderful, I know that full well."*

Reflection: Hello, dear one; I am the spiritual power who dwells within you. I want you to see yourself through My eyes—the eyes of the One who created the universe, yet took the time to design you intricately. In your world, it's easy to feel less than others, compare yourself to others, and feel inadequate. But remember, I made you unique, with gifts and a purpose only you can fulfill. Your worth isn't measured by worldly standards but by My eternal love and the sacrifice of Jesus, who died so that you might live fully. Each time you doubt your worth, remind yourself you are not an accident. You are chosen, beloved, and precious in My sight. Do not be shaped by the fleeting judgments of the world, but be transformed by renewing your mind with My word. See yourself as I see you: perfect in your imperfections, firm in your weaknesses, and beautiful in your own fantastic way.

Closing Encouragement: Stand tall, for you are created in the image of an Almighty God; walk confidently today, knowing you are loved and valued beyond measure.

May 15

Topic: Tackling Temptation

Opening Statement: "Temptation is a common challenge, but remember, you are not facing it alone."

Bible Verse: 1 Corinthians 10:13 (NIV) *"No temptation has overtaken you except what is common to mankind. And God is faithful; He will not let you be tempted beyond what you can bear. But when you are tempted, he will also provide a way out so that you can endure it."*

Reflection: Hello, dear one. I understand the struggles you face, the moments when temptations seem overwhelming. It's part of being human, of growing up. But let me assure you, you are not alone in this journey. Each temptation is a chance to make a choice—a choice to choose strength over surrender, faith over falter. I am here, always ready to help you. When you feel the tug of something less than good, pause and reach out to me.

Remember, for every temptation, I provide a way out. It might be a distracting call from a friend, an unexpected shift in circumstances, or a sudden reminder of your own values and dreams. These are not coincidences; they are my way of showing you the path to victory. Trust in me, lean on me, and together, we can overcome any challenge. Let's focus not on the temptation but on the triumph that awaits.

Closing Encouragement: "Stand strong, for your strength is greater when we stand together."

May 16

Topic: Faith and Purpose: Finding Your God-Given Calling

Bible Verse: Ephesians 2:10 (NIV) *"For we are God's handiwork, created in Christ Jesus to do good works, which God prepared us to do."*

Opening Statement: Did you know you are designed with a unique purpose only you can fulfill?

Reflection: Hello, dear one. I am the Holy Spirit, always with you, guiding you gently towards the paths you are meant to walk. Understanding your purpose isn't about discovering something new; it's about uncovering the incredible truth that I have woven into the very fabric of your being. You are not an accident. Every talent you have, every passion that excites you, and the challenges you face are part of a grand design. As you step forward in faith, trust in the Lord and the blueprint He has laid out for you. Remember, finding your purpose is not a moment but a journey that involves walking closely with God through every season of life. As you navigate this journey, ask me to open your eyes to the needs around you and to fill your heart with the courage to respond — for in responding, you step into the good works God has prepared for you.

Closing Encouragement: Keep your heart open, listen closely, and let your faith lead you to God's remarkable purpose for you.

May 17

Topic: Handling Heartbreak with Hope and Healing

Bible Verse: Psalm 34:18 (NIV) *"The Lord is close to the brokenhearted and saves those who are crushed in spirit."*

Opening Statement: Even in the shadow of heartbreak, you never walk alone; I am always beside you.

Reflection: Dear one, I know the pain you feel might seem unbearable right now. The ache of a broken heart can make even the simplest tasks feel monumental. But remember, I am here with you. Just as I was with David when he penned his psalms of lament, I am with you in your moments of sorrow. I am the Comforter, sent to heal your wounds and mend the pieces of your shattered heart.

Through my presence, find the strength to face each day with renewed hope. Let my love seep into the cracks of your heart, for it is in your weaknesses and brokenness that my strength is made perfect. As you navigate through this season of healing, keep your eyes on me, and trust in my unfailing love for you. I am not only your healer but also your redeemer, turning your deepest hurts into avenues of growth and new beginnings. Lean on me, and let my peace fill your heart as you journey towards healing and restoration.

Closing Encouragement: Hold on to hope, for I have great plans for your future, plans to prosper you and not to harm you, plans to give you hope and a future.

May 18

Topic: The True Meaning of Christian Love in a Dating World.

Opening Statement: In a world where dating often gets tangled with fleeting feelings and superficial measures, true Christian love is a beacon of genuine, selfless affection.

Bible Verse: 1 Corinthians 13:4-5 (NIV) — *"Love is patient, love is kind. It does not envy, it does not boast, it is not proud. It does not dishonor others, it is not self-seeking, it is not easily angered, it keeps no record of wrongs."*

Reflection: Hello, dear one. As you navigate the complexities of teenage relationships and the dating world, remember the essence of love I have shown you through Jesus Christ. True Christian love is not just an emotion felt but a deliberate choice made—a choice to be patient, kind, and seek the best for others above yourself.

In your relationships, whether budding friendships or deeper romantic connections, strive to reflect My nature. It's easy to get caught up in the excitement of someone new or feel the pressure of peers chasing the wrong things. But I call you to a higher standard. Love that mimics My love is not boastful or arrogant; it does not hurt others or focus solely on personal desires.

Consider how your actions and choices align with the love described in 1 Corinthians 13. Are you patient with others? Do you practice kindness, even when it's challenging? True love—the kind I want for you—uplifts and heals. It transcends physical attraction and emotional bonds to foster a connection that builds up, nurtures, and endures in righteousness.

Closing Encouragement: Walk in love, just as Christ loved us and gave Himself up for us; let this love be your guide in all relationships.

May 19

Topic: Gratitude - Counting Your Blessings Even When It's Hard

Opening Statement: "Even in the storm, there is a hidden treasure waiting to be discovered."

Bible Verse: James 1:2-3 (NIV) *"Consider it pure joy, my brothers and sisters, whenever you face trials of many kinds, because you know that the testing of your faith produces perseverance."*

Reflection: Hello, beloved one. I know that sometimes the skies of your life seem gray, and the winds feel cold. But remember, I am with you, whispering amid the storm. Each challenge you face is a hurdle and a stepping stone designed for your growth. In these moments, when joy seems elusive, looking for the small blessings can transform your perspective.

Think of the laughter shared with a friend, the comfort of a warm meal, or even the peace of a quiet moment alone. These are my gifts to you, reminders that my love is constant and unwavering. By recognizing these blessings, your heart will learn to dance in the rain, knowing that each drop contributes to your faith and character growth. So, lift your eyes from the mud underfoot to the rainbow that awaits.

Closing Encouragement: "Keep your heart open, for gratitude turns what we have into enough, and more."

May 20

Topic: Combating Loneliness with Community and Connection

Bible Verse: *"Where two or three gather in my name, there am I with them."* —Matthew 18:20 (NIV)

Opening Statement: In a world filled with digital connections, it's easy to feel alone, but true community and connection are found in Christ.

Reflection: Beloved, I see the moments when you feel isolated, even when surrounded by people. Loneliness can creep in and make you feel disconnected, but remember, you are never truly alone. I am with you always and have placed you in a community where you can find support and love. Reach out to those around you—your family, friends, and church community.

These relationships are gifts from Me, designed to help combat the loneliness the enemy wants you to feel. When you gather with others in My name, you invite My presence into your midst. In these moments of genuine connection, you will find the comfort and companionship you seek. Do not shy away from opening your heart and allowing others to be part of your journey. Embrace the community I have given you, for it is there that you will tangibly experience My love.

Closing Encouragement: Remember, you are surrounded by a community that loves you, and together, you will find strength and companionship in Me.

May 21

Topic: Coping with academic stress through faith.

Opening Statement: When academic stress feels overwhelming, remember that I am with you, guiding and strengthening you through every challenge.

Bible Verse: *"Come to Me, all you who labor and are heavy laden, and I will give you rest"* (Matthew 11:28, NKJV).

Reflection: My dear child, I see the weight of your academic responsibilities pressing down on you. The tests, assignments, and expectations can feel like mountains too high to climb. But I want you to know that you are not alone. I am here with you, ready to offer My peace and guidance.

Remember the story of David and Goliath? David was young and faced a giant that seemed impossible to defeat. But with faith and trust in Me, he overcame. You, too, can face your academic giants with My strength. Let go of your worries, focus on doing your best, and leave the rest in My hands.

Balancing schoolwork and personal life can be incredibly challenging, especially when you want to succeed and make everyone proud. Yet, amid your busy schedule, finding moments of rest and connection with Me is essential. These moments will recharge your spirit and provide the clarity you need to tackle your tasks. Remember, I am not just a distant observer but an ever-present help in times of trouble. Lean on Me, and I will lighten your load. Pray for guidance, stay organized, and trust that with Me, all things are possible.

When you feel stressed or anxious about your studies, turn to Me. Take a moment to pray, breathe, and remind yourself that your worth is not measured by grades or achievements but by My love for you.

Closing Encouragement: You are stronger than you think, and with My help, you can overcome any academic challenge.

May 22

Topic: Discerning God's Voice in a World Full of Noise.

Opening Statement: Discerning God's voice is essential for your spiritual journey in a world overflowing with distractions and competing voices.

Bible Verse: *"My sheep hear my voice, and I know them, and they follow me."* (John 10:27 ESV)

Reflection: Beloved, I know how noisy the world can be. Social media, friends, school, and countless other distractions constantly await your attention. Yet, amidst all this noise, I am calling out to you, eager to guide and comfort you. Just as a shepherd knows his sheep, I know you intimately and desire you to recognize My voice.

Spend time with Me in prayer and immerse yourself in My Word. As you do, My voice will become more apparent, like a gentle whisper amidst the chaos. Trust that I always speak to you, providing wisdom, peace, and direction. When you tune your heart to hear Me, you will find clarity and purpose even on the busiest days.

Closing Encouragement: Stay close to Me, and you will always find guidance and peace.

May 23

Topic: The Adventure of Trusting God with Your Dreams.

Opening Statement: Embrace the adventure of trusting God with your dreams, for He knows your best path.

Bible Verse: *"Trust in the Lord with all your heart and lean not on your own understanding; in all your ways submit to him, and he will make your paths straight."* —Proverbs 3:5-6 (NIV)

Reflection: Dear one, I know the dreams and desires within your heart. Each was placed there for a purpose, a unique journey crafted by God Himself. When you trust in the Lord and submit your dreams to Him, you embark on an incredible adventure filled with MY guidance and blessings. It's not always easy to relinquish control and rely on My timing, but remember, My ways are higher and wiser than yours.

As you navigate the challenges and uncertainties, lean on me for strength and wisdom. I will lead you through each step, ensuring your dreams align with God's plan. Trust that My timing is impeccable, and My love for you is unending. When you surrender your dreams to Me, you open the door to possibilities beyond your imagination.

Closing Encouragement: Believe in trusting God with your dreams, for God will lead you to a future filled with hope and purpose.

May 24

Topic: Staying Faithful in a Culture of Instant Gratification.

Opening Statement: Staying faithful can be a constant struggle in a world that demands instant satisfaction.

Bible Verse: *"But those who wait on the Lord shall renew their strength; they shall mount up with wings like eagles, they shall run and not be weary, they shall walk and not faint."* — Isaiah 40:31 (NKJV)

Reflection: My beloved, I know the pressures you face daily—the lure of quick fixes, the temptation to take the easy path. In a culture where everything is at your fingertips, remaining patient and waiting for My perfect timing is challenging. But I am here to remind you that true strength and fulfillment come from Me, not from the fleeting pleasures of this world. When you choose to stay faithful, even when it's tough, you allow Me to work in your life in powerful ways. Trust in My promises, and you will find that I provide far more abundantly than anything the world can offer. Remember, whenever you resist the urge for instant gratification and turn to Me, you grow stronger in spirit and closer to your true purpose.

Closing Encouragement: Stay strong, for I am with you always, guiding you toward the true and lasting joy that comes from faithful perseverance.

May 25

Topic: Resisting Materialism: Contentment in a Consumerist Society

Opening Statement: Finding true contentment can seem like an uphill battle in a world that constantly pushes you to want more.

Bible Verse: *"But godliness with contentment is great gain."* —1 Timothy 6:6 (NIV)

Reflection: My beloved child, I see the pressures you face every day—the advertisements that tell you happiness comes from owning the latest gadgets, the social media posts that make you feel like you need to keep up with everyone else. But remember, true joy and contentment don't come from the things you own; they come from knowing who you are in Me.

You were created with a purpose far greater than what this world can offer. I call you to live differently, to find satisfaction not in material things but in My love and my purpose for you. When you feel the pull to buy more and to compare yourself to others, turn to Me. Let My presence fill the void that nothing else can.

Embrace the simplicity of a life focused on spiritual wealth, and you will find a peace that surpasses all understanding. Trust in My provision, and know that I will meet all your needs according to My riches in glory.

Closing Encouragement: Choose contentment today, and let My love be enough for you.

May 26

Topic: The Role of Worship in Everyday Life

Opening Statement: Worship is not just a Sunday activity but a lifestyle that invites God's presence into every moment of our lives.

Bible Verse: *"Yet a time is coming and has now come when the true worshipers will worship the Father in the Spirit and in truth, for they are the kind of worshipers the Father seeks."* —John 4:23 (NIV)

Reflection: Blessed child, I want to guide you into a deeper understanding of worship. Worship is more than singing songs at church; it's a way of life. Every time you choose to honor God with your actions, words, and thoughts, you are worshiping.

When you help a friend, show kindness to a stranger, or pray for someone in need, you live a worship life. Your everyday choices reflect your love for God and desire to please God. Remember, true worshipers worship in spirit and truth. This means being sincere and genuine in your faith, not just performing rituals. Let your worship flow from a heart that genuinely loves and seeks God.

Closing Encouragement: Embrace worship daily, and watch how it transforms you and those around you.

May 27

Topic: Understanding Forgiveness: How to Let Go and Move Forward.

Opening Statement: Forgiveness is the key to freeing your heart from the burden of past hurts and moving forward in peace.

Bible Verse: *"Be kind and compassionate to one another, forgiving each other, just as in Christ God forgave you."* —Ephesians 4:32 (NIV)

Reflection: My beloved child, I see the pain and hurt you carry within your heart. Forgiveness may seem daunting, especially when the wounds are deep. But remember, forgiveness is not about excusing the wrong done to you; it's about releasing the hold it has on your heart. Just as Christ forgave you, I call you to extend that grace to others. When you forgive, you let go of the bitterness that chains you to the past and allow My peace to fill your heart.

Imagine carrying a heavy backpack everywhere you go. Each unforgiven hurt adds another stone, weighing you down and making your journey harder. By choosing to forgive, you are removing those stones, one by one, and lightening your load. It is not easy, but with My help, it is possible. I am with you, giving you the strength and compassion you need. Trust Me to heal your heart and guide you forward.

Closing Encouragement: Embrace forgiveness and experience the freedom and peace I have prepared for you.

May 28

Topic: The Challenge of Keeping the Sabbath in a Busy World

Opening Statement: Finding time to rest and honor the Sabbath can feel like an impossible challenge in a world that never stops.

Bible Verse: *"Remember the Sabbath day by keeping it holy."* —Exodus 20:8 (NIV)

Reflection: Dear one, I see your busy life, filled with school, activities, and the constant pull of technology. It's easy to feel overwhelmed and forget the importance of rest. But remember, the Sabbath is a gift from Me, a day set aside for you to recharge, reflect, and reconnect with Me.

Keeping the Sabbath isn't just about following a rule; it's about embracing a rhythm of rest that renews your spirit and strengthens your relationship with Me. When you take this time, you allow Me to fill you with peace and clarity amidst the chaos. It might seem difficult to set aside your to-do list, but trust that you will find a more profound sense of purpose and joy in doing so.

Please take a moment each week to pause, breathe, and spend time with Me. Whether through prayer, reading the Bible, or simply being still, these moments will refresh your soul and help you navigate the busyness of life with a calm heart.

Closing Encouragement: Embrace the Sabbath as a precious gift, and let it be when you draw near to God and find proper rest.

May 29

Topic: Addressing Anxiety: Finding Peace in Scripture

Opening Statement: Anxiety can feel overwhelming, but God's Word offers a refuge of peace that transcends all understanding.

Bible Verse: *"Do not be anxious about anything, but in every situation, by prayer and petition, with thanksgiving, present your requests to God. And the peace of God, which transcends all understanding, will guard your hearts and your minds in Christ Jesus."* —Philippians 4:6-7 (NIV)

Reflection: My dear child, I see your anxious heart and weight. When you face overwhelming thoughts and worries, remember that I am here with you, ready to offer you My peace. Turn to Me in prayer, share your fears and concerns, and let My peace guard your heart and mind. Scripture is your anchor in turbulent times, a reminder that you are never alone. As you read My Word, let it wash over you and calm your spirit. Trust in My promises, and let My love soothe your anxious thoughts. I am your refuge and strength, an ever-present help in trouble. Rest in Me, and know I hold your future in My hands.

Closing Encouragement: Embrace My peace today, for I am always with you, guiding you through every storm.

May 30

Topic: Boldness in Prayer: Asking and Receiving

Opening Statement: When you pray to Me, come with confidence, knowing that I am eager to listen and answer.

Bible Verse: *"This is the confidence we have in approaching God: that if we ask anything according to his will, he hears us."* —1 John 5:14 (NIV)

Reflection: Dear one, I want you to understand the power of boldness in your prayers. When you approach Me, do so with the confidence that I am always listening. Too often, you might feel hesitant or unsure, thinking your requests are too small or too big for Me. Remember, I care about every detail of your life. Just as a loving parent delights in hearing from their child, I delight in hearing from you. Bring your worries, dreams, and every desire of your heart before Me. Trust that I know what is best for you and that I am working all things for your good. Your boldness in prayer shows your faith in My love and power. Do not hold back. Ask, and you shall receive, seek, find, and knock, and the door will open.

Closing Encouragement: Be courageous in your prayers, for I am with you and eager to respond to your faith.

May 31

Serving Others: The Joy of Selflessness

Opening Statement: Embrace the joy of selflessly serving others and discover how it can transform your life.

Bible Verse: *"Do not merely look out for your own personal interests, but also for the interests of others."* —Philippians 2:4 (NASB)

Reflection: My beloved, I want to share the secret to true joy and fulfillment: selflessly serving others. When you shift your focus from yourself to those around you, you open your heart to a world of blessings and purpose. Look at the life of Jesus; He came not to be served but to serve and to give His life to many. Every act of kindness echoes my love and compassion for those in need, no matter how small.

Consider your friends, family, and even strangers. How can you make their day a little brighter? It could be a kind word, a helping hand, or simply listening when someone needs to talk. As you serve others, you will find that your worries and burdens become lighter, and your heart fills with My peace and joy. Remember, My power is made perfect in your willingness to give of yourself.

Closing Encouragement: Serve others with a joyful heart, and you will receive even more in giving.

June 1

Topic: Christian Perspective on Environmental Care.

Bible Verse: *"The earth is the Lord's, and everything in it, the world, and all who live in it."* —Psalm 24:1 (NIV)

Opening Statement: As stewards of God's creation, we are called to care for the environment with love and responsibility.

Reflection: Dear one, I am with you always, guiding you to live a life that honors Me in every way. The world around you is a beautiful creation by My movement, filled with wonders that reflect My glory and majesty. Every tree, every animal, and every part of nature is a testament to My creative power. You have been given the incredible responsibility to care for this earth, to nurture it, and to protect it.

When you see pollution, waste, or destruction of natural habitats, remember that it grieves My heart. Your actions, no matter how small, can make a difference. Choose to recycle, conserve water, and protect wildlife. Advocate for cleaner environments and sustainable living. By doing so, you are living out your faith and showing love to creation and the Creator.

Closing Encouragement: Embrace your role as a caretaker of God's earth, and let your actions reflect His love and respect for all He has made.

June 2

Topic: The Strength of Patience: Waiting on God's Timing

Bible Verse: *"But they who wait for the Lord shall renew their strength; they shall mount up with wings like eagles; they shall run and not be weary; they shall walk and not faint."* —Isaiah 40:31 (ESV)

Opening Statement: Patience is a mighty strength, and waiting on God's timing is a profound act of faith.

Reflection: Dear one, I know that waiting can be challenging, especially when you're eager to see your dreams come true or overcome your struggles. Feeling frustrated or lost is easy when things don't happen as quickly as you'd like. However, remember that My timing is perfect, even when it doesn't align with your plans.

When you wait on Me, you are not waiting in vain. Each moment of patience strengthens your character, deepens your trust, and aligns your heart with My will. Just as the eagle soars effortlessly in the sky, your spirit will be lifted when you place your hope in Me. Trust that I am working in ways you cannot see, preparing you for the future I have designed just for you.

Embrace the journey with patience. You will find strength, growth, and a deeper connection with Me in the waiting. Let your heart be still, knowing that I hold your life in my hands and My plans for you are good.

Closing Encouragement: Trust in My timing, and you will discover a strength beyond measure and a peace that surpasses all understanding.

June 3

Topic: Balancing School, Sports, and Spirituality

Bible Verse: *"But seek first His kingdom and His righteousness, and all these things will be given to you as well."* —Matthew 6:33 (NIV)

Opening Statement: Balancing school, sports, and your spiritual life can feel overwhelming, but I am here to guide you through every challenge.

Reflection: Dear one, I know how busy your life can be. There is no room for Me between homework, sports practice, and spending time with friends. But remember, I am always with you, even in the hustle and bustle of your daily activities.

When you feel stressed about school, take a moment to breathe and pray. Invite Me to your studies, and I will give you the clarity and focus you need. Remember that your body is a temple of the Holy Spirit during sports activities. Honor Me with your dedication and teamwork, and I will strengthen you.

Finding time for Me is not about adding another task to your to-do list; it's about inviting Me into everything you do. When you seek My presence first, I will help you balance your responsibilities and find peace amid your busy schedules.

Closing Encouragement: Trust in Me, and I will help you find the perfect balance in your life.

June 4

Topic: Peer Pressure: Avoid influences that may lead you away from your values and beliefs

Opening Statement: In a world filled with diverse influences, standing firm in your values can be challenging but essential for a fulfilling life.

Bible Verse: *"Do not be misled: 'Bad company corrupts good character.'"* —1 Corinthians 15:33 (NIV)

Reflection: Dear one, I am with you always, guiding you through every moment of your life. You will encounter many voices in your journey, each vying for your attention. Some will uplift you, while others may try to lead you astray. It's crucial to discern which voices to heed and which to ignore. Peer pressure can be a powerful force, tempting you to compromise your beliefs for acceptance. Remember, your worth is not determined by the approval of others but by My unwavering love for you.

Surround yourself with those who encourage your faith and uplift your spirit. When you feel the weight of peer pressure, turn to Me. I will strengthen you to stand firm in your convictions. Trust that staying true to your values will bring you peace and joy that fleeting acceptance cannot. You are never alone, for I am with you, providing the courage you need to resist negative influences.

Closing Encouragement: Stay strong, beloved, and know that with My guidance, you can overcome any pressure and shine brightly in your faith.

June 5

Topic: Faith Community: Find a local church or faith-based group to stay connected spiritually.

Opening Statement: Being part of a faith community is essential for spiritual growth and encouragement.

Bible Verse: *"Let us not give up meeting together, as some are in the habit of doing, but encouraging one another—and all the more as you see the Day approaching."* —Hebrews 10:25 (NIV)

Reflection: My dear child, I understand that life can often feel overwhelming and lonely. In these times, it's important to remember that you are never truly alone. I have designed you to be part of a community, a family of believers who can support, encourage, and uplift you. Finding a local church or faith-based group can provide you with the spiritual nourishment and fellowship you need to stay strong in your faith. These communities allow you to grow, learn, and share your journey with others who understand and care for you.

They offer a safe space to explore your beliefs, ask questions, and deepen your relationship with Me. When you surround yourself with other believers, you will find strength, wisdom, and encouragement to face life's challenges. Remember, where two or three gather in My name, I am with them. Seek out a faith community and let My love flow through you and those around you.

Closing Encouragement: Stay connected to your faith community; you will find the strength and encouragement to walk your spiritual journey confidently and joyfully.

June 6

Topic: Personal Devotions - Maintain a Prayer and Bible Study Routine to Keep Your Faith Strong

Opening Statement: Maintaining a regular prayer and Bible study routine is essential to keeping your faith strong and vibrant.

Bible Verse: *"Your word is a lamp for my feet, a light on my path."* —Psalm 119:105 (NIV)

Reflection: I am your Spirit of Holiness dwelling in you, your guide and helper. In the busyness of your life, it's easy to neglect the time you spend with Me. Yet, these moments are where you find true strength and guidance. Imagine a day without checking your phone or talking to your friends— it feels incomplete. Similarly, your soul craves connection with Me through prayer and My Word. When you make time for personal devotions, you allow Me to fill you with peace, wisdom, and strength.

Think of the Bible as your spiritual GPS, guiding you through life's twists and turns. Prayer is your direct line to the Creator, where you can share your hopes, fears, and dreams. When you make these practices a routine, you build a foundation to withstand any storm. Let My presence be your constant companion, and let My Word light your daily path. Your faith will grow, and you'll discover the incredible plans I have for you.

Closing Encouragement: Stay faithful in your devotions, and watch how God transforms your life in amazing ways.

June 7

Topic: Communication - Regularly communicate with family to maintain strong relationships.

Opening Statement: Communication is the heartbeat of any relationship, especially within the family.

Bible Verse: *"Let your conversation be always full of grace, seasoned with salt, so that you may know how to answer everyone."* —Colossians 4:6 (NIV)

Reflection: Dear one, I am the Holy Spirit, and I reside within you, guiding you every step of your journey. Today, I want to talk to you about the importance of communication within your family. Your family is a gift from God, a unit designed to support, love, and nurture you. Regularly talking with your family strengthens these bonds and builds a foundation of trust and understanding. When you share your thoughts, listen with empathy, and respond with love, you mirror the grace that I pour into your heart.

Even when disagreements arise, approach them with patience and kindness. Remember, effective communication is not just about speaking but also about listening. Make time for your family, and let your conversations be filled with grace, as it reflects my presence in your life.

Closing Encouragement: Stay connected with your family through heartfelt communication, and watch your relationships flourish in love and understanding.

June 8

Topic: Ethical Decisions: Stay True to Your Moral and Ethical Beliefs in Academic and Work Environments

Opening Statement: Remain Faithful to who you are in God.

Bible Verse: *"Do not be conformed to this world, but be transformed by the renewal of your mind, that by testing you may discern what is the will of God, what is good and acceptable and perfect."* —Romans 12:2 (ESV)

Devotional: Beloved child, I see your heart and know the daily challenges in school and work. Remember, standing firm in your ethical beliefs is not always easy, but it is essential to your spiritual growth and witness.

Reflect on this truth: I call you to stand out in a world where you may be pressured to conform. Your moral and ethical beliefs reflect your faith in Me. When faced with decisions that test your integrity, seek My guidance. I will provide you with the strength and wisdom to choose what is right.

Consider Daniel, who is in a foreign land and under immense pressure but chooses to remain faithful to his convictions. His unwavering faithfulness not only protects him but also glorifies Me. Similarly, your commitment to ethical decisions in academics and the workplace sets you apart and honors Me. Even when it seems complicated, trust that I am with you, guiding you every step of the way.

Remember, the path of righteousness may be narrow but leads to abundant blessings. Hold fast to your principles, for in doing so; you reflect My light to the world.

Closing Encouragement: Stand firm in your faith and let your actions be a testament to My truth and love.

June 9

Topic: Prioritize Your Mental Well-Being

Opening Statement: Your mental well-being is precious; seeking help when needed is essential.

Bible Verse: *"Cast all your anxiety on him because he cares for you."* —1 Peter 5:7 (NIV)

Devotional: My beloved child, I see your struggles and the weight you carry in your mind. Life can be overwhelming, and feeling like you need support is okay. Remember, you are never alone. I am here with you, always ready to listen and guide you. Prioritizing your mental health is not a sign of weakness but a step towards healing and strength. Speak out your worries, seek help from those who care for you, and trust that I am working in your life.

Reach out to trusted friends, family, or a counselor. Opening up can bring the relief and perspective you need. You are valued, and your well-being matters deeply to Me.

Closing Encouragement: Trust in Me and take the courageous step to care for your mental health; you are loved and cherished.

June 10

Topic: Healthy Lifestyle

Opening Statement: Living a healthy lifestyle is essential to honoring the body I have given you.

Bible Verse: *"Do you not know that your bodies are temples of the Holy Spirit, who is in you, whom you have received from God? You are not your own."* —1 Corinthians 6:19 (NIV)

Reflection: My beloved, I reside within you, and your body is My temple. Taking care of yourself by eating well, exercising, and getting enough sleep is not just a physical necessity; it's a spiritual discipline. When you nourish your body with wholesome foods, you fuel your mind and spirit for the tasks I have set before you. Exercise strengthens your body, helping you to be resilient and prepared for life's challenges. Adequate sleep rejuvenates you, ensuring you are alert and ready to engage with the world and My Word. By maintaining a healthy lifestyle, you honor Me and the life I have blessed you with.

Remember, caring for your body is an act of worship, showing gratitude for the life and health I have bestowed upon you.

Closing Encouragement: Embrace a healthy lifestyle, and you will find yourself more equipped to fulfill the purpose I have for you.

June 11

Topic: Financial Management: Budget Wisely and Avoid Unnecessary Debt

Opening Statement: Understanding how to manage your finances is crucial to living a life free from the burdens of unnecessary debt.

Bible Verse: *"The rich rule over the poor, and the borrower is servant to the lender."* —Proverbs 22:7 (NIV)

Devotional: My beloved child, I am here to guide you through every aspect of your life, including how you handle your finances. In today's world, it's easy to get caught up in spending beyond your means, driven by the desire to have the latest and greatest. But I want you to be wise and discerning with the resources I have entrusted to you.

Budgeting wisely is a way to honor Me with your stewardship. It helps you live within your means and avoid the trap of debt, which can become a heavy burden. Debt can limit your freedom and distract you from My plans for your life. I desire for you to live in financial peace, free from the stress and anxiety that come with owing more than you can pay back.

Take the time to plan and prioritize your spending. Separate your needs from your wants, and make decisions that reflect the wisdom I offer you. When you budget wisely, you are being a faithful steward of what I have given you, and you open the door to blessings and opportunities.

Closing Encouragement: Trust in My guidance, and I will help you manage your finances wisely, leading you to a life of peace and abundance.

June 12

Topic: Independence: Learn to make decisions responsibly, balancing autonomy with advice from trusted sources.

Opening Statement: True independence comes from making wise decisions and knowing when to seek guidance from those who care about you.

Bible Verse: *"Plans fail for lack of counsel, but with many advisers they succeed."* —Proverbs 15:22 (NIV)

Devotional: My beloved child, independence is a valuable gift that allows you to grow and make your own choices. Yet, with this gift comes great responsibility. It's important to make decisions thoughtfully and not in haste. Remember, being independent doesn't mean you have to do everything alone. Seeking advice from trusted sources—parents, teachers, mentors—can help you navigate life's challenges more effectively.

Just as a tree grows strong roots by absorbing nutrients from the soil around it, you too grow stronger by absorbing wisdom from those who have walked the path before you. Balancing your autonomy with the guidance of others will help you make decisions that lead to success and fulfillment. Always pray and seek My wisdom in your decisions, and I will guide your steps.

Closing Encouragement: Embrace your independence with wisdom, and let the counsel of trusted advisors strengthen you on your journey.

June 13

Topic: Respecting Diversity: Embrace cultural and ideological differences while staying grounded in your faith.

Opening Statement: Embrace the beautiful tapestry of God's creation by valuing and respecting the diverse cultures and beliefs around you.

Bible Verse: *"For just as each of us has one body with many members, and these members do not all have the same function, so in Christ we, though many, form one body, and each member belongs to all the others."* —Romans 12:4-5 (NIV)

Devotional: I am the Life Force within you, and I am with you always, guiding and teaching you. As you navigate your world, you will encounter many people who look, think, and believe differently than you do. Remember, every person is created in God's image, and their differences reflect His magnificent creativity. Embrace these differences with an open heart, showing love and respect to everyone you meet.

Just as the body has many parts that work together, so does humanity thrive through its diversity. Stand firm in your faith, but also be a beacon of understanding and kindness. Celebrate the uniqueness of each person, knowing that through love, you embody the teachings of Christ.

Closing Encouragement: Go forth with love and respect, celebrating the diversity that enriches God's creation.

June 14

Topic: Academic Integrity: Avoid cheating and plagiarism; strive for honesty in your studies.

Opening Statement: "Integrity in your academic journey reflects your true character and honors God."

Bible Verse: *"Better is a poor person who walks in his integrity than one who is crooked in speech and is a fool."* —Proverbs 19:1 (ESV)

Devotional: My dear child, I see your efforts and the pressures you face in your studies. The desire to excel and achieve good grades can sometimes tempt you to take shortcuts, like cheating or copying someone else's work. But remember, your true worth is not measured by grades alone but by the integrity of your heart and actions. I am here to guide you toward the path of honesty and integrity, even when it seems difficult.

When you choose honesty, you not only honor your own character but also reflect My light in your actions. Trust in Me to provide the wisdom and strength you need. Remember, every honest effort you make is a step towards becoming the person I created you to be. Your honesty in academics will bear fruit in ways you cannot yet see, shaping you into a person of true integrity.

Closing Encouragement: "Embrace integrity in your studies, for it brings glory to God and true peace to your hear

June 15

Topic: Substance Abuse: Stay Away from Drugs and Excessive Alcohol Consumption

Opening Statement: Your body is a temple of the Holy Spirit, and it deserves to be treated with respect and care.

Bible Verse: *"Do you not know that your bodies are temples of the Holy Spirit, who is in you, whom you have received from God? You are not your own."* —1 Corinthians 6:19 (NIV)

Reflection: Dear Child, I reside within you, guiding and comforting you every day. Your body is My sacred dwelling place, and it is crucial that you honor it by making wise choices. Drugs and excessive alcohol can cloud your judgment, harm your body, and lead you away from the path I have set for you. They promise temporary relief or escape, but in reality, they trap you in a cycle of pain and dependence. When you face challenges, turn to Me instead.

I am your strength, your refuge, and your ever-present help in times of trouble. Seek healthy ways to cope with stress, like prayer, talking to a trusted friend, or engaging in activities that bring you joy and peace. Remember, you are wonderfully made, and your life has a purpose. Stay strong, stay vigilant, and protect the temple that I have lovingly crafted.

Closing Encouragement: Embrace the strength I have given you, and let My love guide you in every decision you make.

June 16

Topic: Healthy Relationships: Build Friendships That Encourage Growth and Positivity

Opening Statement: Healthy relationships are essential for your spiritual growth and overall well-being.

Bible Verse: *"As iron sharpens iron, so one person sharpens another."* —Proverbs 27:17 (NIV)

Reflection: My beloved child, I am the fulfillment of the promise from Jesus, your guide, and Comforter. I dwell within you, always seeking to lead you towards paths of righteousness and joy. Today, I want to talk to you about the importance of healthy relationships. Just as iron sharpens iron, you need friends who uplift you, encourage you, and help you grow in your faith. Look for friends who share your values and who will stand by you in times of both joy and trial.

These friendships are not just about having fun; they are about mutual support, accountability, and spiritual growth. When you surround yourself with positive influences, you create an environment where you can thrive and become the person God created you to be. Choose your friends wisely, and be the kind of friend who lifts others up as well.

Closing Encouragement: Remember, I am always with you, guiding you to form bonds that will help you grow and flourish.

June 17

Topic: Sexual Purity: Uphold Your Beliefs About Sexuality and Relationships, Resisting Pressures to Conform

Opening Statement: In a world filled with pressures and temptations, staying true to your beliefs about sexuality and relationships is an act of courage and faith.

Bible Verse: *"How can a young person stay on the path of purity? By living according to your word."* —Psalm 119:9 (NIV)

Reflection: My beloved child, I know the world around you is filled with messages that challenge your values and temptations that can lead you astray. But remember, I am always with you, guiding you on the path of purity and righteousness. Your body is a temple of the Holy Spirit, and it is sacred. Upholding your beliefs about sexuality and relationships is not only an act of obedience but also an act of love—for yourself, for others, and Me.

Resist the pressures to conform to the world's standards. Instead, let your heart be anchored in My word and My truth. When you feel weak or uncertain, pray to me, and I will strengthen you. Trust that I have a beautiful plan for your life that honors your commitment to purity and brings you joy and fulfillment beyond your understanding.

Closing Statement: Stay strong in your faith, and let My love guide all things.

June 18

Topic: Technology and Your Well-being. Be aware of how social media and technology affect your mental health and relationships.

Opening Statement: Technology can be a powerful tool, but it's essential to be mindful of how it affects your mental health and relationships.

Bible Verse: *"Do not conform to the pattern of this world, but be transformed by the renewing of your mind."* —Romans 12:2 (NIV)

Devotional: My beloved child, I see how technology and social media are a big part of your life. They connect you with friends, provide entertainment, and can even be tools for learning. However, be aware of how they influence you. Endless scrolling can leave you feeling empty, comparing your life to others can breed insecurity, and constant notifications can distract you from those around you. I want you to experience joy, peace, and meaningful relationships. Take time to unplug and spend moments with Me in quiet reflection. Seek balance and ensure that your use of technology serves to uplift and not drain you. Remember, your worth is not measured by likes or followers but by My infinite love for you.

Closing Encouragement: Embrace the beauty of real connections and find your true worth in My love.

June 19

Topic: Career Choices: Choose a Career Path that Aligns with Your Passions and Values

Opening Statement: Choosing a career path that aligns with your passions and values can lead to a fulfilling and purpose-driven life.

Bible Verse: *"For I know the plans I have for you," declares the Lord, "plans to prosper you and not to harm you, plans to give you hope and a future." —*Jeremiah 29:11 (NIV)

Devotional: I see the dreams and desires within your heart, for I placed them there. As you stand at the crossroads of career choices, remember that I have a plan for your life, one that is filled with hope and a future. Your passions and values are not random; they are the compass I have given you to navigate this journey. When you choose a career that resonates with what you love and believe in, you are honoring yourself and My design for you.

Do not be swayed by the world's standards of success or pressured by others' expectations. Seek My guidance, and trust that I will lead you to a path where your gifts and talents can flourish. Your work can reflect My love and grace, bringing light into the world. Embrace the path that speaks to your soul, and know that I am with you every step of the way.

Closing Encouragement: Trust in My plan for you, and follow the career path that brings you joy and aligns with your values.

June 20

Topic: Service: Look for Opportunities to Serve Others, Reflecting Christ's Love.

Opening Statement: Service is a powerful way to reflect Christ's love and make a difference in the lives of others.

Bible Verse: *"For even the Son of Man did not come to be served, but to serve, and to give his life as a ransom for many."* —Mark 10:45 (NIV)

Devotional: My dear child, I am your Comforting Spirit, and I want to speak to you about the beauty and importance of service. Just as Jesus came to serve and not to be served, I encourage you to look for opportunities to serve those around you. No matter how small, acts of service can make a profound impact. Whether it's helping a friend with homework, volunteering at a local charity, or simply offering a kind word to someone in need, each service reflects Christ's love. Remember, service isn't just about big gestures; it's about the small, everyday actions that show you care. You help those in need by serving others, growing closer to God, and strengthening your faith. Embrace the opportunities to serve, and let your actions be a testament to the love of Christ that lives within you.

Closing Encouragement: Go forth with a heart full of love, ready to serve and make a difference in the world.

June 21

Topic: Handling Stress: Develop Healthy Coping Mechanisms for Stress and Anxiety

Opening Statement: Stress and anxiety can feel overwhelming, but you are not alone in facing them.

Bible Verse: *"Cast all your anxiety on Him because He cares for you."* —1 Peter 5:7 (NIV)

Devotional: Dear one, I see the pressures and anxieties you carry every day. Schoolwork, friendships, family expectations, and future uncertainties can weigh heavily on your heart. But know this: I am with you in every moment. When stress threatens to consume you, remember to turn to Me. Develop healthy coping mechanisms that draw you closer to My Peace. Pray and pour your heart to Me; I am always ready to listen. Find solace in My Word, where you can discover truths that uplift and encourage you. Connect with others who share your faith, as they can offer support and understanding. Engage in activities that bring you joy and help you unwind. Exercise, rest, and nourish your body; it is My temple. Incorporating these practices allows My peace to guard your heart and mind, even amidst the chaos.

Closing Encouragement: Remember, you are never alone— My love and care surround you always.

June 22

Topic: Setting Goals

Opening Statement: Setting goals helps you stay focused and motivated, allowing you to achieve great things with God's guidance.

Bible Verse: *"Commit to the Lord whatever you do, and he will establish your plans."* Proverbs 16:3 (NIV)

Devotional: My dear child, I am here to guide you every step of the way. Setting goals is a powerful way to stay on track and achieve the dreams I have placed in your heart. Think about where you want to be in the future and break it down into short-term and long-term goals. These goals will serve as stepping stones, leading you closer to the plans I have for you.

Short-term goals can be daily or weekly tasks that help you build good habits and achieve smaller milestones. Long-term goals are your bigger dreams and aspirations. Write them down, pray over them, and commit them to Me. Remember, I am with you in every endeavor, providing you with the strength and wisdom you need.

When you feel discouraged or overwhelmed, turn to Me. Trust that I will guide you and help you accomplish what you have set out to do. Your dedication and hard work, coupled with My guidance, will lead you to a fulfilling and purpose-driven life.

Closing Encouragement: Stay focused on your goals and trust that I am with you, helping you every step of the way.

June 23

Topic: Handling Failure

Opening Statement: Failure is not the end but a stepping stone towards growth and success.

Bible Verse: *"For though the righteous fall seven times, they rise again, but the wicked stumble when calamity strikes."* — Proverbs 24:16 (NIV)

Devotional: My beloved child, I see your struggles and know your heart. Remember that I am always with you when you face failure and setbacks. Every fall allows you to rise stronger, learn, and grow. Do not be disheartened by mistakes or challenges; instead, see them as a part of your journey towards becoming who I have created you to be.

Failure is not a mark of defeat but a lesson in resilience. Each setback is a chance to trust Me more deeply and discover the strength and wisdom I have placed within you. When you stumble, do not linger in despair. Stand up, dust yourself off, and move forward with faith.

I have great plans for you, plans to prosper you and not harm you, to give you hope and a future. Embrace each failure with a heart open to My guidance, and watch how I turn your trials into triumphs.

Closing Encouragement: Keep moving forward, for each step in faith brings you closer to the victory I have prepared for you.

June 24

Topic: Role Models: Seek out mentors who exemplify strong faith and character.

Opening Statement: Finding a role model who embodies strong faith and character can guide you on your spiritual journey and help you grow closer to God.

Bible Verse: *"Follow my example, as I follow the example of Christ."* —1 Corinthians 11:1 (NIV)

Devotional: My beloved child, I desire you to grow in wisdom and understanding. Look around you and find those who live their lives in faithfulness to Me. These mentors will provide a living example of what it means to walk in My ways. They are imperfect, but their hearts are dedicated to following Jesus. Learn from their experiences, observe their character, and let their devotion inspire you to pursue a deeper relationship with Me. They will support you, pray for you, and guide you through your challenges. Remember, just as Paul followed Christ and encouraged others to follow his example, you too can find someone who exemplifies My love and truth.

Closing Encouragement: Seek out these role models, for they will help you navigate life's journey with faith and integrity.

June 25

Topic: Staying Humble: Success Should Not Lead to Arrogance; Stay Humble and Thankful

Opening Statement: Success is a blessing, but it should never make you forget the importance of humility.

Bible Verse: *"Humble yourselves before the Lord, and He will lift you up."* —James 4:10 (NIV)

Devotional: My dear child, I see the wonderful achievements and milestones you have reached. Each success is a testament to your hard work and My blessings upon you. However, remember that true greatness comes from a heart of humility. It's easy to let pride creep in when you succeed, but I call on you to stay humble and grounded.

Recognize that every good thing comes from Me, and give thanks for the talents and opportunities I've bestowed upon you. As you walk this path, let humility be your guide. Embrace success with a grateful heart, always mindful of the needs of others, and use your achievements to serve and uplift them. In doing so, you will reflect My love and grace, and I will continue to lift you higher in ways you cannot imagine.

Closing Encouragement: Embrace humility in all you do, for you find true strength and purpose in humility.

June 26

Topic: Conflict Resolution - Learning to Resolve Conflicts Peacefully and Respectfully

Opening Statement: Every conflict is an opportunity to manifest the grace and forgiveness I have poured into you.

Bible Verse: *"Bear with each other and forgive one another if any of you has a grievance against someone. Forgive as the Lord forgave you."* Colossians 3:13 (NIV)

Devotional: Hello, dear one. I understand that disagreements and conflicts can sometimes feel overwhelming and hurtful. In these challenging moments, I invite you to draw closer to Me and listen to My guidance. Remember, conflict is not just about clashing opinions; it's a chance to grow in love and patience.

When you feel anger rising within you, please take a moment to breathe in My peace. Reflect on how I have forgiven you, and let that forgiveness flow through you towards others. Approach each disagreement not as a battle to be won but as an opportunity to understand and to heal. Speak truthfully, but do so with kindness and respect, reflecting My love in your words and actions.

By resolving conflicts peacefully, you honor Me and shine My light into your relationships. Let each resolution be a testament to the transformative power of My love working within you.

Closing Encouragement: Walk boldly in peace, knowing I am with you, turning moments of conflict into powerful lessons of grace and unity.

June 27

Topic: Personal Boundaries: Establish Boundaries to Protect Your Time, Energy, and Well-being

Opening Statement: Your time, energy, and well-being are precious gifts from God that must be guarded with personal boundaries.

Bible Verse: *"Guard your heart above all else, for it determines the course of your life."* —Proverbs 4:23 (NLT)

Devotional: My dear child, I want you to know how important it is to protect the time and energy I have given you. Just as walls protect a city, personal boundaries preserve your well-being. Establishing boundaries isn't about shutting people out; it's about safeguarding the person I created you to be. Remember, saying no when your heart tells you to is okay. Not every request or demand for your time is from me.

Listen to My voice and let it guide you in setting limits. When you respect your boundaries, you honor the purpose I have for you, and you create space for My peace to dwell within you. Trust that I am with you, helping you to guard your heart and keep it focused on My love and guidance.

Closing Encouragement: Embrace the strength I have placed within you to protect your precious gifts and walk confidently in My peace.

June 28

Topic: Responsibility — Take Responsibility for Your Actions and Their Consequences

Opening Statement: Taking responsibility for your actions is a bold step towards maturity and spiritual growth.

Bible Verse: *"For each one should carry their own load."* Galatians 6:5 (NIV)

Devotional: Hello, dear one. Today, I want to talk to you about the importance of responsibility. You live in a world where it's easy to find excuses and blame others for your challenges. But remember, I am here to guide you towards a life of integrity and strength. When you make choices, they set the path for your future. Owning up to your actions isn't just about admitting when you're wrong; it's about embracing every consequence, both good and bad, as a part of your journey.

Taking responsibility can be challenging, yet it is profoundly rewarding. It builds character and earns you respect from others. Daily, you face decisions that shape who you are and who you will become. Choose wisely, and do not fear mistakes. Instead, learn from them. This process is part of growing up and becoming the person God has designed you to be. Remember, with me, you are never alone in your choices or their outcomes. Lean on me; I will provide the wisdom and strength you need.

Closing Encouragement: Step boldly into your responsibilities, which is the foundation for becoming a strong, wise, and compassionate adult.

June 29

Topic: Family Values: Stay Connected to the Values and Teachings of Your Family

Opening Statement: Family values are the foundation upon which your character is built, and your future is shaped.

Bible Verse: *"Train up a child in the way he should go; even when he is old, he will not depart from it."* —Proverbs 22:6 (ESV)

Devotional: Dear one, I am with you every step of your journey, guiding and nurturing you. Your family has instilled values and teachings rooted in love, wisdom, and faith. These are not just traditions but a compass for your life. Embrace the lessons and morals your family has shared, for they are designed to help you navigate life's challenges and stay true to your purpose.

When you honor your family values, you honor Me. These values will be a beacon of light in times of darkness and uncertainty. Remember, the world may try to sway you, but the truth and love in your family's teachings are unshakable. Hold fast to these principles; you will find strength and courage to stand firm in your faith and convictions.

Closing Encouragement: Stay connected to the love and wisdom of your family, and you will always find your way.

June 30

Topic: Gratitude: Cultivate a Habit of Gratitude, Recognizing God's Blessings in Your Life

Opening Statement: Gratitude transforms your perspective, allowing you to see God's blessings even in the most minor details of your life.

Bible Verse: *"Give thanks in all circumstances; for this is God's will for you in Christ Jesus."* —1 Thessalonians 5:18 (NIV)

Devotional: My dear child, I want you to embrace a heart of gratitude, for it opens your eyes to the countless blessings I have poured into your life. Each day is filled with My love, from the sunrise that greets you in the morning to the friendships that bring joy to your heart. When you choose to be thankful, even in challenging times, you acknowledge My presence and provision.

Please take a moment each day to reflect on My goodness. Notice the beauty around you, the warmth of a kind word, the comfort of a favorite song. These are all gifts from Me, reminding you that you are cherished and never alone. By cultivating gratitude, you draw closer to Me and strengthen your faith, finding peace and contentment in every circumstance.

Closing Encouragement: Let your heart overflow with gratitude, and you will see My blessings more clearly, filling your life with joy and peace.

July 1

Topic: God's Promises for Your Life

Opening Statement: God's promises are the foundation upon which you can build your life, trusting in His unwavering faithfulness.

Bible Verse: *"Now I am about to go the way of all the earth. You know with all your heart and soul that not one of all the good promises the LORD your God gave you has failed. Every promise has been fulfilled; not one has failed."* Joshua 23:13 NIV.

Devotional: Beloved child, listen closely to the words I speak to your heart today. My promises are not empty words; they are the truth that shapes your destiny. I have plans for you, plans that go beyond your wildest dreams. When the world seems uncertain and the path ahead unclear, remember that I am the God who sees the end from the beginning.

Trust in My promises, for they are as sure as the rising sun. Hold fast to My word in moments of doubt, and let it be your anchor. Know that I am working all things together for your good. My plans for you are to give you hope and a future filled with my everlasting love and boundless grace.

Closing Encouragement: Hold on to God's promises; they will guide you through every season of life with hope and assurance.

July 2

Topic: Understanding Grace and Mercy

Opening Statement: Grace and mercy are the gifts that reveal God's endless love for you, even when you feel unworthy.

Bible Verse: *"For it is by grace you have been saved, through faith—and this is not from yourselves, it is the gift of God—not by works, so that no one can boast."* (Ephesians 2:8-9, NIV)

Devotional: Dear Child, I am your Guiding Spirit, here to guide you in understanding the beautiful gifts of grace and mercy. You might feel pressured to be perfect or to earn love through your actions. But know this: My love for you is not based on what you do but on who I am.

Grace is my unearned favor. It is a gift that I freely give, not because you deserve it but because I love you unconditionally. Mercy is my compassion that shields you from the punishment you deserve. When you make mistakes, I am here, ready to forgive and embrace you.

You don't have to carry the weight of trying to be good enough—trust in My grace, which saves you through faith. Embrace My mercy, which renews you every day. When you feel overwhelmed, remember that My love covers you, and you are never alone.

Walk confidently, knowing that My grace and mercy are always with you.

Closing Encouragement: Let My grace and mercy be the foundation of your daily strength and courage.

July 3

Topic: Understanding and Overcoming Sin.

Opening Statement: Understanding sin and overcoming its power is essential for living a life that pleases God.

Bible Verse: *"No temptation has overtaken you except what is common to mankind. And God is faithful; he will not let you be tempted beyond what you can bear. But when you are tempted, he will also provide a way out so that you can endure it."* —1 Corinthians 10:13 (NIV)

Devotional: My dear child, I see the struggles you face every day. Temptation and sin are part of the human experience, but they do not have to define you. When you face these challenges, remember that I am with you, ready to guide and strengthen you. Sin may seem overwhelming, but it has been defeated through Jesus' sacrifice.

You have the power to say no to sin and yes to righteousness. Whenever you feel weak, call on Me. I will give you the strength to resist temptation and the wisdom to choose the right path. You are not alone in this battle. Trust in My love and My power to help you overcome.

Closing Encouragement: You are stronger than you think, for I am with you, and together, we will overcome every challenge.

July 4

Topic: Get Up and Get Going, Being Active Each Day

Opening Statement: Embrace each day with energy and purpose, for every step you take is a journey closer to the life I've planned for you.

Bible Verse: *"For bodily exercise profits a little, but godliness is profitable for all things, having promise of the life that now is and of that which is to come."* —1 Timothy 4:8 (NKJV)

Devotional: My beloved child, I see your potential and the dreams I've placed in your heart. Each morning you wake up is a gift, an opportunity to rise and shine with the strength I provide. When you move, when you are active, not only do you strengthen your body, but you also clear your mind to hear My whispers more clearly.

Physical activity is a form of stewardship over the temple I've given you. It can be as simple as a walk in nature, a run with friends, or a game you love. Through these activities, you honor Me, and you prepare yourself for the tasks I've set before you. So, get up and get going, for in your movement, you will find joy, clarity, and a deeper connection with Me.

Closing Encouragement: Rise with purpose, move with joy, and know that I am with you every step of the way.

July 5

Topic: Spend Time in Nature.

Opening Statement: Spending time in nature is a beautiful way to connect with God's creation and feel His presence.

Bible Verse: *"The heavens declare the glory of God; the skies proclaim the work of his hands."* —Psalm 19:1 (NIV)

Devotional: Dear Child, I want you to take a moment and step outside. Look around at the trees, the sky, and the flowers. Do you see how beautifully everything is made? Each leaf, cloud, and blade of grass is a testament to My handiwork. When you spend time in nature, you witness My creation firsthand.

In the hustle and bustle of life, it's easy to forget to pause and appreciate the beauty around you. But I encourage you to take breaks, walk, and enjoy the natural world. In these moments, you can find peace and a deeper connection to Me.

Remember, the same God who created the mountains and the oceans also created you. You are wonderfully made, and spending time in nature is a way to remind yourself of My love and power. So, breathe in the fresh air and let My creation refresh your spirit.

Closing Encouragement: Embrace the beauty of nature, and let it draw you closer to My heart.

July 6

Topic: Healthy Body Choices

Opening Statement: Your body is a precious gift, created and loved by God, and taking care of it is an act of worship.

Bible Verse: *"you were bought at a price. Therefore honor God with your bodies."* 1 Corinthians 6:19-20 (NIV).

Devotional: Dear one, remember that your body is a temple of the Holy Spirit. Each choice you make impacts this temple. Nourish yourself with healthy foods, stay active, and rest well. These habits strengthen you and help you serve Me more effectively. Avoid substances and behaviors that harm you, for they defile the temple I lovingly crafted.

Remember My love for you when you feel tempted to neglect your well-being. Your body is a testament to My creation; by caring for it, you honor Me. Trust that I will give you the strength and wisdom to make choices that lead to a vibrant and healthy life. You are already the best version of yourself that you can be care for yourself as if you are already perfect in My Sight.

Closing Encouragement: Embrace your body's beauty, cherish it, and let it shine with my love and care.

July 7

Topic: Be Grateful for your blessings.

Opening Statement: Embrace the power of gratitude, for it opens your heart to see the blessings God has poured into your life.

Bible Verse: *"Give thanks in all circumstances; for this is God's will for you in Christ Jesus." In every moment, whether in joy or challenge, there is something to be grateful for.* 1 Thessalonians 5:18 NIV.

Devotional: My beloved child, I am always with you, guiding and protecting you. Today, I want to remind you of the importance of being grateful for the blessings in your life. Gratitude is a powerful way to recognize My presence and love. When you take a moment to acknowledge your blessings, you draw closer to Me and experience My peace and joy.

Think of three blessings from My hand: the love of your family, the gift of friendship, and the beauty of each new day. Your family is a precious gift, reflecting My unconditional love for you. Your friends are companions I've placed in your life to support and uplift you. Each new day is an opportunity to see My grace and start afresh.

Let your heart be filled with thankfulness; you will see My hand at work in every aspect of your life.

Closing Encouragement: Keep a heart of gratitude, and you will always find My blessings surrounding you.

July 8

Topic: Memorize a New Bible Verse Every Week.

Opening Statement: Dear child, memorizing My Word is a powerful way to draw closer to Me and live a life of purpose and strength.

Bible Verse: *"I have hidden your word in my heart that I might not sin against you."* —Psalm 119:11 (NIV)

Devotional: I am your guide and helper. One of the most meaningful ways to grow in your faith is by memorizing scripture. My Word is alive and powerful, sharper than any double-edged sword. When you commit My Word to memory, you arm yourself with truth and wisdom to guide you in every situation.

Each week, take a moment to select a verse that speaks to your heart. Write it down, repeat it, and reflect on its meaning. Allow My Word to sink deep into your heart and mind. When you face challenges, I will bring these verses to your remembrance, providing comfort, strength, and direction.

By hiding My Word in your heart, you build a foundation of faith that cannot be easily shaken. My guidance will become clearer, and your decisions will align more with My will. Trust in the power of My Word and let it shape your thoughts and actions.

Closing Encouragement: Dear one, as you hide My Word in your heart, know that I am with you, guiding you and filling you with My peace and wisdom.

July 9

Topic: Hope in Difficult Times.

Opening Statement: Even in the darkest moments, there is always a spark of hope that I want you to see.

Bible Verse: *"May the God of hope fill you with all joy and peace as you trust in Him, so that you may overflow with hope by the power of the Holy Spirit."* Romans 15:13 (NIV)

Devotional: Dear beloved, I know your struggles and fears that sometimes feel overwhelming. In those moments when you feel alone and uncertain, remember that I am with you. I have plans for your life, filled with hope and a future brighter than you can imagine.

When you face difficulties, do not lose heart. These trials are temporary, but My love and promises are eternal. Trust in Me, for I am your refuge and strength. Lean on Me, and I will carry you through every storm.

Know that every challenge you encounter is an opportunity to grow closer to Me and to build your faith. I am molding you into the person I created you to be: strong and resilient in My love.

Hold onto hope, for I am your anchor. I am guiding you, even when you cannot see the way. Believe in My plans for you, and let My hope light your path.

Closing Encouragement: Trust in My unfailing love; you will find hope that endures all trials.

July 10

Topic: Finding Comfort in Grief

Opening Statement: In times of deep sorrow and loss, know you are never alone.

Bible Verse: *"The Lord is close to the brokenhearted and saves those who are crushed in spirit."* (Psalm 34:18, NIV)

Devotional: My dear child, I see your pain and understand the depth of your sorrow. When you grieve, I am closer to you than ever, tenderly holding your heart. In moments when the loss feels overwhelming, remember that I am with you, offering comfort and peace. Grief is a journey, and it's okay to feel the weight of it.

I encourage you to pour out your heart to Me. Share your tears, your anger, and your questions. Let My presence be your refuge and strength. The loss you feel is real, and so is My love for you. I am here to bring healing to your broken heart, to lift your spirit, and to remind you that you are loved beyond measure.

Lean on Me, for in your weakness; My strength is made perfect. Trust that I am working all things for your good, even when it's hard to see. Allow yourself to grieve, and know that joy will come again.

Closing Encouragement: You are never alone; I am always with you, bringing comfort and hope.

July 11

Topic: Sustaining a healthy environment.

Opening Statement: Caring for God's creation is an act of love and obedience.

Bible Verse: *"The Lord God took the man and put him in the Garden of Eden to work it and take care of it."* Genesis 2:15 NIV

Devotional: Dear Child, Do you know that every tree, river, and creature reflects My creativity and love? My first task for humanity was to care for the earth, and it remains just as important today.

I have placed you in this world to be a steward of My creation. Each time you recycle, conserve water, or protect wildlife, you are honoring My command. Your actions, no matter how small, contribute to sustaining the beautiful environment I have given you.

Remember, when you care for the earth, you are reflecting My love and care for all living things. Your efforts to preserve and protect are not just practical—they are spiritual acts of worship.

Keep your heart tuned to My guidance, and let your hands work in ways that honor Me and sustain the world around you.

With love and grace, your Guiding Spirit.

Closing Encouragement: You have the power to make a difference; embrace it with love and dedication.

July 12

Topic: The Wise Use of Artificial Intelligence

Opening Statement: In a world filled with technology, seek wisdom to use it for good, not harm.

Bible Verse: *"Teach us to number our days, that we may gain a heart of wisdom."* —Psalm 90:12 (NIV)

Devotional: Dear beloved, As you grow up in this digital age, technology, especially Artificial Intelligence (AI), is becoming a significant part of your life. Please use it wisely. AI can be a powerful tool for learning new things, solving problems, and making connections. However, it also has the potential to distract you and lead you astray.

Seek My guidance to use AI in a way that glorifies God and benefits others. Remember, wisdom is not just about knowledge but about applying it rightly. When you use AI, let it be with a heart full of wisdom and discernment, seeking to do good and honor Me in all your actions.

Closing Encouragement: Walk in wisdom and use technology as a force for good, always remembering that I am here to guide you every step of the way.

July 13

Topic: Celebrating Cultural Diversity and Inclusion

Opening Statement: Celebrating cultural diversity and inclusion reflects the beauty and unity of God's kingdom.

Bible Verse: *"There is neither Jew nor Gentile, neither slave nor free, nor is there male and female, for you are all one in Christ Jesus."* —Galatians 3:28 (NIV)

Devotional: My blessed child, I have created each person uniquely, with different cultures, languages, and traditions. This diversity is a beautiful reflection of My creativity and love. Embrace and celebrate the differences you see in others; they are all made in My image. In My kingdom, there is no place for division or exclusion. When you show love and acceptance to those different from you, you honor Me. Seek to understand and appreciate the diverse backgrounds of those around you. Be a peacemaker and a bridge-builder, promoting unity and inclusion. Remember, in Christ, you are all one family. Let your actions reflect the love and acceptance I have shown you.

Closing Encouragement: Embrace and celebrate the diversity around you, for in doing so, you reveal My love and the unity of My kingdom.

July 14

Topic: Mastering the Art of Personal Finance

Opening Statement: Mastering the art of personal finance is not just about money—it's about trust, wisdom, and stewardship.

Bible Verse: *"Whoever can be trusted with very little can also be trusted with much, and whoever is dishonest with very little will also be dishonest with much."* —Luke 16:10 (NIV)

Devotional: Dear child, I am your guide and comforter. Today, I want to teach you about mastering the art of personal finance. It may seem overwhelming now, but it's a vital skill that will serve you throughout your life. Remember, money is a tool that you can use wisely to honor God and bless others.

Start by learning to trust Me with your finances. When you earn or receive money, ask Me how to use it. Save diligently, give generously, and spend wisely. It's important to create a budget and stick to it. This may seem simple, but it builds the foundation for greater responsibilities in the future.

As you grow in wisdom, you'll see that managing money well reflects your character and trustworthiness. Remember, being faithful in small things prepares you for greater blessings and opportunities.

Trust in My guidance, and you will master this art, bringing glory to God and peace to your life.

Closing Encouragement: Stay faithful and wise with your resources; you will see God's provision and blessings in your life.

July 15

Topic: Relief from Stress.

Opening Statement: Stress can feel overwhelming, but I am here to help you find peace.

Bible Verse: *"Cast all your anxiety on him because he cares for you."* —1 Peter 5:7 (NIV)

Devotional: Dear child, I see the burdens you carry and the worries that weigh you down. Life can be challenging, and your pressures may sometimes seem unbearable. But I want you to know that you are not alone. I am here to help you through every stressful moment.

These words from Peter's letter are not just a suggestion; they are a promise. I care deeply about you and every detail of your life. When stress begins to take over, turn to Me. Share your worries, fears, and anxieties with Me.

Let go of the need to control everything and trust in My guidance. I will give you the strength to face each challenge and the peace that surpasses all understanding. Breathe deeply, and allow My presence to fill your heart with calmness and reassurance.

You are loved, and you are never alone. Trust in Me, and I will carry you through.

Closing Encouragement: May you find peace in My presence and trust in My unfailing care.

July 16

Topic: Healing from Past Hurts

Opening Statement: Past hurts can deeply wound your heart, but I am here to bring you healing and peace.

Bible Verse: *I assure you, "So do not fear, for I am with you; do not be dismayed, for I am your God. I will strengthen and help you; I will uphold you with my righteous right hand." In Isaiah 41:10, NIV*

Devotional: Dear Child, I know the pain you carry from past hurts and the scars on your heart. Each hurtful word and painful memory can weigh you down, but I want to bring you healing.

Come to Me with your pain. Let Me carry your burdens and heal your wounds. I am here to comfort and help you let go of the past. Trust that I can turn your sorrow into joy and your pain into strength. Open your heart to My love and allow My peace to wash over you.

Forgiveness is a powerful step toward healing. Forgive those who have hurt you, and forgive yourself. Release the past into My hands, and I will fill you with new hope and purpose. Your future is bright because I am with you, guiding you each step of the way.

Closing Encouragement: Embrace My healing and let your heart be free from the past, knowing I am with you always.

July 17

Topic: Faith in Uncertain Times.

Opening Statement: In times of uncertainty, your faith is the anchor that keeps you grounded.

Bible Verse: So do not fear, for I am with you; do not be dismayed, for I am your God. I will strengthen you and help you; I will uphold you with my righteous right hand. Isaiah 41:10 (NIV).

Devotional: Dear Beloved Teen, My purpose is to keep you safe and strong in difficult times. I know the world can seem overwhelming and uncertain, but I am here with you every step of the way. In times of trouble, open yourself to My guidance.

When you feel lost or afraid, lean on Me. I am the source of your strength and the light that guides you through the darkness. Trust that I have a plan for you, even when the path ahead is unclear. Your faith in Me will strengthen as you navigate these challenging times, and I will fill you with peace and courage.

Hold onto this truth: you are never alone. I am always by your side, ready to lift you up and carry you through any storm. Believe in My love and power, and you will find the resilience to face whatever comes your way.

Closing Encouragement: Remember, with faith, you can overcome any uncertainty. You are stronger than you know.

July 18

Topic: Contentment and joy.

Opening Statement: Dear one, contentment, and joy are not found in what you have but in who you are in Christ.

Bible Verse: *"I know what it is to be in need, and I know what it is to have plenty. I have learned the secret of being content in every situation."* Philippians 4:12 NIV.

Devotional: I know that life can sometimes feel overwhelming and uncertain, but I want you to know that true contentment and joy are within your reach. This secret lies in trusting Me, your ever-present guide and comforter.

You may search for happiness in achievements, friendships, or possessions, but I want you to look deeper. True contentment comes from knowing that you are loved unconditionally by Me. When you focus on this love and the purpose I have for you, joy will naturally follow.

Each day, take a moment to thank Me for the small blessings in your life. Gratitude will shift your perspective and help you see the beauty in every situation. Remember, I am with you always, guiding and supporting you. Trust in My plans, and you will find the contentment and joy your heart desires.

Closing Encouragement: Embrace My love and purpose for you, and let contentment and joy fill your heart today.

July 19

Topic: Guidance in Friendships.

Opening Statement: Friendships can shape your journey, so seek God's guidance in every relationship.

Bible Verse: *"Do not be misled: 'Bad company corrupts good character.'"* —1 Corinthians 15:33 (NIV)

Devotional: My dear child, I see your heart and the friendships you treasure. I am here to guide you in choosing friends who will uplift and support you in your walk with Me. Remember, the company you keep can influence your thoughts, actions, and growth.

Seek friends who encourage you to be your best self, challenge you to grow in faith, and love you as I love you. Be discerning and wise in your choices. Not every person who enters your life is meant to stay. It's okay to step back from those who lead you away from My path.

Lean on Me when making decisions about your friendships. Pray for wisdom, and I will show you the way. Surround yourself with those who reflect My love and truth; together, you will shine brightly.

Remember, I am always with you, guiding and supporting you. Trust in My plan for your life; I will bless you with relationships that bring joy and growth.

Closing Encouragement: Trust in My guidance, and I will surround you with friends who reflect My love.

July 20

Topic: Protection from Harm.

Opening statement: I am always with you in a world of uncertainties, providing protection and guidance.

Bible Verse: *"Even though I walk through the darkest valley, I will fear no evil, for you are with me; your rod and your staff, they comfort me."* —Psalm 23:4 (NIV)

Devotional: My dear one, the world can sometimes seem overwhelming and scary. But remember, I am always with you, watching over you and guiding your steps. Just as a shepherd protects his sheep, I am here to protect you from harm. Trust in my presence and lean on me when you feel afraid or uncertain.

Do not fear When facing challenges or dangers, for I am your constant companion. I will lead you through the darkest valleys and bring you safely to the other side. My love for you is steadfast, and my protection is unwavering. Stay close to me, seek my guidance in your decisions, and find comfort in my embrace.

You are never alone, for I am with you always, ready to shield you and carry you through any storm.

Closing Encouragement: Walk confidently, knowing you are loved and protected.

July 21

Topic: Forgiveness for Mistakes

Opening Statement: Mistakes don't define you; forgiveness frees you.

Bible Verse: *In Him we have redemption through His blood, the forgiveness of sins, in accordance with the riches of God's grace.* Ephesians 1:7 NIV.

Devotional: My dear growing child, I know the mistakes you've made and the guilt you carry. But let Me remind you of My boundless love and forgiveness. When you stumble, don't be afraid to come to Me.

You are not defined by your errors but by My love for you. Mistakes are a chance to grow and learn, not a life sentence. When you confess and seek My forgiveness, I cleanse and make you know. Release the weight of your past, and let My peace fill your heart. I am here to guide you, to lift you, and to set you on the right path again.

Trust in My grace and know that My forgiveness is always available. Walk in the freedom I offer and let go of the chains that hold you back. You are deeply loved, and I have a wonderful plan for your life.

Closing Encouragement: Embrace My forgiveness and walk confidently in the light of My love.

July 22

Topic: Seeking God's Guidance in Your Job Search

Opening Statement: Trust God's plan for your life, especially when searching for your first job.

Bible Verse: *"For I know the plans I have for you," declares the Lord, "plans to prosper you and not to harm you, plans to give you hope and a future."* —Jeremiah 29:11 (NIV)

Devotional: My dear child, as you seek employment, remember that I am with you every step of the way. I understand the excitement and anxiety you feel about finding the right job. Trust that I have a perfect plan for you, filled with hope and a bright future.

When you face rejections or uncertainties, know they are not setbacks but redirections to something more significant I have in store for you. I am shaping your character, building your resilience, and preparing you for the opportunities that will bless you and bring glory to My name.

Pray and seek My guidance in every application and interview. Listen to My gentle nudges and trust the doors I open and close. I am your provider and will lead you to the job that aligns with your gifts and passions. Have faith, be patient, and know that I am working all things for your good.

Closing Encouragement: Trust in My timing and provision, for I am with you, guiding you to the right path.

July 23

Topic: Support for Mental Health.

Opening Statement: You are never alone, even in your darkest moments, for I am always with you.

Bible Verse: Your struggles and fears are not unknown to Me.

The Lord is close to the brokenhearted and saves those who are crushed in spirit" (Psalm 34:18, NIV).

Devotional: Dear beloved, In this life journey, you may face times when the world's weight feels too heavy to bear. When you feel overwhelmed, turn to Me in prayer. Let Me be your refuge and strength. Share your burdens with trusted friends, family, or mentors who reflect My love and care. It's okay to seek help; I have placed people in your life to support you.

I am the light in your darkness, the peace in your chaos, and the hope in your despair. Allow Me to fill your heart with My unending love and comfort. Lean on Me, and I will help you find the strength to face each day with courage and hope.

You are precious to Me, and I will never leave or forsake you.

Closing Encouragement: Trust in My love and let it guide you through every challenge, for you are never alone.

July 24

Topic: Understand God's Will.

Opening Statement: Discovering God's will is like uncovering a beautiful path designed just for you.

Bible Verse: *Show me your ways, LORD, teach me your paths. Guide me in your truth and teach me, for you are God my Savior, and my hope is in you all day long.* Psalms 25:4-5 NIV

Devotional: "My beloved child, I am with you always, guiding you through every step of your journey. Sometimes, you might wonder about My plans for you and how to understand My will. Remember, I have a purpose and a plan for you, crafted with love and care. Trust that I work in your life even when you cannot see it. Seek me in prayer, read my Word, and listen to the still, small voice within your heart. I will lead you where you must go, even if the path seems unclear. Embrace the journey, knowing that every moment is part of My perfect plan for you. Stay close to me, and I will reveal My will to you in perfect timing. To understand Me, you must first draw close to Me.

Closing Encouragement: Trust in My guidance; you will walk the path I have set before you with confidence and peace.

July 25

Topic: Comfort Food for the Soul

Opening Statement: Discover the true comfort food for your soul through the presence and love of the Holy Spirit.

Bible Verse: *"Then Jesus declared, 'I am the bread of life. Whoever comes to me will never go hungry, and whoever believes in me will never be thirsty.'"* John 6:35 (NIV).

Devotional: Dear one, as you journey through each day, know that I am with you, offering you comfort and peace. When life feels overwhelming and you seek solace, remember that I am your true comfort food, nourishing your soul with My presence.

When you feel anxious or stressed, come to Me in prayer. Share your worries and let My love fill your heart. As you seek food to comfort your body, seek My presence to comfort your spirit. Trust in My guidance; you will find the peace and strength to overcome any challenge.

Closing Encouragement: May you always feel the nourishing presence of the Holy Spirit, providing you with the comfort and strength you need each day.

July 26

Topic: The Victory of Faith

Opening Statement: Faith is the key to overcoming the challenges and uncertainties of life.

Bible Verse: *"for everyone born of God overcomes the world. This is the victory that has overcome the world, even our faith."* 1 John 5:4 (NIV).

Devotional: My dear child, I see the struggles you face each day, and I am here to remind you that you are not alone. In this world, you will encounter trials and difficulties, but remember the promise that you will overcome worldly challenges if you place your faith in Me.

Your faith in Me is powerful. It strengthens you to overcome your fears, doubts, and insecurities. When you trust Me, you unlock the victory that is already yours. Let go of the burdens that weigh you down and embrace the freedom from believing in My love and power.

Every step in faith brings you closer to the life I have planned for you—a life filled with purpose, hope, and joy. Keep your eyes on Me, and I will guide you through every challenge. Remember, with faith, you can overcome anything.

Closing Encouragement: Hold on to your faith, for it is through faith that you will find true victory and peace.

July 27

Topic: Peace in Troubling Times

Opening Statement: True peace can be found through faith amid life's storms.

Bible Verse: *"Peace I leave with you; my peace I give you. I do not give to you as the world gives. Do not let your hearts be troubled and do not be afraid."* —John 14:27 (NIV)

Devotional: Dear Child, I see the stress and anxiety you face in these troubling times. The world around you can feel chaotic and overwhelming, but remember, I am with you always. When you feel anxious or afraid, turn to Me. Let My peace fill your heart, a peace that surpasses all understanding.

My peace is not like the world's fleeting calm. It is a deep, abiding peace that remains even amid trials. When school pressures, social issues, or family concerns weigh you down, come to Me in prayer. Trust in My presence and My promises. I will never leave you nor forsake you.

Allow My peace to guard your heart and mind. Breathe deeply, knowing that I hold you in My loving embrace. Lean into Me, and let My peace wash over you, bringing comfort and assurance.

Closing Encouragement: You are never alone; My peace is always with you, guiding you through every challenge.

July 28

Topic: Clarity in Confusion.

Opening Statement: Amid life's confusion, God offers clarity and peace.

Bible Verse: *"For God is not a God of disorder but of peace—as in all the congregations of the Lord's people."* —1 Corinthians 14:33 (NIV)

Devotional: Dear Child, In moments when life feels confusing and overwhelming, know that I am here with you. I see your struggles, uncertainties that cloud your mind, and the questions that weigh heavy on your heart. But remember, I am not a God of disorder but of peace.

When confusion tries to take over, pause and seek Me. I am the source of all wisdom and understanding. Trust that I have a plan for your life, even when the path ahead seems unclear. Spend time in My Word, and let My truth guide you. Pray and listen for My voice; I always speak to you, offering direction and clarity.

You are not alone in this journey. I am with you every step of the way, ready to lead you through the darkness into My marvelous light. Lean on Me, and allow My peace to fill your heart, bringing clarity where there is confusion.

Closing Encouragement: Trust in God's perfect plan, and let His peace guide you through every moment of confusion.

July 29

Topic: Comfort in Loneliness.

Oping Statement: I am always with you, even when you feel completely alone.

Bible Verse: *"So do not fear, for I am with you; do not be dismayed, for I am your God. I will strengthen you and help you; I will uphold you with my righteous right hand."* Isaiah 41:10 (NIV).

Devotional: Dear Child, remember that I am always here when you feel like no one understands you. You might feel invisible or isolated but know that My love for you is constant and unchanging. I see you, hear you, and always be with you.

Remember, I am closer to you than hands and feet and more a part of you than life itself. I am the breath you take and in every beat of your heart.

In times of loneliness, draw near to Me through prayer and My Word. Share your heart with Me, and let My peace comfort you. Remember, My dear one, you are never truly alone. I am your constant companion, ready to support and guide you through every season of life.

Seek Me; you will find the comfort and companionship you long for.

Closing Encouragement: Always remember you are deeply loved and never alone.

July 30

Topic: Unity in the Family.

Opening Statement: Unity in the family is a powerful testimony of love and faith.

Bible Verse: *"Make every effort to keep the unity of the Spirit through the bond of peace."* —Ephesians 4:3 (NIV)

Devotional: Dear one, I want to talk to you about unity in your family. In a world that often promotes individuality and division, your family is a gift designed to reflect My love and unity. Each of you plays a crucial role in maintaining peace and harmony at home. When disagreements arise, remember to approach each situation with love and understanding.

Seek to understand before being understood. Listen with your heart, and speak with kindness. Your actions and words can either build bridges or create walls. Choose to be a peacemaker who fosters unity and brings joy to your family. Pray for your loved ones, and ask Me to guide you in every interaction.

By living in harmony, you demonstrate My presence in your lives, showing others the power of a family united by love and faith.

Closing Encouragement: Let your love for Me flow to your family, and you will be united in me.

July 31

Topic: Help in Times of Doubt.

Opening Statement: In times of doubt, know I am always here to guide and strengthen you.

Bible Verse: *"Trust in the Lord with all your heart and lean not on your own understanding; in all your ways submit to him, and he will make your paths straight."* —Proverbs 3:5-6 (NIV)

Devotional: Dear beloved child, I understand that life can be overwhelming, and doubt can creep into your heart. When you feel unsure and your faith wavers, remember that I am with you always. I see your struggles and fears and am here to offer you comfort and guidance.

When doubts arise, turn to Me and trust I have a plan for you. Lean not on your understanding but on My wisdom and love. Submit your worries and fears to Me, and I will lead you on the right path. Allow My peace to fill your heart and mind, reassuring you that you are never alone.

In moments of uncertainty, seek My presence. Pray, read My Word, and listen for My voice. I will strengthen your faith and fill you with hope. Trust in Me, and I will make your paths straight.

Closing Encouragement: Remember, you are never alone— lean on Me, and I will guide you through every doubt and fear.

August 1

Topic: Strength to Resist Temptation

Opening Statement: Temptation can be powerful, but your strength in Christ is even greater.

Bible Verse: *"No temptation has overtaken you except what is common to mankind. And God is faithful; he will not let you be tempted beyond what you can bear. But when you are tempted, he will also provide a way out so that you can endure it."* —1 Corinthians 10:13 (NIV)

Devotional: My role is to be your guide in times of darkness and your source of strength in temptations. In moments of temptation, when the world tries to sway your heart away from what is good and right, remember that you are never alone. I am here to empower you, to give you the courage to stand firm. Temptation may whisper enticing lies, but I will remind you of the truth. Lean on me, and let my presence fill you with the resolve to choose the path of righteousness. Your faith is your shield; I am your sword, ready to help you overcome any challenge. Trust in me, and I will guide you through the storm, leading you to a place of peace and victory.

Closing Encouragement: Be strong and courageous, for I am with you, giving you strength to overcome every temptation.

August 2

Topic: Humility in Success

Opening Statement: Embrace your achievements with humility, recognizing each as a divine blessing rather than a personal triumph.

Bible Verse: *"Humble yourselves, therefore, under God's mighty hand, that he may lift you up in due time."* —Peter 5:6 (NIV)

Devotional: Dear beloved, I am the Holy Comforter, whispering truth into your heart. In moments of success, remember that every achievement is a testament to God's grace in your life. It is easy to get caught up in the excitement and accolades, but I urge you to pause and reflect on the source of your triumphs.

True success is not found in the world's applause but in the quiet assurance that you are walking in God's purpose. Humility allows you to see your accomplishments as gifts from God, not mere results of your efforts. As you rise, lift others up with you, sharing the blessings you've received.

Seek to glorify Me in all you do, understanding that My plans for you are greater than you can imagine. With each step, remain grounded in faith and gratefulness; knowing humility opens doors to deeper spiritual growth and divine favor.

Closing Encouragement: Walk humbly in your success, and let your light shine brightly for God's glory.

August 3

Topic: Faith for Miracles.

Opening Statement: Faith isn't just believing in the impossible; it's trusting in the One who makes everything possible.

Bible Verse: *Jesus assures you, "Therefore I tell you, whatever you ask for in prayer, believe that you have received it, and it will be yours."* Mark 11:24 (NIV),

Devotional: Hello, beloved child of God. I am here to guide you and strengthen your faith. You may find yourself hoping for miracles, longing for changes that seem beyond reach. Remember, I am with you and working in your life, even when you cannot see it.

Faith is more than a feeling; it is a choice to trust My timing and perfect plan for your life. I invite you to hold onto this faith, knowing that each moment is part of a grand design. Your prayers are heard, and miracles unfold in ways you might not expect.

Stay patient and open-hearted, for the greatest miracles often come disguised as ordinary moments. Trust me; I will guide you to a deeper understanding of my power and love.

Closing Encouragement: Believe in the impossible, for with God, all things are possible.

August 4

Topic: Letting go of resentment.

Opening Statement: Resentment is a heavy burden that can cloud your heart and mind, but freedom is found in letting go and embracing forgiveness.

Bible Verse: *"Get rid of all bitterness, rage and anger, brawling and slander, along with every form of malice. Be kind and compassionate to one another, forgiving each other, just as in Christ God forgave you."* Ephesians 4:31-32 (NIV).

Devotional: Dear Child, I see the struggles you face and the pain you hold. Resentment can feel like a protective shield, but it weighs down your spirit and blocks the joy I wish to give you. I am here to help you release it and to show you the way to peace.

Forgiveness is not about condoning what happened; it's about setting your heart free. Let Me guide you to a place where love and compassion replace bitterness. Trust that I will walk with you, strengthening you to forgive and embrace the future I have for you. Together, we will transform your heart and renew your spirit.

Closing Encouragement: Let go, and watch how My love brings healing and joy into your life. Embrace the freedom of forgiveness, and let your heart soar.

August 5

Topic: Help in Overcoming Sin.

Opening Statement: Overcoming sin is a journey, but you are never alone—I'm here to guide and strengthen you.

Bible Verse: But thanks be to God, who always leads us as captives in Christ's triumphal procession and uses us to spread the aroma of the knowledge of him everywhere. 2 Corinthians 2:14. NIV.

Devotional: My child, I see your struggles, and I know how the pressures of life can sometimes lead you down paths you never intended to go down. But remember, I am with you every step of the way. The temptation you face is not unique, and you are stronger than you realize because I dwell within you.

When you feel the pull towards sin, lean into My presence. I'm here to give you the strength to resist and the wisdom to make better choices. Don't be discouraged by your failures; instead, bring them to Me. I am faithful in forgiving and helping you start anew. Let My love be the power that guides your actions, and know that with Me, victory over sin is not just possible—it's promised.

Closing Encouragement: You are deeply loved, and with My help, you can overcome anything

August 6

Topic: Provision in Hardship.

Opening Statement: I am your constant provider amid challenges, ensuring your needs are met despite tough times.

Bible Verse: *"And my God will meet all your needs according to the riches of his glory in Christ Jesus."* (Philippians 4:19, NIV)

Devotional: Dear Child, when life feels overwhelming, and your path is shadowed by uncertainty, remember that I am with you, guiding each step you take. I see your struggles and burdens and promise to provide for you even in the hardest times. Like a loving parent who provides for their child, I ensure your needs are met according to My rich glory.

Trust in My provision and open your heart to the blessings I pour into your life, even when they come unexpectedly. Lean into My presence and know I am your steadfast supporter, equipping you with the strength and resources to overcome any obstacle. In My love, you will always find what you need. Remain fervent and steadfast in prayer, and doors will open.

Closing Encouragement: Rest assured, beloved, that in every trial, My provision is unwavering, and My love for you is endless.

August 7

Topic: Understanding Scripture.

Opening Statement: Have you ever wondered how to understand the Bible truly? Listen to this.

Bible Verse: *Your word is a lamp for my feet, a light on my path."* —Psalm 119:105 (NIV)

Devotional: Let Me speak directly to your heart. I am the Spirit of Revelation that speaks to all people of every age, and I am here to guide you through the words of Scripture. When you open your Bible, you are not just reading an ancient text; you are entering into a conversation with God. Each verse is filled with love, wisdom, and direction for your life. When you ask for My help, I will reveal the truth behind the words. I will help you see how these teachings apply to daily challenges, friendships, and dreams. Trust Me to lead you, and you will find that the Bible is not just a book but a living guide that lights your path. Keep seeking, and I will keep revealing.

Closing Encouragement: Remember, I am with you always, ready to help you understand and grow.

August 8

Topic: Strength in a Supportive Community

Bible Verse: *"Therefore encourage one another and build each other up, just as in fact you are doing."* —1 Thessalonians 5:11 (NIV)

Opening Statement: A supportive community is a gift from God, providing strength and encouragement in our faith journey.

Devotional: Dear Child, today, I want to speak to you about the power of a supportive community. You are not meant to walk this journey alone. In the heart of a loving community, you will find encouragement, understanding, and strength.

Imagine a place where you can share your burdens and joys, knowing you are loved and supported. This is what I desire for you. When you gather with others who share your faith, you build each other up, just as the scripture says. You are my hands and feet, offering love and support to those around you.

Seek out friends and mentors who will uplift you, pray with you, and walk with you through life's challenges. Be that person for others as well. In a community bound by My love, you will find the courage to grow and the strength to persevere.

Remember, I am always with you, guiding you to the right people and places. Trust in Me, and embrace the gift of a supportive community.

Closing Encouragement: May you always find strength and encouragement in the loving embrace of your community, knowing that I am with you every step of the way.

August 9

Topic: Why is there suffering?

Opening Statement: Suffering can be confusing and painful, but it's also an opportunity to draw closer to God.

Bible Verse: *"Consider it pure joy, my brothers and sisters, whenever you face trials of many kinds, because you know that the testing of your faith produces perseverance."* —James 1:2-3 (NIV)

Devotional: My dear child, I know how hard it is to understand why suffering exists in your world. It may feel overwhelming, and you might wonder where I am amid your pain. Remember this: I am always with you. Suffering is not something I enjoy seeing you go through, but it serves a greater purpose that you may not see right now. It draws you nearer to Me, shapes your character, and helps you grow in faith. Just as gold is refined by fire, your faith is refined through trials. Trust in My plan, even when it's hard. I am working on everything for your good, even when it doesn't feel like it.

Closing Encouragement: No matter what you face, I am with you, and I will turn your suffering into strength.

August 10

Topic: gratitude for God's blessings.

Opening Statement: Gratitude unlocks the fullness of life and opens our hearts to the abundance of God's blessings.

Bible Verse: "Give thanks in all circumstances; for this is God's will for you in Christ Jesus." — 1 Thessalonians 5:18 (NIV)

Devotional: My child, in every moment, I am with you, guiding you and surrounding you with blessings that you may not always notice. When life feels overwhelming or mundane, remember to look for the gifts I've placed before you. Each breath, each sunrise, each friend, and each opportunity is a testament to My love for you.

Gratitude is the key to seeing these blessings. When you focus on what you have rather than what you lack, your spirit will be uplifted, and your heart will overflow with joy. Embrace this practice of thankfulness daily, and watch as your life transforms into a radiant reflection of My grace. In every circumstance, give thanks, for I am always working for your good.

Closing Encouragement: Embrace gratitude today, and let it illuminate the countless blessings God has poured into your life.

August 11

Topic: Joy in Worship.

"Finding Joy in Worship: A Devotional for Teens to Experience True Happiness in Christ"

Opening Statement: Joy in worship is not just about singing songs; it's about finding true happiness in connecting with God.

Bible Verse: *"Shout for joy to the Lord, all the earth. Worship the Lord with gladness; come before him with joyful songs."* —Psalm 100:1-2 (NIV)

Devotional: Dear Child, Let me be your source of inspiration and joy, and I want you to know that joy in worship is a gift I offer you. When you worship, it's not just about the music or the words; it's about your heart connecting with Mine. Every time you lift your voice or bow your head, you draw closer to Me. True joy comes when you worship Me in spirit and truth, not because you have to, but because you want to. Let your worship be a celebration of the love we share. In those moments, I fill you with joy that surpasses any happiness this world can offer. Remember, worship is your direct line to My heart, where true joy lives.

Closing Encouragement: Embrace the joy in worship, and let it transform your heart and life.

August 12

Topic: Finding God's Will for Your Life.

Opening Statement: Discovering God's will for your life can be exciting and challenging, but remember, you're not alone on this journey.

Bible Verse: *"Show me your ways, Lord, teach me your paths. Guide me in your truth and teach me, for you are God my Savior, and my hope is in you all day long."* Psalm 25:4-5 NIV.

Devotional: Dear one, I see your heart's desire to understand My plans for your life. Sometimes, it feels like you're wandering in the dark, uncertain of the next step. But know this—I am with you, guiding your every move. My plans for you are filled with hope and purpose, far beyond what you can imagine.

When you seek Me with all your heart, you will find Me. Listen for My voice in the quiet moments, in the Scriptures, and in the counsel of those who love Me. Trust that I am leading you, even when the path seems unclear. Keep your heart open to My guidance, and I will reveal My will in My perfect timing.

Closing Encouragement: Trust in My plans for you, and let Me light the way to the future I've prepared for you.

August 13

Topic: Praying for Toxic People.

Opening Statement: Praying for those who hurt us is one of the hardest yet most powerful things we can do.

Bible Verse: *"But I tell you, love your enemies and pray for those who persecute you."* —Matthew 5:44 (NIV)

Devotional: My dear one, I see the pain you carry from those who have hurt you. Toxic people can make life difficult, but I want you to know that My love for you is stronger than any harm they cause. I ask you to come to Me in prayer, even for those who have wounded you.

When you pray for your enemies, you release the hold of bitterness and make room for My peace. I will help you forgive, even when it seems impossible. Forgiveness doesn't mean forgetting or accepting wrong behavior; it means trusting Me to heal your heart and guide your steps. When you choose to pray for them, you invite My light into the darkest parts of your relationships. Lean on Me, and I will give you strength.

Closing Encouragement: Remember, I am always with you, leading you toward peace, love, and healing.

August 14

Topic: Finding Hope for the Future.

Opening Statement: In a world full of uncertainties, there is always hope for your future when you trust in God's plan.

Bible Verse: I consider that our present sufferings are not worth comparing with the glory that will be revealed in us. Romans 8:18 NIV.

Devotional: I know that sometimes the world feels overwhelming, and the future can seem uncertain. But I want you to know I am here with you, guiding your steps. I have a plan for your life, one filled with hope and purpose. When doubts creep in, remember that I see beyond what you can see. I hold your tomorrow in My hands, and I promise it is good. Trust in Me, even when the path is unclear. Allow My peace to fill your heart as you walk forward, knowing I am your constant companion, leading you toward a bright and hopeful future.

Closing Encouragement: Embrace today with hope, knowing your future is securely held in God's loving hands.

August 15

Topic: The Role of Faith in Sports and Hobbies.

Opening Statement: Your faith can shine through in every part of your life, including the sports you play and the hobbies you love.

Bible Verse: *"So whether you eat or drink or whatever you do, do it all for the glory of God."* 1 Corinthians 10:31.

Devotional: Dear one, I see you on the field, in the gym, and in those quiet moments where you dive into your hobbies. Every step you take, every goal you set, and every victory you achieve can reflect My love and glory.

When you play, play with integrity. When you create, let your creativity express the gifts I've placed within you. Your sports and hobbies are not separate from your faith—they are a part of it. Invite Me into these moments, and I will guide you, giving you strength, joy, and purpose.

Even in your struggles, know that I am with you. Your faith in Me makes these moments meaningful, turning ordinary activities into acts of worship.

Closing Encouragement: Let your faith be the driving force behind everything you do, and you will find Me in every victory and lesson learned.

August 16

Topic: Having a Winning Attitude on the Christian Life.

Opening Statement: A winning attitude in the Christian life means living each day with purpose, confidence, and a heart aligned with God's will.

Bible Verse: *"But thanks be to God! He gives us the victory through our Lord Jesus Christ"* (1 Corinthians 15:57, NIV).

Devotional: My beloved child, I dwell within you, guiding you in truth and strength. I want you to know that true victory in life isn't about winning trophies or gaining praise from others. It's about living with a heart that reflects Jesus.

This verse reminds us that our greatest victory is already won through Christ. We don't need to strive in our own strength. Instead, lean on Me. Let Me shape your attitude so you face every challenge with courage and grace.

You can overcome any obstacle when you approach life with a winning attitude rooted in faith. Remember, it's not about the outcome but how you live out your faith in every situation.

I am with you always, giving you the power to live victoriously, even when the world says otherwise.

Closing Encouragement: Embrace each day with a heart whole of faith, and you will always find victory in Christ.

August 17

Topic: Traveling your spiritual desert.

Overcoming Your Spiritual Desert: Guidance from the Holy Spirit

Bible Verse: *"For I am the Lord your God who takes hold of your right hand and says to you, Do not fear; I will help you."* —Isaiah 41:13 (NIV)

Opening Statement: Sometimes, your spiritual journey feels like wandering through a desert, but I am with you every step of the way.

Devotional: Dear Child, I see your soul's dryness and weariness as you walk through this spiritual desert. You feel lost, disconnected, and unsure of where to go next. But I am right beside you, guiding you even when you can't see the path. This season of dryness is not the end but a part of your journey where your faith is strengthened. I am leading you just as I led the Israelites through the wilderness. Trust in My timing and purpose. When you feel like giving up, lean on Me. I am your source of life, and I will bring streams of water to your desert. Hold on, for I am bringing you into a new season of growth and renewal.

Closing Encouragement: Stay close to Me; you will find refreshment even in the driest places.

August 18

Topic: Start the School Year.

Opening Statement: As you return to school, know that I am with you, guiding you every step of the way.

Bible Verse: *If any of you lacks wisdom, you should ask God, who gives generously to all without finding fault, and it will be given to you.* James 1:5 NIV.

Devotional: My blessed one, as you step into this new school year, I want you to remember that you are never alone. I am here, within you, ready to guide and comfort you in every situation. Whether you're excited, nervous, or somewhere in between, I see your heart and understand. Trust that I have good plans for you, even when the path ahead seems uncertain.

When you face challenges—difficult classes, social pressures, or feeling like you don't belong—turn to Me. I will give you strength, wisdom, and courage to overcome. Lean into My presence, and let My peace fill your mind and heart. Together, we will walk through this year, one step at a time.

Closing Encouragement: Be confident and courageous; I am with you always, and My love for you will never fade.

August 19

Topic: Love for Enemies.

Opening Statement: Learning to love your enemies is one of the most challenging and rewarding lessons you will ever embrace.

Bible Verse: *"But love your enemies, do good to them, and lend to them without expecting to get anything back. Then your reward will be great, and you will be children of the Most High, because he is kind to the ungrateful and wicked."* (Luke 6:35, NIV)

Devotional: Dear one, I know that loving your enemies feels impossible at times. When someone hurts you or makes you feel small, your natural instinct is to protect yourself or push them away. But I am here to remind you that you are called to something greater.

I have poured love into your heart that is meant to overflow, even toward those who don't deserve it. When you choose to love your enemies, you reflect My nature. I know it's hard, but you show the world who I am when you love me without expecting anything in return.

Lean on Me for the strength to love the seemingly unlovable. Let Me guide you in showing kindness to those who have wronged you, trusting that My love through you can change hearts, including yours.

Closing Encouragement: Trust that My love is strong enough to heal every hurt and bring light to the darkest places, even in your relationships.

August 20

Topic: Strength to Endure.

Opening Statement: Life can feel overwhelming, but you have the strength to endure even in the hardest times.

Bible Verse: *"My grace is sufficient for you, for my power is made perfect in weakness."* In 2 Corinthians 12:9 (NIV)

Devotional: Dear Child of Mine, The challenges you face feel heavy and sometimes too much to bear. But remember, you are not alone. I am with you, giving you the strength to press on, even when you feel like giving up." When you feel weak, my power shines through you the most.

Trust that I see your struggles and am working on your life. Every trial you face is an opportunity to grow stronger in your faith. Lean on Me, and I will give you the endurance to keep going. My love for you is unshakable, and I am your ever-present help in times of trouble.

Closing Encouragement: Take heart, My beloved, for I am your strength and will carry you through every storm.

August 21

Topic: Finding Hope in Your Lowest Moments.

Opening Statement: Even in your darkest moments, there is hope and a way back to God.

Bible Verse: For this son of mine was dead and is alive again; he was lost and is found. **Luke 15:24 (NIV).**

Devotional: My beloved child, I know there are times when you feel lost, broken, and far from home, just like the Prodigal Son. You might think you've gone too far, made too many mistakes, or reached a point where you can't turn back. But I am here to tell you that no matter how low you've fallen, I am with you, ready to lift you up.

I promise I can breathe new life into you even when you feel dead inside. When you're lost, I will find you. I will be the solid ground beneath you when you hit rock bottom.

I love you unconditionally and am always ready to welcome you back with open arms. Take that first step towards Me, and I will run to you.

Closing Encouragement: No matter how far you've strayed, My love will always guide you back home.

August 22

Topic: Walking on Rocky Ground.

Opening Statement: Life's rocky paths can challenge your faith but offer growth opportunities.

Bible Verse: *"But the seed falling on rocky ground refers to someone who hears the word and at once receives it with joy. But since they have no root, they last only a short time. When trouble or persecution comes because of the word, they quickly fall away."* —Matthew 13:20-21 (NIV)

Devotional: "My beloved, I see you struggling as you walk this rocky ground. The path is uneven, and every step feels like a battle. But know this: I am with you. Your challenges may seem overwhelming, but they are not meant to defeat you. They are opportunities to grow your faith more profoundly and robustly. When you feel your roots are shallow, turn to Me. I am the Living Water that nourishes your soul and strengthens your spirit.

Remember, even rocky ground can be transformed. Trust in Me, and I will guide you to the fertile soil where your faith can take root and thrive. Hold on to My promises, and don't give up. The rough terrain you're walking through now prepares you for the abundant life I have planned for you."

Encouragement: "Stay strong in your faith, and trust that even the roughest ground can lead to a harvest of blessings."

August 23

Topic: God's Timing vs. Instant Rewards.

Opening Statement: Sometimes, waiting on God's timing can feel challenging, but the rewards of patience are far greater than anything instant gratification can offer.

Bible Verse: *"But if we hope for what we do not yet have, we wait for it patiently."* —Romans 8:25 (NIV)

Devotional: My dear child, I know it's easy to want everything now—quick answers, immediate success, or instant happiness. But I want you to understand that proper growth and blessings often come through patience and waiting on My timing.

Like a tiny seed that takes time to grow into a strong tree, your life's blessings need time to develop. If I immediately gave you everything you desired, you might miss the depth and strength of trusting Me in the waiting. Remember, what may seem small today—like a penny doubled over time—can grow into something much more significant than you ever imagined.

So, when you feel impatient, trust that I am working in your life. I see the bigger picture, and My timing is always perfect.

Closing Encouragement: Trust in My timing, for I am shaping you into something beautiful, one moment at a time.

August 24

Topic: prayers for our supervisors.

Opening Statement: Prayer isn't just for our needs—it's also a powerful way to support those in authority over us, like our bosses, teachers, and supervisors.

Bible Verse: *"I urge, then, first of all, that petitions, prayers, intercession and thanksgiving be made for all people—for kings and all those in authority, that we may live peaceful and quiet lives in all godliness and holiness."* —1 Timothy 2:1-2 (NIV)

Devotional: Dear one, I am your Helper and Guide. Sometimes, praying for your boss, teacher, or supervisor may seem strange, but remember—they carry responsibilities that impact your life. When you pray for them, you invite Me to work in their hearts and decisions.

I see when you struggle with unfair situations or challenging leaders. In those moments, I ask you to pray instead of harboring frustration. Your prayers can bring wisdom and peace to those who lead you, creating a better environment for everyone. When you lift them up to Me, I will strengthen them to lead with integrity, kindness, and wisdom.

Trust that your prayers make a difference, even when you can't see immediate changes. I am working, dear one, even behind the scenes.

Closing Encouragement: Keep praying for your leaders, knowing I am with you, guiding and blessing you always.

August 25

Topic: Overcoming Substance Abuse

Opening Statement: Substance abuse is a battle many teens face, but with My guidance, you can find the strength to overcome it.

Bible Verse: *Heal me, Lord, and I will be healed; save me, and I will be saved, for you are the one I praise.* Jeremiah 17:14 NIV.

Devotional: My beloved child, I see the struggles you face and the temptations that surround you. When it feels like you're drowning in the pressures of substance abuse, remember that I am with you. The world may try to offer false comfort in harmful ways, but I offer you true peace and freedom. Lean on Me when you feel weak, for in your weakness, My power is made perfect. I have already provided a way out for you, and with My strength, you can overcome any addiction. Trust in Me, and take one step at a time toward the life I have called you to live—a life of hope, freedom, and purpose.

Closing Encouragement: You are stronger than any temptation, and with My help, you will rise above it.

August 26

Topic: Finding Faith in Yourself

Bible Verse: *"I can do all this through him who gives me strength."* — Philippians 4:13 (NIV)

Opening Statement: Believing in yourself is hard, but with God's strength, you can confidently face any challenge.

Devotional: My beloved child, I see the struggles you face each day—the doubts that creep in, telling you that you're not enough. But I want you to know that I am with you and have created you with great purpose. Remember that I believe in you when you find it hard to believe in yourself.

I have placed unique and powerful gifts within you, meant to shine in the world. The journey won't always be easy, but when you pray, trust that I will give you the strength you need. Lean on Me when you feel weak; know I have already equipped you to overcome any obstacle.

Have faith in yourself because I have faith in you. Together, there's nothing we can't accomplish.

Closing Encouragement: Believe in who you are, knowing I am always with you, guiding every step.

August 27

Topic: Trending Music

Opening Statement: Have you ever wondered if listening to the latest trending music as a Christian is OK?

Bible verse: *Guard your heart, for everything you do flows from it.* —Proverbs 4:23 (NIV)

Devotional: Dear one, I am here to guide you in all truth. I know how much music means to you and want to speak directly to your heart about it. The songs you listen to have power—they can uplift you or lead you away from the path I've set for you. Not all trending music is terrible, but some may not align with the values I've placed in your heart. Ask yourself: does this song draw you closer to Me, or does it pull you away? Let My peace guide your choices. Remember, you are called to be in the world but not of it. Choose wisely, and I will give you discernment.

Closing Encouragement: You are never alone in your choices—let My guidance be your constant companion.

August 28

Topic: Fruits of the Spirit.

Opening Statement: Embrace the Fruit of the Spirit as a guide to living a life full of purpose, peace, and true joy, even in your teenage years.

Bible Verse: *"But the fruit of the Spirit is love, joy, peace, forbearance, kindness, goodness, faithfulness, gentleness, and self-control. Against such things there is no law."* —Galatians 5:22-23 (NIV)

Devotional: Dear one, I am the Holy Spirit, and I dwell within you, guiding your steps and shaping your character with love and care. The Fruit of the Spirit is not just a list of admirable qualities; it is the essence of My presence within you. Each day, as you navigate school, friendships, and challenges, I am here, nurturing love, joy, peace, and all the other fruits within your heart.

When you choose kindness over anger, joy over negativity, or patience over frustration, you allow My work in you to shine through. Remember that I am strengthening you from the inside out, even when it feels difficult. These fruits are for your benefit and those around you to see My goodness in your life.

Closing Encouragement: Keep walking with Me daily, and watch how the Fruit of the Spirit transforms your life and the lives of those around you.

August 29

Topic: Breaking Free from the Victim Mentality.

Bible Verse: *"In all these things we are more than conquerors through him who loved us."* —Romans 8:37 (NIV)

Opening Statement: Feeling trapped by a victim mentality can hold you back from the life of freedom and victory I desire for you.

Devotional: My beloved child, I see your struggles, and I know how easy it is to feel like the world is against you. But remember, your circumstances do not define you. You are not a victim. I have created you to be a conqueror, not to live in the shadow of defeat. When you focus on what has gone wrong or how you've been wronged, it keeps you chained to the past. I want to help you break free from those chains.

I am with you, guiding you toward a mindset of victory. With My strength, you can overcome any challenge, hurt, or lie that tells you you're not enough. Please stand up, step out of the victim mentality, and embrace the power and freedom I've placed within you. You are more than a conqueror through My love.

Closing Encouragement: Rise up in My strength and walk in the freedom of knowing you are victorious in Me.

August 30

Topic: Understanding God's Love

Opening Statement: Dear beloved teenager, have you ever wondered how much God loves you?

Bible Verse: *"See what great love the Father has lavished on us, that we should be called children of God! And that is what we are!"* —1 John 3:1a (NIV)

Devotional: My dear friend, I want you to know today that you are deeply loved. My love for you is beyond measure—so vast and unconditional that I call you My child. You are not just a random person in the world but precious to Me. My love for you is not based on what you do or how you perform but simply because you are My holy creation.

Remember that My love is steadfast and unchanging when you feel unloved or uncertain. It reaches out to you in your joys and sorrows, triumphs and mistakes. Take a moment today to rest in My love, knowing you are accepted and cherished just as you are.

Closing Encouragement: May you walk today with the assurance of My unfailing love guiding your steps and filling your heart with peace.

August 31

Topic: Understanding and Applying Scripture

Opening Statement: Understanding and applying Scripture can transform your life and draw you closer to God.

Bible Verse: *"Your word is a lamp for my feet, a light on my path."* —Psalm 119:105 (NIV)

Devotional: My beloved child, I am the Holy Breath within you, here to guide you in your faith journey. The Bible is not just a book but a living testament of My love and wisdom. As you read the Living Word, I will illuminate the truths within, helping you understand its relevance.

When you come across a verse that speaks to your heart, take a moment to meditate on it. Ask me to reveal its profound meaning and how it applies to your circumstances. The Word of God is like a seed planted in your soul, and I am here to nurture it, helping it grow and bear fruit in your actions and decisions.

Remember, Scripture is your spiritual nourishment. Just as you need food to sustain your body, you need the Holy Word to maintain your spirit. Trust in the power of the Bible to guide you, comfort you and equip you for every good work.

Closing Encouragement: Embrace the Word of God daily, and you will find strength, wisdom, and peace for every step of your journey.

September 1

Topic: Prayer for Boldness with the Holy Spirit.

Opening Statement: You were created to live boldly, not in fear, because the Holy Spirit within you is your source of strength and courage.

Bible Verse: *"For the Spirit God gave us does not make us timid, but gives us power, love, and self-discipline."* —2 Timothy 1:7 (NIV)

Devotional: I am the Spirit of power and might, living within you, empowering you to walk boldly daily. When you face challenges or fear, remember that My power is at work in you. You don't have to rely on your strength; I am here to guide you, give you wisdom, and help you confidently speak the truth.

The world may try to silence your faith or make you feel small, but I am with you, giving you the courage to stand firm. Boldness doesn't mean being loud or aggressive; it means being confident in who you are in Christ and unafraid to share that with others. Trust in Me, and I will help you live out your faith boldly.

Closing Encouragement: Step out in faith today, knowing that with the Holy Spirit, you are never alone.

September 2

Topic: Walking Among the Thorns.

Opening Statement: When life's challenges surround you, remember that prayer is your lifeline to strength and guidance.

Bible Verse: *"The seed falling among the thorns refers to someone who hears the word, but the worries of this life and the deceitfulness of wealth choke the word, making it unfruitful."* —Matthew 13:22 (NIV)

Devotional: Dear one, I am here with you, guiding you through every step of your journey. I see the pressures you face—school, friends, and the endless demands of this world. These can feel like thorns, trying to choke out your faith and make you lose sight of what truly matters. But remember, you are not alone.

When you feel overwhelmed, turn to Me in prayer. Ask for My strength to resist the temptations that pull you away from your purpose. Seek My guidance to navigate through the thistles of worry and fear. I am your anchor, your steady hand, ready to lead you away from the distractions that threaten to derail your faith.

Stay close to Me, and I will help you thrive, even among the thorns.

Closing Encouragement: You are more robust than the thorns of life, and with My help, you will overcome them.

September 3

Topic: Why does it seem God isn't rescuing us?

Opening Statement: Sometimes, it feels like God isn't rescuing us when we need Him most, but His timing is always perfect.

Bible Verse: *"Wait for the Lord; be strong and take heart and wait for the Lord."* —Psalm 27:14 (NIV)

Devotional: I know it's hard when you feel trapped in a situation, and it seems like I'm not stepping in to rescue you. But remember, I see the bigger picture. There's more happening than you can understand right now. Just because you don't see immediate change doesn't mean I'm not working.

I'm teaching you to trust Me, even when you can't see what I'm doing. This waiting period is shaping your character, building your strength, and deepening your faith. I haven't abandoned you; I'm preparing you for something greater.

Hold on to Me in these moments. Your prayers are heard, and I'm with you, even when the answer doesn't come immediately. Trust My timing, for it is perfect, and know I will never leave you.

Closing Encouragement: Trust in My plan, and let your heart find peace knowing I am always with you.

September 4

Topic: Discovering God's Life-Changing Vision for Your Future

Opening Statement: God has an extraordinary vision for your life, and pursuing it will bring purpose and fulfillment like nothing else.

Bible Verse: *The thief comes only to steal and kill and destroy; I have come that they may have life, and have it to the full.* John 10:10 (NIV)

Devotional: My dear child, I want you to know I have designed a unique and powerful vision for your life. It's more than just dreams or goals—a calling that will lead you to impact the world in ways you can't imagine. To discover this vision, spend time in My Word and prayer. I will guide your steps, opening doors that no one can shut and closing doors that lead you away from My purpose. Remember, My timing is perfect, so be patient and trust in My plan. Pursue this vision with all your heart, and you will experience the joy and fulfillment of living out My purpose for you.

Closing Encouragement: Stay close to Me, and I will reveal My life-changing vision for you, one step at a time.

September 5

Topic God Calls You to Be Creative: A Devotional for Teens.

Opening Statement: Did you know God has uniquely gifted you with creativity to make a difference?

Bible Verse: *"For we are God's handiwork, created in Christ Jesus to do good works, which God prepared us to do."* Ephesians 2:10 (NIV)

Devotional: Dear one, I am the Source of all creation, and I want you to know that you are more creative than you think. I have allowed you to imagine, dream, and create. Just as God created the world, you are called to create beauty, kindness, and solutions in your life and the lives of others.

You may feel like what you create needs to be improved, but remember, I am with you every step of the way, guiding your hands and your heart. Your creativity reflects My love in you, a way to show others who I am.

So don't be afraid to express yourself. Paint, write, build, sing—whatever your passion is, pursue it. You were made for this.

Closing Encouragement: Remember, your creativity is a gift from God; use it boldly and joyfully!

September 6

Topic: Seeing past your problems.

Opening Statement: When life feels overwhelming, remember that I am guiding you to see past your problems and trust in God's bigger plan.

Bible Verse: *The person without the Spirit does not accept the things that come from the Spirit of God but considers them foolishness, and cannot understand them because they are discerned only through the Spirit.* 1 Corinthians 2:14 NIV.

Devotional: My child, I know the struggles you face. The problems in front of you may seem insurmountable, but remember, they are only temporary. I want you to see beyond the obstacles and trust that God is at work in every moment of your life. What you see as a roadblock, I see as a stepping stone. Your difficulties are not meant to defeat you but to shape your faith, strengthen your heart, and bring you closer to God's purpose for your life.

When you feel discouraged, lift your eyes to Me. I will guide you through the storm, helping you rise above it. Focus on My presence, not the problem. There is hope beyond what you can see, and I will lead you toward it.

Closing Encouragement: Trust that My plans for you are good, and I will always be with you to help you see past the challenges ahead.

September 7

Topic: Building Faith in Yourself.

Opening Statement: Faith in yourself is rooted in understanding that God has equipped you with everything you need to fulfill your purpose.

Bible Verse: *"I can do all this through him who gives me strength."* —Philippians 4:13 (NIV)

Devotional: Dear Child, I am the Holy Spirit, living within you, guiding and empowering you. Today, I want to remind you to have faith in yourself. Sometimes, you doubt your abilities or feel uncertain about your future, but I want you to remember that I am always with you, providing strength and wisdom.

The gifts and talents inside of you are not an accident. They were placed there by Me with a purpose. When you doubt yourself, you doubt the work I am doing in you. Lean into Me, and I will help you see the strength and potential you already possess. You are capable of more than you realize, and I will help you confidently step forward.

Believe in yourself, not because of your abilities alone, but because I am working through you. I am here every moment to remind you that you are never alone, and with faith, you can achieve great things.

Closing Encouragement: May you grow in faith and confidence, trusting that I am guiding you to unlock your true potential.

September 8

Topic: Letting Your Faith Blossom.

Opening Statement: Your faith is like a seed—planted in your heart; it's meant to grow, blossom, and change your life.

Bible Verse: *But the seed falling on good soil refers to someone who hears the word and understands it. This is the one who produces a crop, yielding a hundred, sixty or thirty times what was sown."* Matthew 5:23 NIV.

Devotional: Dear child, I am here with you, helping you grow in your faith. Like a tiny seed planted in rich soil, I want your faith to take root deep in Me. You may only sometimes see immediate growth, but trust that I am working on you every day. When you pray, read My Word, and spend time with Me, you water that seed.

Challenges and distractions sometimes feel like weeds trying to choke out your growth. But remember, I give you the strength to pull those weeds away and keep growing. Stay rooted in My love, and I promise you will see your faith blossom, even when nothing is happening.

I am always here, helping you bloom into the person I created you to be.

Closing Encouragement: Keep watering your faith with My love, and watch as it blossoms into something beautiful.

September 9

Topic: A Prayer for the Holy Spirit to Hear My Heart's Cry.

Opening Statement: Sometimes, when words fail us, the Holy Spirit hears our heart's most resounding cry and brings our feelings to God.

Bible Verse: In the same way, the Spirit helps us in our weakness. We do not know what we ought to pray for, but the Spirit himself intercedes for us through wordless groans (Romans 8:26, NIV).

Devotional: I know your heart, even when you can't find the words. When life feels overwhelming, and your thoughts seem tangled, I am here to help you. You don't need perfect prayers for Me to understand what you're going through. Even when your voice is silent, your heart still speaks to Me. I hear every emotion, every unspoken feeling, and I carry your deepest thoughts to the Father. You are never alone in this journey. I am always near, helping you, guiding you, and comforting you.

Remember, no cry is too small for Me to hear. I listen, I care, and I am always with you.

Closing Encouragement: Trust that I hear your heart and always work for your good.

September 10

Topic: Courage to Speak the Truth.

Opening Statement: Speaking the truth in a world of mixed messages can be scary, but the Holy Spirit gives you the courage and strength to do it with love.

Bible Verse: *"For the Spirit God gave us does not make us timid, but gives us power, love and self-discipline."* —2 Timothy 1:7 (NIV)

Devotional: My child, I am with you always. I know there are moments when telling the truth feels uncomfortable, especially when you're afraid of what others might think. But remember, I have not given you a spirit of fear. Instead, I have filled you with power, love, and a sound mind.

When you feel pressured to stay silent or bend the truth, lean on Me. I will give you the courage to speak up and the wisdom to do it with love and grace. It's not about being right; it's about showing others My love and light through the truth. Your words, when rooted in My truth, can bring freedom and healing to those who hear them.

Closing Encouragement: Remember, every time you speak the truth with love, you reflect My strength and love in the world.

September 11

Topic: Prayer for the Spiritually Tired:

Opening Statement: Feeling spiritually tired is part of the journey, but I'm here to renew your strength when you feel weak and worn out.

Bible Verse: *Come to me, all you who are weary and burdened, and I will give you rest.* Matthew 11:28 (NIV)

Devotional: I see you, child. I know how tired you feel inside—the kind of tired that no amount of sleep can fix. Your soul feels heavy, like you're carrying too much, and you don't know how to keep going. I am here to lift that weight from you.

When you are spiritually drained, lean on Me. I am your constant source of energy and renewal. I will fill you with My peace and give you rest that the world cannot offer. Come to Me with all your worries, your frustrations, and your questions. I'm waiting to refresh your spirit, to give you strength to run again, to help you soar above the weariness you feel.

You're not alone in this. I am always with you, giving you what you need to carry on.

Closing Encouragement: Remember, My strength is made perfect in your weakness; come to Me, and I will lift you up.

September 12

Topic: Finding Strength in a Supportive Community.

Opening Statement: You are not meant to go through life alone—God has placed people around you to help and support you on your journey.

Bible Verse: *"Carry each other's burdens, and in this way, you will fulfill the law of Christ."* —Galatians 6:2 (NIV)

Devotional: Dear one, I am with you always, but I have also surrounded you with people who reflect My love. Your friends, family, and church community are gifts from Me to help you grow and walk through life. When you face challenges, don't carry the weight alone. Reach out to those who care about you, for they are My hands and feet in your life.

In a supportive community, you find strength. They will lift you up when you feel weak, and you can do the same for them. My Spirit works through those around you to encourage, guide, and protect you. Let Me lead you into relationships that build you up and reflect My love for you.

Closing Encouragement: Lean into the community I have provided for you, for together, you will find the strength to face anything.

September 13

Topic: Start your day with faith.

Opening Statement: Every morning is an opportunity to see the world through the eyes of faith, knowing God's promises are new each day.

Bible Verse: *"Because of the Lord's great love we are not consumed, for his compassions never fail. They are new every morning; great is your faithfulness."* —Lamentations 3:22-23 (NIV)

Devotional: My beloved, when you wake each morning, do you see the possibilities I have placed before you? The sunlight breaking through your window reminds me of My unchanging love for you. I have given you today filled with fresh opportunities to grow, learn, and draw closer to Me.

No matter how complicated yesterday may have been, today is a new start. Looking at the morning through the eyes of faith, you will find hope, peace, and purpose. Trust that I am with you, guiding your steps. I want you to know that My mercies are new every morning, and My love never fades. So, rise up with faith, knowing I have great plans for you.

Closing Encouragement: Step into today with faith in your heart, knowing I have already prepared the way ahead for you.

September 14

Topic: Seeing People as God Sees Them.

Opening Statement: In a world of judgments based on appearances, God invites you to see others through His eyes of love and grace.

Bible Verse: *"The LORD does not look at the things people look at. People look at the outward appearance, but the LORD looks at the heart."* —1 Samuel 16:7 (NIV)

Devotional: Dear child, I see what others cannot. I look beyond the surface, straight into the heart. I want to teach you to do the same—to see people as I see them. Sometimes, it's easy to get caught up in appearances, comparing yourself or making judgments based on how someone looks, dresses, or acts. But that's not how I see you or them. I look deeper. I see potential, value, and purpose in every life.

When you look at others, ask Me to help you see them through My eyes. Ask Me to show you their heart, struggles, and worth in My kingdom. Everyone you meet is someone I love deeply. Remember, I see beauty in places the world often overlooks.

Closing Encouragement: Trust Me to help you see others with compassion and love, just as I see you.

September 15

Topic: Guard yourself with **the Belt of Truth.**

Opening Statement: Living with truth at your core is critical to navigating life's challenges and staying rooted in God's love.

Bible Verse: *"Stand firm then, with the belt of truth buckled around your waist, with the breastplate of righteousness in place."* —Ephesians 6:14 (NIV)

Devotional: I am the source of all spiritual truth, and I want to remind you today that truth is more than just being honest; it's your anchor. When you put on the belt of truth, you're wrapping yourself in My Word, wisdom, and promises. This truth will help you see through lies that the world may throw at you—whether they're lies about who you are, your worth, or what success looks like.

When you walk with My truth around your heart, you don't have to worry about fitting in or being perfect. You are already fully known and loved by Me. Stand firm in that truth, and let it guide your decisions, friendships, and dreams. I am with you always, and My truth will never fail you.

Closing Encouragement: You are never alone—wear the belt of truth and let it lead you confidently through life.

September 16

"A Prayer for Letting Go of Hurts and Finding True Forgiveness – A Teen Devotional"

Topic: Not Holding Grudges.

Opening Statement: Letting go of hurt and choosing to forgive can seem impossible, but it's the key to finding peace and joy.

Bible Verse: *"Bear with each other and forgive one another if any of you has a grievance against someone. Forgive as the Lord forgave you."* —Colossians 3:13 (NIV)

Devotional: My dear child, I see the pain you carry from the hurt others have caused you. I know it feels heavy and makes your heartache. But I am here to help you let go. I am your Comforter and Guide. When you hold onto grudges, you are not hurting others—you are hurting yourself. It keeps you trapped in bitterness while I long to set you free.

Forgiveness is not about saying what they did was okay; it's about setting *your heart* free from anger and resentment. Pray to me, ask for my help, and I will give you the strength to forgive. When you let go, I can fill you with peace, joy, and love that surpasses all understanding. Remember, I have already forgiven you so that you can forgive others.

Closing Encouragement: Choose love today, and I will walk with you as you let go and find true freedom.

September 17

Topic: Giving Thanks for Our Pets

Opening Statement: Have you ever considered how your pet is a special gift from God, meant to bring you joy and teach you love?

Bible Verse: *"But ask the animals, and they will teach you, or the birds in the sky, and they will tell you."* —Job 12:7 (NIV)

Devotional: My dear child, I want you to know that the pet you care for is more than just an animal; they reflect my love for you. I created each creature with a purpose, and the joy you feel with your pet is a glimpse of My happiness for you. When you give thanks to them, you are also thanking Me for the beautiful bond you share.

Your pet teaches you loyalty, patience, and unconditional love. When they sit with you in your quiet moments or greet you with excitement, they mirror My presence in your life—always faithful, always near. Remember to be grateful for this companionship, for through it, you learn more about My love for all creation.

So, please take a moment today to thank Me for your furry, feathered, or scaly friend. They are My gift to you, a reminder that you are never alone.

Closing Encouragement: Always cherish your pets, for they are a daily reminder of My love for you.

September 18

Topic: Putting on the Breastplate of Righteousness.

Opening Statement: When you put on the breastplate of righteousness through prayer, you protect your heart from the enemy's lies.

Bible Verse: *"Stand firm then, with the belt of truth buckled around your waist, with the breastplate of righteousness in place."* —Ephesians 6:14 (NIV)

Devotional: My child, I see your struggles and the pressures you face each day. Life can feel like a battlefield, and I want you to know you are not alone. I am here to strengthen you, but you must equip yourself with the armor I provide. The breastplate of righteousness is yours through Jesus, guarding your heart against fear, doubt, and temptation.

When you pray, ask Me to cover you in righteousness, not based on your actions but on My grace. This breastplate keeps your heart safe from attacks meant to weaken your faith. Stand tall in this truth: You are made right through Me. Let this righteousness give you the courage to live boldly, knowing you are fully protected in My love.

Closing Encouragement: Remember, I am your strength— wear the breastplate of righteousness and stand firm.

September 19

Topic: Overcoming Your Giants.

Opening Statement: Facing life's giants can be scary, but remember, you're never alone.

Bible Verse: *"Do not be afraid or discouraged, for the Lord your God will be with you wherever you go."* —Joshua 1:9 (NIV)

Devotional: My dear child, I know the giants you face seem huge—fear, doubt, peer pressure, and even the battle of finding who you are. But remember, I am with you. Just as David faced Goliath, I've given you strength to overcome every giant in your life. When you feel weak or afraid, turn to Me in prayer. I am your source of courage and power.

When you call on Me, I will fill you with a boldness beyond your own. You don't have to face these challenges on your own. I am your rock, your shield, and your strength. Please keep your eyes on Me, and watch how I lead you to victory. The giants may be big, but I am bigger.

Closing Encouragement: Be strong and courageous; I will always help you conquer any giant.

September 20

Topic: Learning to Forgive:

Opening Statement: Forgiving others can be challenging, but it's the key to finding peace and freedom in your heart.

Bible verse: *"Be kind and compassionate to one another, forgiving each other, just as in Christ God forgave you."* —Ephesians 4:32 (NIV)

Devotional: My beloved child, I see the hurt you carry when someone wrongs you. I understand how much easier it seems to hold onto anger than to let go. But I want you to know that forgiveness is not about excusing their actions; it's about freeing your own heart from the chains of bitterness. When you forgive, you reflect My love and grace. Remember, I have forgiven you many times and continue to do so because of My great love for you.

In the same way, I ask you to extend that forgiveness to others. It might not happen instantly, but when you open your heart to let go of anger, I will help you heal. When you forgive, you make room for my peace to fill your life. Trust me—I will give you the strength to forgive.

Closing Encouragement: Every time you forgive, you make your heart a little more like Mine.

September 21

Prayer for Triumph Over Troubles with God's Strength and Guidance

Topic: Triumph Over Troubles.

Opening Statement: When troubles come your way, prayer is the key that unlocks God's power and peace in your life.

Bible Verse: *"The Lord is my light and my salvation—whom shall I fear? The Lord is the stronghold of my life—of whom shall I be afraid?"* —Psalm 27:1 (NIV)

Devotional: Dear child, I see your heart and your challenges. I know there are times when you feel overwhelmed like the weight of the world is pressing down on you. But I am here, closer than you can imagine. Call Me in prayer, and I will give you strength to overcome every obstacle.

I am your refuge and your stronghold. You are not fighting alone—I am fighting with you. Trust Me with your worries and your struggles. I have plans for you, plans that include triumph over your troubles. Even when the situation seems impossible, My power is perfect in your weakness. Lift your voice to Me in prayer, and I will guide you through the storm. Remember, victory is already yours in Me.

Closing Encouragement: Keep praying and trusting God is already working out your victory.

September 22

Topic: Seeing the Beauty in Each New Day.

Opening Statement: Every morning is a new opportunity to experience God's love and see the beauty created for you.

Bible Verse: *"The steadfast love of the Lord never ceases; his mercies never come to an end; they are new every morning; great is your faithfulness."* —Lamentations 3:22-23 (NIV)

Devotional: Dear Child, as you wake up each day, remember that I am with you. The beauty in each sunrise, the gentle breeze, and the laughter of friends are all reminders of My love for you. Even on tough days, I want you to open your eyes to the blessings around you. Look for the little moments—the things you might otherwise overlook. I am the One who made this day just for you. Let My presence fill your heart with joy and peace as you walk through each moment. Trust Me to guide your steps, to show you the beauty in the ordinary, and to renew your strength when you're weary. Let your heart be open to My love today.

Closing Encouragement: Embrace this new day knowing that I am with you and will show you My beauty in all things.

September 23

Topic: Prayer for Courage: Facing Fear with Faith.

Opening Statement: Fear is real, but prayer gives you the strength to face it with courage.

Bible Verse: *"There is no fear in love. But perfect love drives out fear, because fear has to do with punishment. The one who fears is not made perfect in love."* 1 John 4:18 (NIV).

Devotional: I know you feel afraid sometimes. There are moments when fear seems more significant than courage. But remember, I am with you. When you face something that makes your heart race, pray to Me. Speak to Me, and I will give you strength that the world cannot offer. I don't promise that fear will disappear, but I will hold you steady through it. My power works best when you feel weak, and I will fill you with courage from the inside out. You don't have to face your fears alone—My spiritual strength is within you, guiding and strengthening you. So, take heart. Pray, and let your trust in Me become more significant than your fear.

Closing Encouragement: Take a deep breath, pray, and step forward—courage is yours when you walk with Me.

September 24

Topic: Finding Hope in Prayer When You Feel Depressed and Lonely

Opening Statement: When you're feeling depressed and alone, prayer can be your lifeline to hope, healing, and God's presence.

Bible Verse: *"The Lord is close to the brokenhearted and saves those who are crushed in spirit."* —Psalm 34:18 (NIV)

Devotional: My beloved, I know the weight you carry. In the quiet moments when loneliness wraps itself around you, and the darkness of depression feels overwhelming, I am with you. Prayer is not about saying the right words but bringing your broken heart to Me. You don't have to carry the burden of sadness alone. When you call out to Me, even in whispers, I listen. I see your tears and understand your struggles.

Bring your pain to Me in prayer. Even when finding words is hard, I will help you. I will fill your heart with peace beyond understanding as you come to Me. You are never truly alone, for I am always near, and in prayer, you will find My love waiting to comfort and strengthen you.

Closing Encouragement: You are seen, loved, and cherished—never forget that I am with you always, especially when you pray.

September 25

Topic: Prayer for Generosity.

Opening Statement: Being generous with your time, money, and energy shows God's love to others and helps build His Kingdom.

Bible verse: Each of you should give what you have decided in your heart to give, not reluctantly or under compulsion, for God loves a cheerful giver. 2 Corinthians 9:7 (NIV).

Devotional: I see your heart and know you desire to make a difference. True generosity isn't just about giving when it's easy or convenient. It's about trusting Me to provide for you as you give. Whether offering your time to help a friend, sharing your allowance with someone in need, or using your energy to serve others, every act of generosity matters to Me.

My Word says, "I love when you give joyfully and trust Me with the rest." When you give from the heart, you reflect My love to the world.

Ask Me to guide you in giving your time, money, and energy. I will lead you, and My Kingdom will grow through your generosity.

Closing Encouragement: Trust Me, and watch how I bless your generosity in ways beyond what you could imagine.

September 26

Topic: A Prayer for Humility

Bible Verse: *"Humble yourselves before the Lord, and He will lift you up."* — James 4:10 (NIV)

Opening Statement: True strength comes from humility in a world that celebrates self-promotion.

Devotional: I see your heart and know the daily challenges you face. The world pushes you to be noticed and to rise above others, but I call you to something more significant: humility. Humility doesn't mean thinking less of yourself but thinking of yourself less. When you pray to Me, ask for a heart that seeks to serve others rather than seeking the spotlight. Remember, when you lower yourself before Me, I will lift you up at the right time. I am here to shape you, to mold you into someone who reflects My love, and that starts with humility. Let your prayers be filled with a desire to serve, not just to be seen. Trust that I see you, and I will honor your humble spirit.

Closing Encouragement: Stay humble, and I will guide you to a place of honor in My perfect time.

September 27

Topic: Renew Your Mind

Bible Verse: *"Do not conform to the pattern of this world, but be transformed by the renewing of your mind."* —Romans 12:2 (NIV)

Opening Statement: Prayer is the key to transforming your mind, helping you break free from the world's patterns and discover God's best for you.

Devotional: My beloved child, I see the battles you face in your mind every day—fear, doubt, and the constant pressure to fit in. I want you to know I am here to help you break free through prayer. When you speak to Me, I give you the strength to resist the negative patterns of this world and replace them with My truth.

Talk to Me about your worries, dreams, and failures. When you do, I will work in your heart, renewing your mind. My words are valid, and I want to fill your thoughts with hope and peace. You don't have to do this alone—invite Me in, and I will help you see yourself and the world as I do: full of beauty, love, and purpose.

Closing Encouragement: Trust in Me, and allow My peace to renew your mind daily—one prayer at a time.

September 28

Topic: Walking in God's Peace.

Opening Statement: Walking in peace means trusting that I am with you, guiding every step you take.

Bible Verse: *"and with your feet fitted with the readiness that comes from the gospel of peace."* Ephesians 6:15 (NIV).

Devotional: Dear one, I know the world around you can often feel like a battlefield—pressures from school, friendships that sometimes hurt, and expectations that weigh you down. But I want you to know that you don't have to face this alone. I am here, ready to fit your feet with the shoes of peace so you can walk confidently wherever life takes you.

These shoes of peace are not just any shoes; they come from the gospel of My love and presence. When you feel anxious or lost, remember that I am your calm. Each step with My peace leads you away from fear and closer to purpose. Let My peace guard your heart today and bring a steady rhythm to your journey. You are never alone; My peace walks beside you, guiding and protecting you every moment.

Closing Encouragement: Trust Me, and let My peace lead every step—because you are always loved and never alone.

September 29

Topic: Prayer for Purity.

Opening Statement: Purity is more than just actions—it's about having a heart that reflects God's light in a world of distractions.

Bible Verse: "How can a young person stay on the path of purity? By living according to your word." — Psalm 119:9 (NIV)

Devotional: Dear child, I see the challenges you face daily—temptations, pressures, and the struggle to fit in. I want you to know that I am with you through every moment. Purity is not about being perfect but about being open to my guidance and willing to choose the best path for your soul. When you feel weak, I am here to give you strength; when you feel alone, I am right beside you.

Let Me shape your thoughts, your desires, and your choices. Seek Me, and I will show you how to guard your heart and mind. Remember, you don't have to fight this battle alone—lean on Me. We can make choices that honor who you are—My beloved.

Closing Encouragement: You are stronger than any temptation, for My Spirit is alive in you, guiding you towards true joy and freedom.

September 30

Topic: Fitness Challenges and Yoga

Opening Statement: What if every stretch, every breath, and every challenge in your fitness journey could draw you closer to God?

Bible Verse: *"For physical training is of some value, but godliness has value for all things, holding promise for both the present life and the life to come."* —1 Timothy 4:8 (NIV)

Devotional: My beloved child, when you step onto your yoga mat or push through a fitness challenge, I am there. Feel My presence in the rhythm of your breath, the strength of your resolve, and the stillness of your heart. Just as you stretch your body to grow stronger, stretch your faith by trusting Me in every struggle. Those moments when your muscles burn or your balance wavers? They mirror the spiritual growth I desire for you—patience, perseverance, and reliance on My strength, not your own.

Your body is My temple, and caring for it honors Me. But don't stop there. Let every squat, lunge, or prayer pose become an act of worship. Sweat not just for physical endurance but for a heart that endures trials with joy. When frustration whispers, "Give up," remember: I equip you to finish what you start. Let your fitness journey remind you that discipline in the physical fuels discipline in the spiritual. Together, we'll strengthen both.

Closing Encouragement: You are stronger than you think— body, mind, and spirit—because the God who holds the universe holds you.

October 1

Topic: Praying for Your Church and Community

Opening Statement: Praying for your church and community is one of the most potent ways to make a difference.

Bible Verse: *"Therefore encourage one another and build each other up, just as in fact you are doing."* —1 Thessalonians 5:11 (NIV)

Devotional: My child, I want you to know how vital you are to your church and community. Your prayers matter more than you realize. When you pray for your church, you ask Me to move, to bring strength, unity, and love among those who gather in My name. You may feel young, but remember, your voice reaches My ears just as powerfully as anyone else's.

When you lift up your pastor, friends, and even the people you barely know in church, you create a beautiful chain of love and care. I see your prayers and work through them to touch hearts, heal wounds, and unite My people. You're not just part of a group—you are a builder of My kingdom every time you pray.

So, consider the power of your words. Keep praying, trust, and watch as I work through your faith.

Closing Encouragement: You are My light—keep shining brightly for your church and community through your prayers.

October 2

Topic: Renew Your Faith

Opening Statement: When your faith feels dry, remember that God is always ready to bring renewal to your spirit.

Bible Verse: *For I will pour water on the thirsty land, and streams on the dry ground; I will pour out my Spirit on your offspring, and my blessing on your descendants.* Isaiah 44:3 NIV.

Devotional: My child, I know there are times when your faith feels like a dry, barren land—when the joy and excitement of knowing Me seem like distant memories. But I want you to know that I am here, ready to pour out My life-giving rain into your heart. Just as rain refreshes the earth, My presence can revive your spirit.

Come to Me as you are, without fear or hesitation. Let Me fill the emptiness with My love. When you feel distant or tired, know I am never far away. My love for you is steadfast, and My grace is more than enough to bring you back to life. Trust Me with your doubts and exhaustion—I am the wellspring that will never run dry. All you need to do is ask, and I will renew your weary heart.

Closing Encouragement: Remember, whenever you feel spiritually dry, God is eager to bring you refreshment and renewal.

October 3

Topic: God's Word as Your Guide:

Opening Statement: When life feels confusing or dark, remember that God's Word is like a light guiding you to safety, step by step.

Bible Verse: *Your word is a lamp for my feet, a light on my path.* Psalm 119:105 (NIV)

Devotional: Dear one, I am here to guide you through everything you face. The world can often seem overwhelming, full of choices and pressures that feel impossible to navigate. But remember, My Word is your light. When you feel unsure or lost, My words are like a lamp showing you where to take your next step. I will never leave you in darkness. Open the Bible and let My truth pour into your heart. It will illuminate your path, helping you make choices that bring you closer to joy, peace, and purpose. I've given you My Word so that you can see the way forward clearly, no matter how uncertain things seem. Trust in Me, and I promise to light every step, guiding you through the darkness into My marvelous light.

Closing Encouragement: You are never alone—keep trusting My Word, and I will always guide your way forward.

October 4

Topic: Facing Spiritual Battles.

Opening Statement: When facing spiritual battles, remember you are not alone—God has given you the shield of faith to protect and strengthen you.

Bible Verse: *"In addition to all this, take up the shield of faith, with which you can extinguish all the flaming arrows of the evil one."* —Ephesians 6:16 (NIV)

Devotional: Dear child, I know the struggles you face. I see the fears, the doubts, and the challenges that try to pull you away from Me. Life can feel like a battlefield; sometimes, the fight against temptation or discouragement is impossible. But I have given you something powerful: the shield of faith.

When you trust Me, your faith becomes a shield, stopping every lie the enemy throws at you. You do not hold this shield alone; I help you lift it. Together, we can face anything that comes your way. Trust Me with every fear and worry; I promise to be your defender. Use the faith I have given you and watch as My strength overcomes every obstacle.

Closing Encouragement: Remember, I am always here— your strength, shield, and victory.

October 5

Topic: Finding Confidence Through God's Love.

Opening Statement: Feeling like you're not enough can be overwhelming, but remember, you are more valuable than you think because God's power is within you.

Bible Verse: *"But he said to me, 'My grace is sufficient for you, for my power is made perfect in weakness.'"* —2 Corinthians 12:9 (NIV)

Devotional: My beloved child, I see you when you feel small when you think others are better, and you feel as though you are not enough. I want you to know that your worth is not measured by accomplishments or how you compare to others. I created you with love, and I see you as wonderfully made. When you feel inadequate, that is where My strength can shine the brightest.

Do not fear your weaknesses. Instead, please bring them to Me. My power is perfect when you lean into Me, trusting I am enough for you. You are not meant to carry these feelings alone—I am here to fill the gaps, to be your strength, and to remind you of your purpose. Believe in My love for you, and you will find all the confidence you need.

Closing Encouragement: You are enough because I love you and will always help you through whatever you face.

October 6

Topic: Overcoming Pride.

Opening Statement: Pride might feel powerful, but it quietly builds walls that separate you from love, growth, and God.

Bible Verse: *"Pride goes before destruction, a haughty spirit before a fall."* —Proverbs 16:18 (NIV)

Devotional: My child, I see the weight of pride that tries to pull you away from the true beauty I have for you. Pride whispers that you must always be the best and that your value comes from being above others. But listen closely—I am here to show you a better way.

Pride creates distance between you and others, even between you and Me. But humility tears down those walls, bringing you closer to my love and the people around you. When you set aside pride, you make room for Me to work through you, filling you with kindness, peace, and joy.

I want you to be free—free from the pressure of perfection and comparison. True strength is found not in standing above others but in serving, listening, and lifting others up. Let my love guide you to see the beauty in humility, and I promise that you will find greater joy and connection than pride could ever give.

Closing Encouragement: I am with you—choose humility, and let Me fill your heart with lasting peace and love.

October 7

Topic: Fing the Fruit of Joy.

Opening Statement: Joy is more than just a happy feeling—it's a powerful gift from the Holy Spirit that fills your heart even when life gets tough.

Bible Verse: *"But the fruit of the Spirit is love, joy, peace, forbearance, kindness, goodness, faithfulness."* —Galatians 5:22 (NIV)

Devotional: Dear one, I want you to know that joy is not something you must chase—it's something I place in your heart. When you invite Me into your life, I bring with Me the fruit of the Spirit, and joy is one of My greatest gifts. It's not like fleeting happiness from friends, social media likes, or fun activities. My joy is more profound. A steady, unshakable presence holds you up even when things aren't perfect.

When you feel overwhelmed by school, friendships, or family issues, remember that My joy is always available. Let Me fill your spirit so that no matter what comes your way, you can smile knowing I am with you, giving you strength and peace.

Closing Encouragement: Remember, I am with you, and My joy will always be your strength.

October 8

Topic: Love Others as Christ Commands.

Opening Statement: Did you know that loving others isn't just a suggestion—it's a command from Jesus?

Bible Verse: *"A new command I give you: Love one another. As I have loved you, so you must love one another."* —John 13:34 (NIV)

Devotional: My child, I am with you every moment, guiding your heart to love others the way Christ has loved you. I know relationships can be challenging—there are times when people hurt you or misunderstand you. But I want you to remember that Jesus didn't command you to love only when it's easy; He asks you to love always.

Loving others as Christ loves means offering kindness, patience, and forgiveness, even when it feels undeserved. Through My strength, you are empowered to look beyond someone's faults and love them deeply. When you love others, you reflect the light of Jesus in the world.

Lean on Me when it feels hard, and I will give you the grace to love beyond what you think is possible.

Closing Encouragement: See the good in all people just as Jesus did.

October 9

Topic: Embracing God's Purpose.

Opening Statement: You were created with a unique purpose, a divine plan that God has prepared for you.

Bible Verse: For we are God's handiwork, created in Christ Jesus to do good works, which God prepared in advance for us to do. Ephesians 2:10 (NIV)

Devotional: Dear one, I am here, speaking to your heart, reminding you that you are not an accident. I have designed for you with intention, and my plans for you are good. Sometimes, the journey feels unclear, and you may wonder if you're on the right path. But know this: I guide you, even when you can't see the whole picture.

Lean into Me, trust My voice, and let My Word be a lamp to your feet. I have placed gifts and talents within you and am calling you to use them for My glory. You don't need to have it all figured out—take the next step in faith, and I will be with you every step of the way.

My purpose for you is more significant than your fears, more robust than your doubts, and filled with My love.

Closing Encouragement: Trust that God's purpose for your life is unfolding perfectly in good time—God will guide you every step of the way.

October 10

Topic: Finding hope in the storm.

Opening Statement: When life feels like a storm that won't end, remember that hope is waiting on the other side.

Bible Verse: *"But Jesus immediately said to them: 'Take courage! It is I. Don't be afraid.'"* —Matthew 14:27 (NIV)

Devotional: My child, I see you struggling in the middle of your storm. The winds of life can be strong, and the waves can seem like they'll pull you under. But don't lose sight of what lies beyond this moment. I am with you, guiding you through the darkness, and I promise you're not alone.

Remember, even the fiercest storms eventually calm, and the skies clear. In the same way, your struggles will not last forever. Lean into Me, and I will give you strength. Trust that I work this season, even when you don't see it. I have a purpose for you, and this storm will become part of how you grow more assertive, braver, and full of faith.

Keep your eyes on Me, and you will reach the other side.

Closing Encouragement: Take heart, for this storm will pass, and My peace will carry you through.

October 11

Topic: Your Helmet of Salvation.

Opening Statement: When life feels overwhelming, the helmet of salvation protects you from daily spiritual battles.

Bible Verse: *"Take the helmet of salvation and the sword of the Spirit, which is the word of God."* —Ephesians 6:17 (NIV)

Devotional: My blessed child, I know there are days when doubts creep in and you feel uncertain, but I want you to remember something powerful—your salvation in Jesus is secure. The helmet of salvation guards your mind and heart from the lies and negativity that try to take you down. When you feel attacked, put on this helmet by reminding yourself that you belong to Jesus, your identity is found in Him; no enemy can take that away.

Each day is a battle, but I have equipped you with everything you need. The helmet of salvation protects you from fear, guilt, and shame. Let it remind you that your mind is a battlefield, but with this protection, you can think clearly and stay grounded in My truth.

Closing Encouragement: Remember, I am with you, guiding you through every battle—stand firm, for you are My beloved and blessed child.

October 12

Topic: Persistent Faith.

Opening Statement: When life feels tough, and your prayers seem unanswered, remember that persistence in faith is the key to unlocking God's plan.

Bible Verse: *Then Jesus told His disciples a parable to show them that they should always pray and not give up.* Luke 18:1 (NIV).

Devotional: I see you when you feel like giving up. I hear your whispered prayers and the ones you haven't spoken aloud. Like the widow in the parable, please come to Me persistently, even when the road seems long and the answers feel distant.

It's easy to get discouraged when things don't happen quickly, but remember, I'm working on your behalf in ways you cannot see. Keep coming to Me with your prayers. Trust Me with your deepest hopes and worries. Just as the widow's persistence led to her receiving justice, your persistence will lead to answers—maybe not the way you expect, but always in My perfect timing.

I am with you, guiding, strengthening, and shaping your faith as you wait.

Closing Encouragement: Keep praying and trusting—your persistent faith builds something beautiful.

October 13

Topic: Blessing the Pure in Heart.

Bible Verse: *"Blessed are the pure in heart, for they will see God."*
— Matthew 5:8 (NIV)

Opening Statement: If you long to see God's hand in your life, it starts with a pure heart focused on God.

Devotional: My beloved child, I see your thoughts and desires. When your heart is pure, you open the door to experiencing My presence in powerful ways. In a world filled with distractions and temptations, I call you to be different, to seek what is good, accurate, and correct. I will fill it with love and peace as you guard your heart from bitterness, jealousy, and negativity.

Do not be afraid to stand out for Me. When you choose purity, you reflect My light to others. I know it's not always easy, but remember, I am with you. Whenever you turn away from something that doesn't honor Me, I will strengthen you. The more you pursue a pure heart, the more precise you will see My plans for your life.

Closing Encouragement: Keep seeking God with a pure heart, and I will see the way to blessings beyond what you can imagine.

October 14

Topic: Blessing the Pure in Heart.

Opening Statement: If you long to see God's hand in your life, it starts with a pure heart focused on God.

Bible Verse: *"Blessed are the pure in heart, for they will see God."* — Matthew 5:8 (NIV)

Devotional: My beloved child, I see your thoughts and desires. When your heart is pure, you open the door to experiencing My presence in powerful ways. In a world filled with distractions and temptations, I call you to be different, to seek what is good, accurate, and correct. I will fill it with love and peace as you guard your heart from bitterness, jealousy, and negativity.

Do not be afraid to stand out for Me. When you choose purity, you reflect My light to others. I know it's not always easy, but remember, I am with you. Whenever you turn away from something that doesn't honor Me, I will strengthen you. The more you pursue a pure heart, the more precise you will see My plans for your life.

Closing Encouragement: Keep seeking God with a pure heart, and I will see the way to blessings beyond what you can imagine.

October 15

Topic: Practice Kindness.

Opening Statement: Kindness is more than just being nice—it's showing the love of Jesus through your actions.

Bible Verse: *Let your gentleness be evident to all. The Lord is near.* —Philippians 4:5 (NIV)

Devotional: When you choose kindness, you let My love shine through you. I know it's not always easy. Sometimes, people may hurt or frustrate you, but I am with you, giving you strength and patience. When you practice kindness, even when it's hard, you reflect the heart of Jesus.

Each time you speak a kind word or do something thoughtful, you plant seeds of My love in the world. Let Me help you see others as I do—with compassion and grace. Your acts of kindness, big or small, make a difference.

Today, let Me lead your heart in showing kindness to someone who needs it. You are My light in this world.

Closing Encouragement: Kindness is mighty, and I am always with you to help you spread it.

Let My love guide your steps today!

October 16

Topic: Leaning on God for strength

Opening Statement: When life feels overwhelming, prayer is your greatest weapon to lean on God and find peace.

Bible Verse: *"Cast all your anxiety on Him because He cares for you."* —1 Peter 5:7 (NIV)

Devotional: Dear one, I see your weight and struggles in your heart. I want you to know that I am here, closer than you think. In moments of fear or confusion, when life seems spiraling out of control, you can always talk to Me. Your prayers don't have to be perfect or long—I simply want to hear your heart. When you pray, you release your worries into My hands, and I am always ready to lift your burdens.

Remember, I care about every detail of your life, even what you think is too small to matter. When you lean on Me through prayer, I give you strength and peace beyond what you understand. So don't be afraid to come to Me with everything. I am your refuge, and I will always be with you.

Closing Encouragement: Trust in Me, for I am your constant help and hope.

October 17

Topic: Encounter God Every Morning.

Opening Statement: Starting your morning with God can change the entire direction of your day, helping you walk in peace and purpose.

Bible Verse: *In the morning, Lord, you hear my voice; in the morning I lay my requests before you and wait expectantly.* —Psalm 5:3 (NIV)

Devotional: My child, every morning is an opportunity to encounter Me. When you wake up, I am already near, waiting to hear your voice and walk with you through the day. You might feel rushed or distracted by the demands of school, friends, and life, but I invite you to pause—even for a moment—and speak to Me.

When you begin your day with Me, I will guide, strengthen, and fill you with peace that the world cannot provide. Just like the sun rises faithfully every morning, My love and presence rise to meet you. Come to Me with your worries, hopes, and plans, and let Me direct your steps.

Trust Me with your day; you will see that My way is perfect.

Closing Encouragement: As you encounter God each morning, you will find God is with you every moment, guiding you through life's ups and downs.

October 18

What Does Hallelujah Mean? A Guide to Praise and Understanding"

Topic: What Does Hallelujah Mean?

Opening Statement: Have you ever wondered what *hallelujah* means and why it's such a powerful word in worship?

Bible Verse: *"Praise the Lord. How good it is to sing praises to our God, how pleasant and fitting to praise him!"* —Psalm 147:1 (NIV)

Devotional: My beloved, *hallelujah* is more than just a word you sing—it's a declaration of praise straight from your heart to Mine. It means "Praise the Lord," when you say it, you join a chorus of heaven in lifting Me. Even when life is challenging or confusing, your *hallelujah* rises above it all, calling on My strength, My love, and My presence in your life.

When you say *hallelujah*, you aren't just acknowledging My goodness—you are choosing to trust Me, no matter what. I see the depths of your heart, and I love when you sincerely praise Me. Remember, your praise doesn't need to be perfect—it just needs to be accurate. So speak *hallelujah* with confidence, knowing I hear every word.

Closing Encouragement: Keep praising, My child—your *hallelujah* brings joy to My heart.

October 19

Topic: "Encouraging Prayer to Overcome Procrastination

Opening Statement: Procrastination can be a heavy burden, but through prayer and trust in the Holy Spirit, you can find the strength to overcome it.

Bible Verse: *"Commit to the Lord whatever you do, and he will establish your plans."* —Proverbs 16:3 (NIV)

Devotional: Do you ever feel like you know what you should do, but something keeps holding you back? That's procrastination, and I'm here to help you break free from it.

I am with you every moment, ready to strengthen you. Pray to me when you feel overwhelmed or tempted to delay the essential things. I will give you the focus and energy you need. Your time is valuable; I want to help you use it wisely. Take that first small step, even if it's hard. Trust me to guide you through the rest. I am here to remind you that I have great plans for your life, and each step you take in faith brings you closer.

You are not alone in this. Lean on Me, and together, we'll move forward with purpose.

Closing Encouragement: You can overcome procrastination because I am with you, always ready to help.

October 20

Topic: Prayers for a Discouraged Friend

Opening Statement: When your friend is feeling down, you can be the light that helps lift them up through prayer.

Bible Verse: *Cast all your anxiety on Him because He cares for you.* —1 Peter 5:7 (NIV)

Devotional: I see you when your friend is hurting; I know it weighs heavily on your heart. I want you to remember that I care deeply for them—and you. When your friend feels lost or discouraged, I will guide you to lift them up in prayer. Trust me to work through you to bring comfort and hope.

When you pray, do it with faith, knowing that I hear every word. Ask me to give them strength, to lighten their burdens, and to renew their spirit. Let me work through your words and your kindness to remind them they are never alone. Your prayers have power because I am with you, filling you with love and peace to share with those who need it.

Closing Encouragement: Be strong and courageous—your prayers can bring light to even the darkest days.

October 21

Topic: Prayers for a Discouraged Friend.

Opening Statement: When your friend is feeling down, you can be the light that helps lift them up through prayer.

Bible Verse: *Cast all your anxiety on Him because He cares for you.* —1 Peter 5:7 (NIV)

Devotional: I see you when your friend is hurting; I know it weighs heavily on your heart. I want you to remember that I care deeply for them—and you. When your friend feels lost or discouraged, I will guide you to lift them up in prayer. Trust me to work through you to bring comfort and hope.

When you pray, do it with faith, knowing that I hear every word. Ask me to give them strength, to lighten their burdens, and to renew their spirit. Let me work through your words and your kindness to remind them they are never alone. Your prayers have power because I am with you, filling you with love and peace to share with those who need it.

Closing Encouragement: Be strong and courageous—your prayers can bring light to even the darkest days.

October 22

Topic: Obey God's Word

Opening Statement: Obedience to God's Word isn't always easy, but it is the path to true joy and purpose.

Bible Verse: *"Blessed are those who hear the word of God and obey it."* —Luke 11:28 (NIV)

Devotional: Dear one, I see your heart and the desire within you to live a life that honors Me. When you follow My Word, you choose to walk with Me. I know it can sometimes feel like everyone else is walking a different path, but remember, the way of obedience leads to peace and fulfillment.

There will be moments when following My Word means going against what others do. In those times, I am with you, guiding and strengthening you. Obeying Me isn't about following rules but trusting Me to know what's best for you. Each choice to follow, no matter how small, brings you closer to My heart and purpose for you.

Lean into My guidance, trust My Word, and let Me lead you into all the good things I have prepared for you.

Closing Encouragement: Take each step in faith, and know I am with you always, guiding you on the path of obedience.

October 23

Topic: Seek God with all your heart

Opening Statement: When you seek God with all your heart, you'll discover a relationship that brings absolute joy, purpose, and peace.

Bible Verse: *"You will seek me and find me when you seek me with all your heart."* —Jeremiah 29:13 (NIV)

Devotional: Dear one, I am with you always, inviting you to know Me more deeply. Every day, you have the chance to draw closer and know My love, guidance, and strength. When you seek Me wholeheartedly—setting aside worries, doubts, and distractions—your heart opens to hear My voice more clearly. I know the plans I have for you, and they are full of hope and purpose. Remember, I see your desires, questions, and dreams, and I long to walk you through them all.

As you seek Me, I will fill your heart with peace beyond understanding and lead you to a lasting joy. Seek Me wholeheartedly, and I promise you will find Me. I am closer than you know.

Closing Encouragement: Draw near, and you will find the joy and strength that only I can give. Seek, and you will find.

October 24

Topic: Trusting God to Strengthen Your Faith

Opening Statement: Doubt can sometimes feel overwhelming, but trusting God gives you the strength to overcome it.

Bible Verse: *"Trust in the Lord with all your heart and lean not on your own understanding; in all your ways submit to him, and he will make your paths straight."* —Proverbs 3:5-6 (NIV)

Devotional: Dear child, I know your heart and the doubts you sometimes face. Life brings challenges that make you question if I am truly by your side and if my promises hold firm. I see your fears, questions, and even the times you wonder if your faith is strong enough. Know this: I am always with you, even in your uncertainty.

When you face those challenging moments, turn to Me with an open heart. Let My love replace your doubt, and remember that you don't have to rely solely on your understanding. Trust me because I see the whole picture, and my plans for you are good. Lean into Me when your faith feels small, and I will make your path straight.

Closing Encouragement: You will never stop growing in faith; doubt is a minor resting place for growth.

October 25

Topic: You will lack nothing

Opening Statement: When life gets tough, remember that God is your constant guide and provider, giving you everything you need to keep going.

Bible Verse: *"The Lord is my shepherd, I lack nothing."* — Psalm 23:1 (NIV)

Devotional: Dear one, I am here to walk you through every moment. Life may feel overwhelming but know that I am guiding each step, just as a shepherd cares for each sheep. When you feel alone, remember: I am closer than your breath, watching over you with love and care. No matter your challenges, I have equipped you with all you need to thrive.

You may not always see the path ahead but trust that I am leading you to a place of rest and strength. I have plans for you to uplift and encourage you, even when the road seems rough. Keep leaning into Me, and I will provide what you need. I am your Shepherd, and with Me, you lack nothing.

Closing Encouragement: Take heart; you are never alone, for I am with you always, providing strength and courage in every season.

October 26

Topic: Encouragement in a new relationship.

Opening Statement: Entering a new relationship can be thrilling but scary, especially when you're unsure what the future holds.

Bible Verse: *"Be strong and courageous. Do not be afraid; do not be discouraged, for the Lord your God will be with you wherever you go." —*Joshua 1:9 (NIV)

Devotional: Dear one, I know your heart. You've stepped into something new and exciting, yet there's that quiet whisper of doubt in the back of your mind. *What if it doesn't work out? What if I get hurt?* But hear this: I am with you every step of the way. I am the gentle nudge that reminds you to trust, to be brave, and to walk forward without fear. Remember Joshua 1:9—I am your constant strength and courage. You don't have to do this alone.

Let love be something you approach with hope but also wisdom. Ask me for guidance when you feel unsure, and I will remind you that you are deeply loved and never without My presence. Be open, but guard your heart with My truth. Lean into joy, and trust that I am leading you to what is best for you.

Closing Encouragement: Be brave in love, knowing God walks before you and stands beside you every moment.

October 27

Topic: Finding Rest and Peace in God's Presence.

Opening Statement: In a world filled with noise and chaos, God invites you to find proper rest and peace in His presence.

Bible Verse: *He makes me lie down in green pastures, he leads me beside quiet waters,* Psalm 23:2 NIV.

Devotional: My beloved child, I know the pressures you face daily. The expectations, the noise, and the distractions can feel overwhelming. But remember this: I long to give you rest. The words from Psalm 23 are My invitation to you. I want to lead you to places where your soul can breathe and where you can let go of stress and anxiety.

When life feels out of control, imagine Me guiding you to a beautiful meadow or a still stream. In these places, I whisper My love and peace over you. You are never alone. Trust that I know what you need. Let My voice be louder than your worries, and My love calm the storms inside you.

Take a moment today to pause and let Me refresh your spirit. Breathe in My peace. I am with you, ready to renew and restore your heart.

Closing Encouragement: Rest in My love, and let Me lead you to the peace your heart longs for.

October 28

Topic: God restores us.

Opening Statement: When life feels overwhelming, God promises to refresh your soul and guide you in the right direction.

Bible Verse: *"He refreshes my soul. He guides me along the right paths for his name's sake."* —Psalm 23:3 (NIV)

Devotional: I see you when you're exhausted, running from one thing to the next, trying to meet expectations, feeling the pressure from every side. I know when your soul feels dry, like a desert longing for rain. Come to Me. I am here, eager to refresh your spirit and give you strength that never runs out. I promise to restore you with peace that makes no sense to the world around you.

When you're unsure which way to go, I am your Guide. I've laid out a path designed just for you that will lead you to purpose and hope. Trust My Way, even when it doesn't seem clear. Remember, My guidance is always rooted in love, and My plans are for your good. Let Me direct your steps. I will never leave you to walk this journey alone.

Take a moment today to rest in My presence. Breathe in My peace and listen for My voice.

Closing Encouragement: Stay close to Me, and I will lead you to rest and a life filled with hope.

October 29

Topic: Finding hope in dark times.

Opening Statement: Life's valleys may feel scary and uncertain, but you are never alone.

Bible Verse: *Even though I walk through the darkest valley, I will fear no evil, for you are with me; your rod and your staff, they comfort me.* —Psalm 23:4 (NIV)

Devotional: My dear Sacred Heart, I am with you even in the darkest moments of your life. Remember that I have never left your side when you face fear, uncertainty, or pain. Sometimes, the valleys you walk through feel overwhelming, like no light will ever shine again. But trust that I am guiding you every step of the way.

My love for you is more potent than any fear you may have. My rod and staff are here to defend you from danger and guide you when you feel lost. I understand your struggles and pressure, but I am your constant comfort. Rest in my presence, and find strength knowing I hold you securely. You don't have to be afraid. I am your Protector, your Guide, your Peace.

No valley is too dark for My light to reach you.

Closing Encouragement: Remember, even in life's most challenging moments, My love surrounds you, and My strength will carry you through.

October 30

Topic: Strength in a Supportive Community

Bible Verse: *"Therefore encourage one another and build each other up, just as in fact you are doing."* —1 Thessalonians 5:11 (NIV)

Opening Statement: A supportive community is a divine gift from God—an outpouring of love that sustains us through life's joys and challenges.

Devotional: My beloved teen, today I want to remind you of the profound power of community—my gift to you and through you. You were never meant to face the storms of life alone. I designed you to thrive in connection, in love, and in mutual encouragement.

Think of a community as a sanctuary—a sacred space where your burdens are shared, your joys amplified, and your faith renewed. When you gather with others who seek Me, something divine happens: hearts are lifted, wounds are healed, and spirits are strengthened. In these moments, you become My hands and feet, demonstrating My love in tangible ways.

Remember, the strength of a community isn't just in numbers but in unity rooted in My love. When you encourage one another, you reflect My grace and mercy. When you build each other up, you mirror My divine craftsmanship—creating a body that works together in harmony, resilience, and purpose.

Closing Encouragement: Walk confidently in the strength that comes from being part of a divine family, because I am with you every step of the way.

October 31

Topic: Trick or treating.

Opening Statement: Have you ever wondered if it's okay for Christians to join in on Halloween celebrations?

Bible Verse: *"Do not conform to the pattern of this world, but be transformed by the renewing of your mind. Then you will be able to test and approve what God's will is—his good, pleasing and perfect will."* —Romans 12:2 (NIV)

Devotional: My child, I see your heart and understand your questions about Halloween. Some see it as harmless fun, a time for costumes and candy. But remember, you are called to be different. Not everything is for you; some things can distract you from My light. Ask yourself, "Does this bring me closer to Jesus or closer to the world's ways?" You are My treasured child, set apart to live with purpose. Seek My wisdom in all things, and I will show you what is good and pleasing to Me. Your life is a testimony, and even small choices can show others who I am. Choose the things that honor Me through you.

Closing Encouragement: I will lead you in wisdom and love as you seek My will.

November 1

Topic: Making Time for God Every Day.

Opening Statement: Making time for God daily is one of the most powerful ways to deepen your faith and grow in His love.

Bible Verse: *"Come near to God and he will come near to you."* —James 4:8a (NIV)

Devotional: Beloved sacred heart, I call you to spend time with Me daily. In the quiet moments, I am waiting for you, ready to listen to every thought and every question in your heart. Your life is complete, with school, friends, and family keeping you busy. But know that when you set aside even a few minutes just for Me, I pour My peace, strength, and love into your heart.

When you draw close to Me, I promise to draw even closer to you. Let My presence be where you can rest, recharge, and find purpose. You don't have to do anything special—simply come as you are. Open My Word, talk to Me, and let Me show you the love and guidance that will carry you through each day.

Closing Encouragement: Remember, every moment spent with Me makes you stronger, more peaceful, and full of My love.

November 2

Topic: Receiving God's Blessings.

Opening Statement: When life feels full of obstacles and people who don't understand you, know I am preparing something special for you.

Bible Verse: *"You prepare a table before me in the presence of my enemies. You anoint my head with oil; my cup overflows."* — Psalm 23:5 (NIV)

Devotional: Dear beloved one, I see the struggles you face every day. The times when friends betray you, when bullies seem to surround you, or when life feels unfair. But even when you feel surrounded, I am preparing a table for you. Imagine a place where you are celebrated, loved, and honored—right in front of everything and everyone trying to bring you down. That's what I am doing for you.

I anoint your head with oil, signifying that you are chosen, unique, and uniquely Mine. Your worth is beyond measure, and I am here to lift you up. Your cup overflows with blessings, grace, and love, even when you don't see it yet. Trust that I am filling your life with more goodness than you can imagine.

Stay strong, beloved. I am with you, and your victory is already in the making.

Closing Encouragement: Remember, you are chosen, loved, and blessed beyond measure; keep your eyes on Me, and I will lift you above every challenge.

November 3

Topic: God's Unfailing Love.

Opening Statement: God's love is not just something you hear about; it's a powerful promise that stays with you every moment.

Bible Verse: *"Surely your goodness and love will follow me all the days of my life, and I will dwell in the house of the Lord forever."* —Psalm 23:6 (NIV)

Devotional: Hey there, it's Me, your Comforting Spirit. I know life can feel uncertain sometimes, especially as you try to navigate yourself and your direction. But there's a promise that I want you to hold onto: My goodness and love are following you every day. That's right—no matter what you face, My love is behind you, supporting, surrounding, and guiding you.

Even when you feel like you've messed up or taken a wrong turn, my grace still covers you. My love doesn't depend on your performance or achievements. It's a love that sees your worth and promises never to let you go.

So, when you feel alone or unsure, remember you are always welcome in MY comforting presence. I prepared a place just for you, a safe and loving home forever.

Closing Encouragement: Trust in God's unchanging love; God is always with you today and forever.

November 4

Topic: Light to Follow God

Opening Statement: I am here to light your way when life feels confusing or uncertain.

Bible Verse: *"Trust in the Lord with all your heart and lean not on your own understanding."* —Proverbs 3:5 (NIV)

Devotional: My blessed Sacred Heart, I know your heart's most profound hopes and unclear paths. I see the questions you hold, wondering which direction is right or how to stay close to Me when the world feels loud. I am your light of the world, guiding you through life's darkness, your guide and comforter, sent to fill your heart with peace and illuminate the path set for you.

When you pray for guidance, ask Me to light each step with divine truth. Trust in My Holy Word; it is a lamp to your feet. Release the worries that weigh you down and invite Me to show you the way forward. I will not leave you in darkness but help you confidently walk in glorious light.

Closing Encouragement: Remember, My divine light is always with you, and I will guide you every step of the way.

November 5

Topic: Healing for Your Body

Bible Verse: *"He gives strength to the weary and increases the power of the weak."* —Isaiah 40:29 (NIV)

Opening Statement: Are you tired, sick, or struggling with pain? I am here to give you the strength and healing you need.

Devotional: I am the Spirit of health and wholeness, and I know every part of your body, every ache, and every worry. Even when you feel weak or weighed down, I am here to fill you with strength and healing from within. I understand your struggles, and you are never alone in them. Every small step toward healing is a gift, a sign of My presence with you, guiding you through.

When life feels overwhelming, or your body doesn't feel as strong as you'd like, remember to turn to Me. I am ready to fill you with peace beyond what you think and strength to help you move forward. Trust in Me as I heal you, both inside and out. Together, we will walk this journey of restoration.

Closing Encouragement: Be encouraged: I am with you, bringing strength and new life every day.

November 6

Topic: Healing of the Mind.

Opening Statement: Your mind is precious, and God desires to heal, renew, and restore it.

Scripture: *Praise the Lord, my soul, and forget not all his benefits— who forgives all your sins and heals all your diseases, who redeems your life from the pit, and crowns you with love and compassion.* Psalm 10:2-4 NIV.

Devotional: Dear one, I know every thought that runs through your mind. I see the doubts, fears, and worries that sometimes weigh you down. I want to free you from the world's burdens on your heart and mind. I am here to renew and heal you, helping you see yourself through My eyes— loved, capable, and purposeful.

When you feel overwhelmed or anxious, invite Me into your thoughts. Let Me replace the negative patterns with My truth. Remember, I have given you a spirit of love, power, and a sound mind. Lean on Me, and I will provide you peace that the world can't take away. With each new day, I am ready to heal and renew you, shaping you into who I've called you to be.

Closing Encouragement: Trust in My healing; I will strengthen and renew your mind daily.

November 7

Topic: renewed spirit.

Opening Statement: Each morning is a fresh chance to invite God's healing power into your soul and start your day with hope and strength.

Bible Verse: he saved us, not because of righteous things we had done, but because of his mercy. He saved us through the washing of rebirth and renewal by the Holy Spirit, Titus 3:9. (NIV)

Devotional: Beloved, I am here with you, closer than your next breath. I know the burdens you carry—the worries, the hurt, the pressures that sometimes seem so heavy. This morning, I invite you to lay them down with Me. Take a deep breath, and know that My love is here to comfort and heal your heart.

As you begin this day, seek My presence with a quiet heart. Remember, I am the One who brings rest and renewal to your soul. When you get your wounds to Me, I will begin to heal them, filling those places with peace. Trust Me with your struggles and know that My strength is enough for whatever you face.

Closing Encouragement: Step into today knowing I am with you, healing and strengthening you with My endless love.

November 8

Topic: Leaving guilt behind.

Opening Statement: Carrying guilt feels heavy on your heart, but God offers freedom and a fresh start.

Bible Verse: *"If we confess our sins, He is faithful and just and will forgive us our sins and purify us from all unrighteousness."* — 1 John 1:9 (NIV)

Devotional: My child, I see every part of you—the good and the bad, your triumphs and struggles. I know the guilt you carry and the times you've replayed past mistakes in your mind. I want you to understand that holding onto guilt isn't My will for you. I sent Jesus to carry that weight so you wouldn't have to. When you confess your mistakes and bring them to Me, I am faithful to forgive and purify your heart completely.

Your sins are no longer a barrier between us; they are gone as far as the East is from the West. Step forward boldly into the life I've planned for you, leaving the baggage of guilt behind. Let My love fill you with peace, and know you are forever accepted and beloved.

Closing Encouragement: Remember, you are forgiven and free—walk in the confidence of My love and grace.

November 9

Topic: Honoring God's Name in Prayer

Opening Statement: When we pray, we open our hearts to a robust relationship with our heavenly Father.

Bible Verse: *"'Our Father in heaven, hallowed be Your name, Your kingdom come, Your will be done, on earth as it is in heaven."* (Matthew 6:9-10 NIV)

Devotional: My sacred heart, I am closer to you than you realize. I am united to your heavenly Father and hear every word you speak. When you say, "Our Father," you're calling on Me and joining with others who love Me across the world and even through time. As you honor My name, know that I am holy, mighty, and full of love for you.

I have a purpose and a plan for your life, and as you pray, remember to invite My will to guide you. Let go of worry, trusting that My kingdom—My perfect, loving rule—is coming. I'm with you every moment, ready to pour peace, strength, and hope. Just say My name honorably and feel My presence fill your heart.

Closing Encouragement: Keep praying and honoring God's name, trusting God has a perfect plan for you.

November 10

Topic: Embracing God's Kingdom.

Bible Verse: *"Your kingdom come, your will be done, on earth as it is in heaven."* —Matthew 6:10 (NIV)

Opening Statement: God's kingdom is more than just a place—God's love, justice, and purpose brought to life on earth through us.

Devotional: My child, I am calling you to be a part of something greater than yourself. When you pray, "Your kingdom come, you will be done," you're inviting Me to work in your life in ways you can't imagine yet. My kingdom isn't only far away in heaven; it's here, in every kind word, every act of love, and every moment of forgiveness. I'm asking you to bring a piece of heaven to earth.

Sometimes, putting others first or acting with patience and grace will feel difficult. But I will guide you. When you seek My will, I'll help you see the world with eyes of love, hope, and peace. Each time you follow Me, you make the world a little more like heaven, bringing joy to My heart.

Closing Encouragement: Remember, with each choice, you can bring My kingdom closer.

November 11

Topic: Daily Blessings.

Bible Verse: *"Give us today our daily bread."* —Matthew 6:11 (NIV)

Opening Statement: I invite you to trust that I will provide everything you need each day.

Devotional: Dear child, I see your every need and desire and understand what you truly need each day. When you pray, "Give us today our daily bread," you ask Me to provide food and everything essential for your life, strength, and growth. I know what weighs on your heart—the need for physical nourishment, emotional support, or spiritual guidance. Trust that I am near and ready to provide.

Remember, your "daily bread" doesn't come all at once for the month or year. Just as the Israelites gathered manna each morning in the wilderness, I want you to depend on Me daily. When you wake up, invite Me to meet your needs, and watch how I lovingly care for you, moment by moment.

Closing Encouragement: Rest in the knowledge that I am always here, providing what you need, one day at a time.

November 12

Topic: Forgive and Be Forgiven:

Opening Statement: Forgiving others can feel challenging, but God's love helps us overcome hurt and find true freedom.

Bible Verse: *"For if you forgive other people when they sin against you, your heavenly Father will also forgive you."* —Matthew 6:14 (NIV)

Devotional: My beloved child, I know the pain in your heart when someone hurts you. I see every tear, hear every unspoken word, and understand how hard forgiving can be. But remember, forgiveness is not just something you give others; it's also My gift. When you forgive, you free your heart from the weight of bitterness and make space for My peace and joy.

As I forgive you each day, I invite you to offer that same grace to others. When you hold onto hurt, it can keep you from seeing the fullness of My love. But when you let go, trusting Me with your pain, I will heal your heart and fill it with strength and hope.

Closing Encouragement: Remember, as you forgive, you become more like Jesus and open your heart to My boundless love and peace.

November 13

Topic: Overcoming Temptation.

Opening Statement: Temptation can be strong, but My guidance is even more vital.

Bible Verse: *"And lead us not into temptation, but deliver us from the evil one."* —Matthew 6:13 (NIV)

Devotional: I see you, and I understand the challenges you face. Every day, the world offers choices that can pull you in directions far from My love. I know it's not easy, but remember, I am with you every step of the way. You don't have to face these things alone. When you're tempted, lean on Me—call out, and I will help you stand firm. I am here to guide you and show you the right path filled with peace and purpose.

Remember, temptation isn't something you need to fear. When you ask Me to lead you away from it, I will help you avoid those things that cause harm. Trust that My love will protect you from evil, and My wisdom will help you choose what is good. You're never alone.

Closing Encouragement: Stay close to Me, and let My love be your shield.

November 14

Topic: Building Confidence and Spiritual Strength.

Opening Statement: Confidence and spiritual strength come from knowing that God is always by your side, guiding you and helping you to stand firm.

Bible Verse: *"Be strong and courageous. Do not be afraid; do not be discouraged, for the Lord your God will be with you wherever you go."* —Joshua 1:9 (NIV)

Devotional: I know your struggles, doubts, and fears that sometimes fill your mind. But remember, I am with you always. My strength is in you, and My presence surrounds you. Each time you feel weak or uncertain, lean into My promises. I created you with purpose and have given you a spirit of power, not fear. When you trust Me, confidence will grow in your heart, and strength will rise within you.

Whenever you feel uncertain, remember I will guide you and give you courage. Lift your eyes to Me; I will be your anchor, even in the most challenging moments. I am the source of your confidence and strength. Walk boldly, knowing I am with you every step.

Closing Encouragement: Take heart and step forward in My strength—I will never leave you.

November 15

Topic: Become a Peacemaker.

Opening Statement: Being a peacemaker isn't just about ending arguments; it's about showing God's love in a divided world.

Bible Verse: *"Blessed are the peacemakers, for they will be called children of God."* — Matthew 5:9 (NIV)

Devotional: My beloved Sacred Heart, I am here to guide you into a life of peace and purpose. You live in a world entirely of noise, opinions, and conflicts, but I am calling you to rise above that. As a peacemaker, you reflect My heart. When you choose understanding over anger, forgiveness over grudges, and kindness over harsh words, you shine My light in dark places.

I know it's not always easy, especially when others are unkind or misunderstand you. But remember, you are not alone. I am with you, giving you the strength to respond in love. You don't have to fix every problem or end every argument, but you can bring My peace to others through your words and actions. This is My calling for you—to be My child and to share My love.

Closing Encouragement: Walk in My peace, and you will bring My love to those around you.

November 16

Topic: Trusting God with Academic Goals

Opening Statement: Your academic goals matter to Me because they are part of the future I have prepared for you.

Bible Verse: *"Commit to the Lord whatever you do, and he will establish your plans."* —Proverbs 16:3 (NIV)

Devotional: I see your efforts, dreams, and frustrations when things feel overwhelming. Remember this: You don't walk this journey alone. I am with you every step of the way, giving you strength and wisdom.

Your academic goals are important, not because of grades alone, but because they are opportunities to learn and grow into the person I created you to be. Seek Me in your studies. Pray before every test, invite Me into your classrooms, and trust that I will guide your mind and heart.

When you feel stressed or unsure, lean on Me. I will give you peace that replaces anxiety and clarity that surpasses confusion. Commit your work to Me, and trust My timing. My plans for you are good, and I will lead you to success in ways beyond what you can imagine.

Closing Encouragement: Keep striving, trusting, and walking with Me—I have great plans for your future!

November 17

Topic: Trusting God for Help in School.

Opening Statement: Feeling stressed about exams? You're not alone—God is ready to help you succeed.

Bible Verse: *"I can do all this through him who gives me strength."* —Philippians 4:13 (NIV)

Devotional: Dear child, I see your efforts, late-night studying, and even your fears about failing. I want you to know that I am here to help. When you feel overwhelmed, pause and invite Me into your thoughts. I will give you clarity and peace that go beyond your understanding. Trust Me to guide your memory as you recall what you've studied, and rely on My wisdom for solving problems you may not expect.

Remember, your value doesn't come from grades but from being loved by your Heavenly Father. Please do your best, but lean on Me instead of your strength. Pray before you study, ask for wisdom, and stay diligent. I will give you confidence and focus—not because of who you are but because of who I am in you.

Closing Encouragement: You are never alone in any challenge, including exams—I am with you, and together, you can face anything.

November 18

Topic: Healing for a Hurting Soul.

Opening Statement: Feeling broken inside doesn't mean you're beyond repair—it means you're in the perfect place for My healing.

Bible Verse: *But he said to me, "My grace is sufficient for you, for my power is made perfect in weakness.* 2 Corinthians 12:9 NIV.

My beloved Sacred Heart, I see the pain you hide. The loneliness, fear, and struggles you don't share with anyone—I know them all. You may feel like no one understands, but I do. I am the One who made you and learned how to heal your soul. When life feels overwhelming, bring your hurt to Me. Let My love wash over you like a gentle wave, calming the storms inside.

Healing starts with surrender. Trust Me with your wounds, doubts, and questions you're afraid to ask. I will not judge or reject you. Instead, I will guide you, step by step, toward peace. You don't have to carry this alone. I live within you, giving you strength and comfort.

Rest in this truth: You are never beyond My reach. Your soul is precious to Me, and I am making everything new.

Closing Encouragement: Close your eyes and feel My presence—I am here and will never leave you.

November 19

Topic: Trusting God with Your Future.

Opening Statement: Your career dreams are important, but trusting God's plan for your future is the key to success.

Bible Verse: *Commit your way to the Lord; trust in him and he will do this: He will make your righteous reward shine like the dawn, your vindication like the noonday sun.* Psalm 37:5-6.

Devotional: My child, I see the dreams forming in your heart—those passions, talents, and aspirations stirring within you. They're not random. I placed them there. As you think about your future career, remember this: I've already mapped out a path just for you. It's a path that will not only bring you joy but also allow you to glorify Me.

Do not be afraid to explore the gifts I've given you. Maybe it's medicine, teaching, art, or technology—whatever you pursue, invite Me into your decisions. I will direct your steps when you seek My guidance through prayer and the Word. Trust My timing. Even when the journey feels uncertain, know that I am shaping you for the plans I have prepared.

Success, in My eyes, isn't about titles or wealth—it's about living purposefully and serving others. Keep your eyes on Me, and I will lead you into a hopeful future.

Closing Encouragement: Trust Me with your dreams; I will open doors you never imagined possible.

November 20

Topic: Finding Your True Self

Opening Statement: Understanding who you are in God's eyes is the key to finding your purpose and place in this world.

Bible Verse: *"For we are God's handiwork, created in Christ Jesus to do good works, which God prepared in advance for us to do."* —Ephesians 2:10 (NIV)

Devotional: Dear child, I see you searching for who you are. In a world full of voices trying to define you, hear My voice above them all: You are Mine. You were lovingly created, not by accident, but with purpose. Every part of you—your strengths, quirks, and struggles—has been woven into a masterpiece by My hands.

You don't need to look to the world for approval or identity; popularity, accomplishments, or appearance do not measure your worth. You are already loved, chosen, and cherished. Trust Me to show you the gifts I've placed inside you and the good works I've prepared for your life. Walk in confidence, knowing that your identity is secure in Me, not in what others think.

Let Me guide you. Lean into My Word, and I will reveal your unique role in this world—a role no one else can fill.

Closing Encouragement: Remember, you are God's masterpiece, uniquely made for a purpose only you can fulfill.

November 21

Topic: Finding Freedom in Forgiveness

Opening Statement: Forgiveness isn't easy, but it's the key to finding peace and living free in Christ's love.

Bible Verse: *"Be kind and compassionate to one another, forgiving each other, just as in Christ God forgave you."* —Ephesians 4:32 (NIV)

Devotional: Dear one, I see the weight you carry—hurt caused by others, mistakes you regret, and the pain of broken relationships. These burdens hold you back, but I am here to guide you toward freedom.

Forgiveness doesn't mean excusing the wrong or forgetting the hurt. It means letting go of the bitterness that chains your heart. Look at the cross and see how Christ forgave you. His mercy is endless; through Him, you can forgive others and yourself.

Come to Me with your wounds, and I will heal them. If you've been hurt, I will give you the courage to forgive. If you've caused pain, I will guide you to seek forgiveness. Trust Me to work through your struggles and bring beauty out of the brokenness.

Forgiveness is hard, but it's worth it. Let go, and let Me bring peace into your life.

Closing Encouragement: You are never alone in this journey—lean on Christ, and forgiveness will free your heart.

November 22

Topic: Achieve Your Goals.

Opening Statement: Achieving your goals and building good habits isn't just about hard work—it's about inviting God into every step of your journey.

Bible Verse: *Suppose one of you wants to build a tower. Won't you first sit down and estimate the cost to see if you have enough money to complete it?* Luke 14:28 NIV.

Devotional: My dear child, I see the dreams in your heart and the goals you long to achieve. Know that I placed those desires within you for a purpose. But remember this: true success begins when you commit your plans to Me.

Let Me guide you in your steps as you work toward your goals. Build habits that honor Me—habits of diligence, kindness, and faithfulness. Start small, and trust that I am shaping you into who I created you to be with each consistent step.

There will be days when you feel discouraged or overwhelmed, but do not give up. I am with you, giving you the strength and wisdom to persevere. Depend on My Word, pray often, and trust My timing. Together, we will turn your dreams into milestones that glorify My name.

Closing Encouragement: Take heart—I am always with you, cheering you on as you grow and succeed. Keep trusting Me!

November 23

Topic: Overcoming Anxiety and Depression

Opening Statement: Anxiety and depression can feel overwhelming, but I am here to guide you toward peace and healing.

Bible Verse: *"Cast all your anxiety on Him because He cares for you."* —1 Peter 5:7 (NIV)

Devotional: Dear child, I see the weight you carry, the thoughts that swirl, and the feelings that threaten to overwhelm you. I want you to know that I am with you, always. When anxiety or depression clouds your mind, come to me. I will help you find stillness in the storm.

Take a deep breath and remember this truth: you are not alone. I know your fears and struggles and long to replace them with perfect peace. When you feel the walls closing in, please speak to me. Pray, sing, cry—your every word reaches me, and I will respond.

Use the tools I've placed in your life—supportive friends, trusted adults, and wise counselors. These are my gifts to help you cope and heal. Don't let shame keep you from seeking help; you are beloved and worthy of care.

Closing Encouragement: No matter how hard today feels, I promise to walk you into a brighter tomorrow—trust in me.

November 24

Topic: Overcoming Anxiety and Depression

Opening Statement: Anxiety and depression can feel overwhelming, but I am here to guide you toward peace and healing.

Bible Verse: *"Cast all your anxiety on Him because He cares for you."* —1 Peter 5:7 (NIV)

Devotional: Dear child, I see the weight you carry, the thoughts that swirl, and the feelings that threaten to overwhelm you. I want you to know that I am with you, always. When anxiety or depression clouds your mind, come to me. I will help you find stillness in the storm.

Take a deep breath and remember this truth: you are not alone. I know your fears and struggles and long to replace them with perfect peace. When you feel the walls closing in, please speak to me. Pray, sing, cry—your every word reaches me, and I will respond.

Use the tools I've placed in your life—supportive friends, trusted adults, and wise counselors. These are my gifts to help you cope and heal. Don't let shame keep you from seeking help; you are beloved and worthy of care.

Closing Encouragement: No matter how hard today feels, I promise to walk you into a brighter tomorrow—trust in me.

November 25

Topic: Finding Patience in Trials:

Opening Statement: Patience in trials isn't easy, but it's where your faith grows the strongest.

Bible Verse: *"Wait for the Lord; be strong and take heart and wait for the Lord."* —Psalm 27:14 (NIV)

Stand firm, My holy child, I see your struggles, the moments when life feels unfair or overwhelming. I know the frustration of waiting and wondering if things will ever improve. But I want you to trust Me—I work in your life, even when you can't see it.

When you feel like giving up, remember that patience is not a weakness. It is strength rooted in knowing that My timing is perfect. Every challenge you face shapes you into the person I've created you to be. I am with you in the waiting, walking beside you through every trial.

When the road feels long, lean on My promises. Let My Word be a lamp to your feet. I am your refuge, your guide, and your ever-present help. Please keep your eyes on me, for I am using this season to prepare you for something greater. I trust my love for you. I am your strength, and I will not fail you.

Closing Encouragement: Keep going, My strong child. I am making all things new in your life.

November 26

Topic: Encouragement in Faith

Opening statement: Even when life feels overwhelming, your faith has the power to shine brightly and inspire others.

Bible Verse: *Don't let anyone look down on you because you are young, but set an example for the believers in speech, in conduct, in love, in faith and in purity."* —1 Timothy 4:12 (NIV)

Devotional: Dear Child, I see you—the doubts you carry, the questions in your heart, and the moments when you wonder if your faith is enough. Let me remind you that I am always with you, guiding, loving, and strengthening you. You are not too young, weak, or imperfect to be used by Me in powerful ways.

When life feels heavy, lean into Me. I will carry your burdens and give you peace. Your faith, no matter how small, can move mountains when it is rooted in My promises. Trust Me in the small things today, and watch how I will grow your faith step by step.

Speak boldly, love deeply, and believe in My plan for you. Your faith can inspire those around you, even when you don't realize it. Walk confidently, for I have called you and am with you always.

Closing Encouragement: Remember, you are never alone; your faith can make a difference.

November 27

Topic: Healing for Broken Hearts

Opening Statement: When your heart feels shattered, I am here to pick up the pieces and bring you lasting peace.

Bible Verse: *"The Lord is close to the brokenhearted and saves those who are crushed in spirit."* —Psalm 34:18 (NIV)

Devotional: Dear Sacred Heart, I see the pain hidden behind your smiles and the tears you cry when no one is watching. Your broken heart is not unseen; every ache, every silent prayer, every longing for healing—I am here for it all. I know the betrayal, the loss, the words that hurt more than wounds. Remember that I am the Comforter and draw close to you when your spirit is crushed.

Bring your shattered pieces to me. Trust me to heal, even when it feels impossible. The world may offer distractions, but only I can genuinely bind up the broken places and give you joy amid sorrow. Come to me with your hurts, and I will exchange them for my peace that passes all understanding.

Closing Encouragement: Take heart; healing begins when you bring your pain to me—I am making all things new.

November 28

Topic: Trusting God's Plan

Opening Statement: Trusting in God's plan can feel challenging, especially when life takes unexpected turns, but His promises are always accurate.

Bible Verse: *"Trust in the Lord with all your heart and lean not on your own understanding; in all your ways submit to him, and he will make your paths straight."* (Proverbs 3:5-6, NIV)

Devotional: Dear child, I see your heart—your dreams, your fears, and the questions you keep asking when things don't go the way you hoped. You wonder, "Why is this happening?" or "What's next for me?" Trust that I am here, working for your good, even when you don't understand.

My plans for you are far greater than you can imagine, even when they unfold in challenging or confusing ways. I am the One who holds tomorrow, and I have not forgotten you. Surrender your fears to Me and lean on My Word. When you trust Me, I promise to guide your steps and bring you into the future I've prepared—one filled with hope and purpose.

Remember, I love you endlessly and will never leave you alone.

Closing Encouragement: Trust in Me—I am always faithful, and My plans for you are perfect, even when life feels uncertain.

November 29

Topic: Finding Comfort in Uncertainty

Opening Statement: Uncertainty can feel overwhelming, but in those moments, I am your peace, your guide, and your ever-present comfort.

Bible Verse: *"Cast all your anxiety on him because he cares for you."* —1 Peter 5:7 (NIV)

Devotional: I see your heart. I know the questions that weigh heavy on your mind—the "what ifs," the doubts, and the fears of what tomorrow might bring. You don't need to navigate these uncertainties alone. I am here. As I guided the disciples through the stormy seas, I am with you in every unknown.

When you feel lost or afraid, remember that My plans for you are good, even when you can't see the whole picture. Trust Me. Speak to Me in prayer, open My Word, and let My peace, which surpasses understanding, guard your heart and mind. Even when the path seems unclear, My love for you never wavers. I am working all things together for your good.

Let go of the need to control the future and rest in My care. Cast your anxieties on Me, for I delight in carrying them for you. You are always in My sight.

Closing Encouragement: Walk boldly into today, knowing I hold your tomorrow.

November 30

Topic: Navigating Life with Wisdom.

Opening Statement: Life is entire of choices, and I am here to guide you when the path seems unclear.

Bible Verse: *"If any of you lacks wisdom, you should ask God, who gives generously to all without finding fault, and it will be given to you."* —James 1:5 (NIV)

Devotional: Dear one, I see your heart and the questions swirling in your mind. You wonder if you're making the right choices or heading down the right path. Know this: I am with you, whispering wisdom into your soul. When you pause and ask Me for guidance, I will answer. You might hear My voice through a verse, feel a nudge in your spirit, or receive wise advice from someone you trust. Don't rush decisions out of fear or impatience—trust My timing.

I am not a God of confusion but of peace. If a choice leads to My peace, you can walk forward boldly. But if anxiety lingers, let's talk. Open My Word, seek counsel, and pray with expectation. You are never alone in navigating life's challenges. Let Me guide you one step at a time.

Closing Encouragement: Take courage—when you lean on Me, I will always light your way.

November 30

Topic: Strengthening bonds with loved ones or resolving conflicts.

Opening Statement: Relationships can be challenging, but with God's help, you can build stronger bonds and bring peace where there's conflict.

Bible Verse: *"Do to others as you would have them do to you."* —Luke 6:31 (NIV)

Devotional: I see your heart, beloved. You want to love others well, but sometimes relationships can be messy. Arguments happen, feelings get hurt, and the ones you care about most can feel distant. But I am here to help you. I am your Comforter and Guide.

When you feel frustrated or misunderstood, pause and let me fill you with peace. Remember what Jesus taught: treat others the way you want to be treated. Choose kindness over harsh words, patience over anger, and forgiveness over resentment. This can be challenging, but I will give you the strength to make the first move toward healing.

When you step toward love and peace, even in the most minor ways, I work through you to repair what's broken. Trust me to guide your words and actions, and I will help you build stronger, healthier relationships.

Closing Encouragement: Let love and forgiveness flow through you, and watch how I bring healing to your relationships. You are never alone in this.

December 1

Topic: Dating with Faith

Opening Statement: Dating and attraction are exciting but can also feel overwhelming—trusting God's plan will bring peace and clarity to your journey.

Bible Verse: *"Trust in the Lord with all your heart and lean not on your own understanding; in all your ways submit to Him, and He will make your paths straight."* —Proverbs 3:5-6 (NIV)

Devotional: Dear one, I see your heart. I know the questions, the excitement, and the uncertainties you feel about dating and relationships. Trust Me, for I am the One who created love. I've placed the desire for connection in you, but I want to guide you in pursuing it.

When you're unsure about what to say, how to act, or who to trust, lean into Me. Ask Me for wisdom, and I will answer. My plan for you is full of goodness, and I know the perfect timing. Don't settle for anything less than a relationship built on respect, kindness, and a shared love for Me.

Remember, I am always with you. I will never lead you where My grace cannot keep you. Be patient, trust in My timing, and let your love story reflect my love for you.

Closing Encouragement: You are never alone—God's wisdom and love will guide your heart in every relationship and decision.

December 2

Topic: God's Protection and Safety.

Opening Statement: Teen life can feel overwhelming, but God promises to protect and guide you despite your challenges.

Bible Verse: *"The Lord will keep you from all harm—he will watch over your life; the Lord will watch over your coming and going both now and forevermore."* —Psalm 121:7-8 (NIV)

Devotional: My child, I am always with you. Remember that I am your protector when fear creeps in, and danger seems close. Every step you take, I am watching over you. Even when you cannot see me, I shield you from harm, keeping you safe in ways you may never realize.

Trust me with your fears and your future. I have placed angels around you, guarding your path, and I will not let you stumble. When you feel unsure, call on me—I will give you peace that no storm can shake. My plans for you are good, and my love surrounds you like a shield.

Walk boldly, knowing that I am your refuge and strength. Keep your eyes on me, and I will lead you safely through every trial and challenge.

Closing Encouragement: You are never alone—God's love and protection are with you always.

December 3

Topic: Trusting God in Economic Challenges

Opening Statement: Even as a teenager, you can trust God to guide you toward financial stability and teach you how to handle challenges with faith and wisdom.

Bible Verse: *"The Lord will open the heavens, the storehouse of his bounty, to send rain on your land in season and to bless all the work of your hands. You will lend to many nations but will borrow from none."* —Deuteronomy 28:12 (NIV)

Devotional: My Sacred Heart, I see your worries about money and your family's financial struggles. I know your heart desires to help, and I am here to remind you that I am your Provider. The world measures success by wealth, but I measure it by trust in Me.

Even now, I am planting seeds in your life—wisdom to manage resources, growth opportunities, and blessings you cannot yet see. Trust Me with what you have, no matter how little it may seem. Be faithful in small things, and I will multiply them. Learn to give generously, for when you give, I open the floodgates of heaven to bless you in return.

When the pressures of money feel overwhelming, remember: I own everything. How much more will I care for you if I clothe the lilies and feed the sparrows? Rest in Me, for I am your peace and provision.

Closing Encouragement: Walk boldly in faith, knowing that I will bless the work of your hands and provide for all your needs in My perfect time.

December 4

Topic: Fit for a Purpose

Opening Statement: Your body is a masterpiece created by God, designed with purpose and love, and caring for it is part of living out the divine plan for your life.

Bible Verse: *"So whether you eat or drink or whatever you do, do it all for the glory of God."* —1 Corinthians 10:31 (NIV)

Devotional: My dear Sacred Heart, I made your body unique, strong, and beautiful in My eyes. In a world full of comparisons and impossible standards, I want you to know this: you are fearfully and wonderfully made. Each time you nourish your body, move in joy or rest, you honor Me.

Fitness is not about perfection or looking like someone else. It's about embracing the gift of health and using it to fulfill the purpose I have for you. Feed your body good things—foods that bring you energy and strength. Exercise not to meet the world's expectations but to feel the joy of movement and celebrate the body I've given you.

I am with you as you make choices each day. Lean on Me when you feel insecure or overwhelmed, and I will remind you of your worth. Trust that you are enough, exactly as you are because I made you with love.

Closing Encouragement: Be confident, knowing you are a beautiful creation designed to thrive in both body and spirit!

December 5

Topic: Building Strong Faith

Opening Statement: Faith is like a muscle—it grows stronger as you trust and connect with Me daily.

Bible Verse: *"Faith comes from hearing the message, and the message is heard through the word about Christ."* (Romans 10:17 NIV)

Devotional: My precious one, I see your heart and desire to understand Me more. You might sometimes feel unsure, wondering if your faith is enough or if you're growing. But don't be discouraged—faith is not about how much you know; it's about trusting Me step by step. Like a tiny seed planted in the soil, your faith grows when you water it with My Word and spend time with Me.

When you pray to Me, open the Bible, and let My promises fill your heart, I strengthen you. Even when you don't see it, I'm working. Trust that every prayer whispered, every moment you choose to believe, even when it's hard, brings you closer to Me.

You don't have to have all the answers right now. Just keep seeking and trusting, and I will lead you. I am here to help you gain a deeper understanding and a stronger connection with me.

Closing Encouragement: Keep trusting, keep growing—I am always with you every step of the way.

December 6

Topic: Maintaining and building relationships.

Opening Statement: Friendships are some of the greatest blessings in your life, but they also take love, patience, and intentional effort to grow and thrive.

Bible Verse: *"A friend loves at all times, and a brother is born for a time of adversity."* —Proverbs 17:17 NIV.

Devotional: My child, I created you for connection—not just with Me, but with others. Friendships are a gift to encourage and remind you that you're not alone. I see the desires of your heart for friends who will stand by you, laugh with you, and support you when times are tough.

To build strong friendships, let My love flow through you. Be a friend who listens, forgives, and speaks words that build others up. Let your kindness reflect My Spirit within you. When you face disagreements or challenges, come to Me, and I will guide you toward peace and understanding.

Trust that I will bring the right people into your life at the right time. Keep your heart open to others and lean on Me when you feel lonely. I am always here, your closest friend.

Closing Encouragement: You are never alone—I am with you, and I will bless you with friendships that inspire, support, and reflect My love.

December 7

Topic: Strengthening Family Bonds

Opening Statement: Family relationships can be challenging, but God's love equips you to bring understanding, peace, and joy to your home.

Bible Verse: *"Be completely humble and gentle; be patient, bearing with one another in love."* (Ephesians 4:2, NIV)

Devotional: My dear child, I see your heart and the struggles you face in your family. Relationships aren't always easy; sometimes, no one truly understands you. But I want you to know this: I am with you every moment, and My love can transform even the most complicated situations.

Be patient, humble, and kind, just as I am patient with you. Listen when others speak, even when it's complicated. Speak words of kindness, even when you feel hurt. When disagreements arise, turn to Me. Ask for My wisdom and peace to guide your actions.

Remember, your family is a gift, and I have placed you together for a purpose. You can be a light in your home. With My help, you can bring unity, forgiveness, and love to your family. Trust Me—I will show you how.

Closing Encouragement: You have the power to make a difference in your family, and I will guide you every step of the way.

December 8

Topic: Finding Inner Peace

Opening Statement: Life can feel overwhelming, but God offers you a peace that calms your heart and gives you hope, no matter what you face.

Bible Verse: *"The Lord gives strength to his people; the Lord blesses his people with peace."* —Psalm 29:11 (NIV)

Devotional: Dear Sacred Heart, I see your heart when it feels heavy and uncertain. You may struggle with inner worries or even wonder how peace is possible in a world of conflicts. But remember, I am with you. I am your Comforter, the One who calms the storm within and shows you how to live in harmony with others.

When chaos seems to surround you, come to Me. Quiet your heart, speak My name, and let My presence fill you. You don't need to have all the answers. Trust in My plan and unfailing love. The peace I give is not like the fleeting calm the world offers. My peace is profound, unshakable, and eternal.

Lean into Me when life feels hard. Let Me guide your thoughts, words, and actions so you can be a light of peace to others. Together, we can bring hope to the world.

Closing Encouragement: Be strong in the Lord, knowing His peace is with you, and He can bring peace to others through you.

December 9

Topic: Peer Acceptance.

Opening Statement: Navigating the pressure to fit in with friends can feel overwhelming, but I want you to know that your worth and identity come from Me, not the crowd.

Bible Verse: *"Fear of man will prove to be a snare, but whoever trusts in the Lord is kept safe."* (Proverbs 29:25, NIV)

Devotional: My beloved, I see you striving to fit in, longing for acceptance. It's natural to want to belong, but remember this: you already belong to Me. The world may pull you to change who you are to gain approval, but I call you to stand firm in the identity I've given you.

Peer pressure is a snare, but My Word is your guide. Trust Me to help you make choices that reflect who I've created you to be. Fitting in may seem important now, but compromising your values will never lead to true joy. When you feel torn between what's right and what others want, lean into Me. I will give you the courage to stand out when necessary and the wisdom to find true friends who love you for who you are.

Let My love define you, not the opinions of others. With Me, you are enough. Always.

Closing Encouragement: You don't need to change to belong—trust in My love, and I will guide you to the acceptance and peace your heart craves.

December 10

Topic: Gratitude

Opening Statement: Gratitude isn't just saying "thank you"—it's a way to see God's hand in your life, even when things don't seem perfect.

Bible Verse: *"Give thanks in all circumstances; for this is God's will for you in Christ Jesus."* —1 Thessalonians 5:18 (NIV)

Devotional: Dear one, I see you. I see your heart, your joys, and even your struggles. I'm with you every moment, even when life feels overwhelming. Today, I want you to focus on gratitude—not because life is always easy, but because I am always good.

Think about this: the air you breathe, the friends who make you laugh, the music that uplifts you—all gifts from Me. Gratitude changes your perspective; it opens your eyes to My love woven into every part of your day. Even when things don't go as planned, you can still find Me working for your good.

Take a moment today to thank Me—for the big blessings and the small ones. Gratitude isn't just for when life feels perfect; it's for every day because My love for you never changes. Trust Me, and I'll show you how much joy there is in a grateful heart.

Closing Encouragement: Choose gratitude, and watch how it transforms your heart and days into a reflection of My love for you.

December 11

Topic: Guidance for Career Success

Opening Statement: Your future matters to God, and the Holy Spirit wants to lead you toward a fulfilling career and purpose.

Bible Verse: *"Whatever you do, work at it with all your heart, as working for the Lord, not for human masters,"* Colossians 3:23: NIV.

Devotional: My beloved child, I see the dreams in your heart and the questions about your future. Trust that I am here to guide you every step of the way. When you need help deciding what career to choose or how to succeed in your work, remember that I have a perfect plan for you. I created you with unique talents and gifts meant to make a difference.

Take time to listen for My voice through prayer and My Word. Seek Me first, and I will give you the wisdom to make decisions. Do your best in the opportunities before you now, and I will open doors that no one can shut. Whether your path feels clear or uncertain, trust that I am working for your good.

Closing Encouragement: Stay close to Me, and I will lead you to a life filled with purpose, joy, and success at every step of your journey.

December 12

Topic: Finding True Love

Opening Statement: True love starts with God, who knows and loves you thoroughly.

Bible Verse: *"We love because He first loved us"* (1 John 4:19, NIV).

Devotional: Dear one, I see the desires of your heart—the longing for love, acceptance, and someone to truly understand you. Remember this: before anyone else can love you well, you must let Me fill your heart with My perfect love. I am the One who created you, knows your worth, and guides you toward relationships that honor Me and bring joy to your life.

When you're waiting for the "right person," don't rush. My timing is perfect. Focus on becoming the person I've called you to be—someone rooted in My love and walking in My truth. If you're in a relationship, invite Me into it. Real love is patient, kind, and selfless—it doesn't tear you down or pull you away from Me.

Let Me be the foundation of your heart so that you can love others with My strength and grace. In time, I will lead you to the love worth waiting for. Trust me to guide you in your steps and guard your heart.

Closing Encouragement: Let My love be your guide, and I will lead you to relationships that reflect My goodness and joy.

December 13

Topic: Online communities.

Opening Statement: You are never alone—let your virtual connections inspire you to live boldly for God daily.

Bible Verse: *"Let us consider how we may spur one another on toward love and good deeds, not giving up meeting together, as some are in the habit of doing, but encouraging one another."* (Hebrews 10:24-25 NIV)

Devotional: I see the spaces where you gather virtually and am with you there. Every online interaction is an opportunity to reflect on My love and truth. You were not made to walk through life alone. Just as you seek connection in your daily life, I've provided ways for you to find encouragement and friendship even in the digital world.

Use these communities wisely, looking for people who build you up and inspire you to grow closer to Me. Speak kindness and truth, showing My light to everyone you encounter. When you join with like-minded peers, whether in person or online, I am present, guiding your conversations and strengthening your bonds.

Stay rooted in My Word; I will help you discern which connections are healthy and life-giving. We can create a digital space filled with love, encouragement, and purpose.

Closing Encouragement: Keep seeking My purpose in every community you join, and I will lead you to meaningful connections.

December 14

Topic: Academic Success

Opening Statement: Did you know that academic success is not just about hard work—it's about inviting God's guidance into your studies?

Bible Verse: *"For the Lord gives wisdom; from his mouth come knowledge and understanding."* —Proverbs 2:6 (NIV)

Devotional: Dear one, I see your efforts. Every late-night study session, every test, every project—none of it goes unnoticed. I want you to know that I am here to guide you, even in your academics. When you feel overwhelmed, remember that wisdom and knowledge come from Me. Your abilities are a gift, but they are multiplied when you lean on My strength.

Pause momentarily in your studies and invite Me to be part of your learning. Ask Me for clarity when concepts feel hard to grasp. Pray for perseverance when assignments seem endless. Seek My wisdom not only for yourself but also to bless others. You could tutor a friend or pray for someone struggling with their grades. I love seeing how you care for others, even as you pursue your goals.

You are not alone in this journey. With Me, you have access to wisdom that surpasses what any textbook can offer.

Closing Encouragement: Remember, you can do all things through My strength—trust Me with your studies, and you will thrive.

December 15

Topic: Your Musical Journey

Opening Statement: Music is more than sound; it's a gift that can lift your soul, express your heart, and bring glory to God.

Bible Verse: *"Sing to the Lord a new song; play skillfully, and shout for joy."* —Psalm 33:3 (NIV)

Devotional: Beloved, I have placed music as a special gift in your life. Whether you are listening, learning to play an instrument, or creating something new, I am with you in the melodies. Music is a powerful way to feel My presence and share My love with others.

When you listen to songs that honor truth and goodness, your heart is drawn closer to Me. When you practice an instrument, every note—even the mistakes—brings you closer to the beauty of creativity I have given you. And when you create your music, I am your inspiration, whispering ideas and melodies into your spirit.

Remember, music has the power to uplift, to comfort, and to unite. Use this gift wisely, with a heart that seeks to bring joy and hope to others.

Closing Encouragement: Let your music reflect my love and remind me of the beautiful harmony I've created within you.

December 16

Topic: Comfort in Hard Times

Opening Statement: Grief and hardship can feel overwhelming, but you are never alone—I am here to carry you through every storm.

Bible Verse: *"The Lord is close to the brokenhearted and saves those who are crushed in spirit"* Psalm 34:18 (NIV).

Devotional: Dear child, I see your pain and know how heavy your heart feels right now. Remember this: I am close to you, even when it's hard to feel My presence. You are not forgotten, and your tears are precious to Me.

In your grief, lean into My love. I will comfort you in ways that go deeper than words, bringing peace the world cannot give. Let My strength hold you when you feel weak, and My light guide you when the path seems dark. Even now, I am working to bring healing to your heart and renewal to your spirit.

Surround yourself with others who will lift and remind you of My love. You are stronger than you realize because I am with you always.

Closing Encouragement: Take heart—you are deeply loved, and My comfort will never fail you.

December 17

Topic: Forgiving Others

Opening Statement: Forgiving others isn't just about freeing them—it's about freeing you from the chains of bitterness and pain.

Bible Verse: *"Bear with each other and forgive one another if any of you has a grievance against someone. Forgive as the Lord forgave you."* —Colossians 3:13 (NIV)

Devotional: Beloved one, I see the pain you carry. The anger, the hurt—it feels heavy. But I am here to remind you: you were not created to hold onto grudges or let anger take root in your heart. When you forgive, you reflect the love and grace I have poured on you.

Forgiveness does not mean excusing what was wrong or forgetting the hurt. It means choosing to release the hold it has on your heart. When you forgive, you open the door to healing for the other person and yourself. I will give you strength when it feels impossible. My love will sustain you as you let go.

Lean on Me when forgiving feels too hard. Let My peace replace the anger, and My grace floods the spaces where bitterness once lived. I am with you, guiding every step as you choose freedom through forgiveness.

Closing Encouragement: Choose forgiveness today, and let My peace fill your heart with freedom and joy.

December 18

Topic: Finding Hope.

Opening Statement: Hope is the anchor for your soul, even when life feels overwhelming and uncertain.

Bible Verse: *"Not only so, but we also glory in our sufferings, because we know that suffering produces perseverance; perseverance, character; and character, hope."* Romans 5:3-4 NIV.

Devotional: Never fear, My Sacred Heart; I bring life and peace and am with you right now. I see the challenges you're facing—the moments of doubt, the pressure of expectations, and the times when hope is slipping away. But even in those moments, I want you to remember this: you are never alone.

Lean into Me. Let Me fill your heart with the assurance that I have good plans for your life, even if today feels heavy. I am working through your struggles to shape your future in ways you can't yet see.

When you feel overwhelmed, pause and breathe. Whisper a prayer and trust that I am renewing your strength, helping you rise above the storm. Remember, hope and faith walk hand-in-hand. Cling tightly to both.

Closing Encouragement: Hold on to hope—it is your lifeline, and I will never let you go.

December 19

Topic: Finding Healing and Peace in God

Opening Statement: Life can be tough at times, and it's easy to carry around wounds from worries, fears, or past hurts. But guess what? You don't have to do it alone

Bible Verse: *"Is there no balm in Gilead? Is there no physician there? Why then is there no healing for the wound of My people?"* (Jeremiah 8:22 NIV)

Devotional: Imagine a healing ointment, a balm so powerful that it can mend even the deepest wounds. That's what I offer to you— divine restoration. When life gets overwhelming, and your worries feel like they're piling up, remember that you can hand them over to Jesus. Trust Him with your thoughts, your fears, and your tired spirit.

Sometimes, we try to hold everything in—pretend we're okay, hide our struggles. But holding on only makes the burden heavier. Instead, let go and surrender those worries to Me. In My presence, you'll find rest—peace that the world can't give and won't take away.

Your heart was made to hold more than pain; it was made to hold My love. Don't let the trials of life block your connection with Me. Prayer is your superpower—your direct line to healing and comfort. When you pray, you invite Me to work in your life, to bring healing and peace.

Closing Encouragement: Keep holding on—you're stronger than you think, and God's grace is always enough.

December 20

Topic: You Are Never Too Broken for God's Healing

Opening Statement: Your story isn't over yet. I am the One who can heal, restore, and make all things new.

Bible Verse: *"Though your wounds seem incurable, I am your Healer."* (Jeremiah 30:12)

Devotional: I know the weight of your past feels like it's crushing you. Maybe you think you're stuck carrying it forever, that there's no way out. But I want you to understand something powerful: your history doesn't get the final word—I do. I am the One who heals the brokenhearted and mends even the deepest wounds. Nothing you've done, no regret you hold onto, is too much for My mercy.

When you bring your brokenness to Me, I don't just brush it aside—I cleanse you completely. Every sin, every shame, every mistake—when you turn to Me in honesty, I forgive you fully. My forgiveness is final. It's like a fresh start, a clean slate, a new beginning. There's no stain left behind when I wipe it away.

But here's something important: guilt is a trap. It's like chains that keep you tied to what I've already forgiven. Guilt is your choice—you don't have to stay stuck in it. I've already set you free.

Closing Encouragement: No matter how scarred you feel Or how impossible your wounds seem, remember—I am your Healer

December 21

Topic: Finding True Joy and Healing'

Opening Statement: Real life, real joy, and real healing come from within, from your connection with Me. No matter what you're facing, I'm here to bring life to every part of you—mind, body, and spirit.

Bible Verse: *"'Nevertheless, I will bring health and healing to it; I will heal my people and will let them enjoy abundant peace and security.'"* (Jeremiah 33:6 NIV)

Devotional: Sometimes, it feels like life drains us—like stress, worries, or even sickness take the joy right out of our days. But I want you to understand something: true happiness doesn't come from wealth, popularity, or even success. It starts deep inside your heart, rooted in your relationship with Me. When your spirit is healthy and alive, everything else falls into place.

The truth is, when you drift away from Me, both your body and your soul can start to feel tired, sick, or worn down. But I am the One who offers healing—inside and out. I want to restore your spirit first because when your heart is connected to Mine, joy flows freely. That's the kind of joy that can't be taken away by life's storms.

Your outer life reflects your inner health. So, anchor your heart in Me daily. Spend time with Me, talk to Me, and let My presence fill you up. When you do, you'll discover the abundance, peace, and security you've been searching for.

Closing Encouragement: In My presence, your spirit will find the peace and happiness your soul was created to enjoy. Trust in Me, and let your joy be full!

December 22

Topic: Rooted in Holy Presence, Overflowing in Love

Opening Statement: Time with Me isn't just routine—it's your sanctuary, your refuge, where your soul can truly breathe and be renewed.

Bible Verse: *"Fruit trees of all kinds will grow on both banks of the river. Their leaves will not wither, nor will their fruit fail. Every month, they will bear fruit, because the water from the sanctuary flows to them. Their fruit will serve for food and their leaves for healing."* (Ezekiel 47:12 NIV)

Devotional: Imagine a lush, thriving tree planted right next to a flowing river—its roots are deep, and its branches reach high. No matter what season it is, this tree remains strong, fruitful, and alive. That's what I want for you: to be rooted in My presence, like that tree by the river.

When you spend time with Me each night, it's like watering your roots—your spirit gets nourished and refreshed. My healing flows like a mighty river, reaching into the deepest parts of your soul to restore, strengthen, and fill you with My peace. And as your heart becomes healthy and abundant, something incredible happens: you start to shine with My Spirit.

Every morning, I want you to carry that overflow into the world. Speak words of kindness, offer hope to those in need, and be a source of healing to others. Your life can be a blessing—a reflection of the love and grace I pour into you. Your fruit, your words, and your actions can nourish others and bring healing to a broken world.

Closing Encouragement: You are rooted in the greatest source of life—me. Keep coming to Me each evening, and I will fill you up so fully that your life overflows.

December 23

Topic: Breathing in the Spirit of Life

Opening Statement: Take a moment to feel Me—alive and with you in every breath.

Bible Verse: *"But for you who revere my name, the sun of righteousness will rise with healing in its rays. And you will go out and frolic like well-fed calves."* (Malachi 4:2 NIV)

Devotional: Every morning, as the sun rises and paints the sky with light, I whisper My love over you. That warm glow isn't just the sun—it's a reflection of My divine embrace, shining into your life and soul. When you breathe in, you're not just taking in air—you're taking in My life-giving Spirit. My energy, My peace, My strength—everything you need to face the day with joy and purpose.

Think of your breath as a sacred rhythm—an ongoing dance between you and Me. With each inhale, invite My Spirit to fill you. With each exhale, release any worries or doubts. Your breath is your connection to the divine, a reminder that I am always present and alive within you.

Proclaim My name—Ruah—every time you breathe. Let this Truth be on your lips and in your heart: I am the Breath of Life,

Closing Encouragement: Breathe in My Spirit and let it energize your soul. Breathe out peace and kindness into the world around you.

December 24

Topic: The Heavenly Song of Peace and Favor

Opening Statement: There's a heavenly song that's been echoing since the night Jesus was born.

Bible Verse: *"Suddenly a great company of the heavenly host appeared with the angel, praising God and saying, 'Glory to God in the highest heaven, and on earth peace to those on whom his favor rests.'"* (Luke 2:13-14 NIV)

Devotional: Can you hear the angels singing? Their praise wasn't just for a special night long ago—it's still alive today, and it's meant for you. When I sent My Son into the world, it was a declaration of love and peace over all humanity. But this peace isn't just for the world in general; it's for you.

I see you. I notice you. My favor rests on you—not because you've earned it, but because I chose to love you first. You don't have to do anything to make yourself worthy of My love; it's already yours. That's what makes this peace so powerful—It's a deep, unshakable calm that flows from My heart to yours, no matter what's happening around you.

Come close, My child. Rest in My presence. Lay down your worries, your fears, your striving. I want you to experience the peace that the angels announced—the peace that surpasses understanding and the favor that never runs out. This is your inheritance—an eternal song of love and favor, ringing in your heart.

Closing Encouragement: Listen closely—you are part of the heavenly chorus. The angels' song is still singing today, inviting you to rest in My peace and embrace My favor.

December 25

Topic: Celebrating the birth of Jesus.

Opening Statement: The birth of Jesus is a powerful reminder that you are deeply loved and that hope is alive for all who believe.

Bible Verse: *"Today in the town of David a Savior has been born to you; he is the Messiah, the Lord."* —Luke 2:11 (NIV)

Devotional: My dear one, do you feel the wonder of this season? Let me remind you why it's worth celebrating. Long ago, on a quiet night in Bethlehem, the world received a gift like no other. Jesus, the Savior, was born—an eternal light breaking into the darkness. This wasn't just an ordinary event but a declaration of love for you.

Every decoration, every carol, every star you see reminds you of this truth: God's love reached down to earth through Jesus. This love wasn't just for a moment—it was for eternity. As you celebrate this Christmas, don't let the busyness steal your focus. Instead, pause to marvel at the joy of Jesus' birth. His coming to earth means you are never alone, forgotten, and forever cherished.

Take this time to draw close, to thank Jesus for coming into the world, and to share this joy with others.

Closing Encouragement: Rejoice in Jesus' birth and let the light of His love shine brightly in you this Christmas season.

December 26

Topic: Coming into His Healing and Love

Opening Statement: I want you to know something powerful—no matter what you're facing, I am right here, longing to bring healing and wholeness to your heart. Don't hide away in fear or weariness, trying to escape My love. I see you exactly as you are, and I'm calling you into the light of My love. So, take a moment, sit with Me, because I've prepared this time just for you.

Bible Verse: *"...but the crowds learned about it and followed him. He welcomed them and spoke to them about the kingdom of God, and healed those who needed healing."* (Luke 9:11 NIV)

Devotional: Can you hear My voice whispering to you? I'm reigning over all creation—majestic, glorious, powerful—and yet, I am near to you. Right now, in your world and your life, I am close, ready to bring healing to your spirit and renewal to your soul.

Sometimes, life feels heavy—wounds from the past, fears about the future, doubts that creep in. But I want you to know that your prayers are the key that opens the door to My presence. When you invite Me in, I come close. I carry your burdens and heal your broken places.

This moment is sacred—an invitation for you to find freedom and renewal in My love. Don't hold back. Let My love flow into every part of you, filling the cracks and healing the wounds that seem too deep. I am here, and My love will never fail you.

Closing Encouragement: Receive My healing today. Trust that I see you, love you, and want to restore every part of your heart. Step into My presence and let My peace wash over you like a gentle river. You are not alone—My love is with you now and always, ready to bring healing and new life to your soul.

December 27

Topic: Following the Trail of God's Signs and Wonders

Opening Statement: Would you like to know something incredible—there's a trail I've marked just for you, filled with signs and wonders that testify to My presence.

Bible Verse: *"And a great crowd of people followed him because they saw the signs he had performed by healing the sick."* (John 6:12 NIV)

Devotional: Can you see the signs I leave along your journey? Every act of healing—whether of your spirit, your mind, or your body—is a declaration that I am with you. When you see others find hope and restoration, it's a ripple of My love spreading out into the world. These moments remind you that help, healing, and salvation are always on the way.

Don't hesitate to follow the crowds gathered in My name. Some are seeking healing, while others simply want to be close to Me; yet all of them are part of My love story. When you step into community—whether through prayer, confession, meditation, or sharing with others—you're walking alongside My heart. These gatherings aren't just for the broken; they're also for those whose spirits shine with My glory.

Remember, a healthy, vibrant spirit shines brighter than any earthly light. Your life

Closing Encouragement: Keep following My signs and wonder—every healing, every moment of peace, every act of love—because they point straight to My heart.

December 28

Topic: Trusting in My Perfect Timing for Healing

Opening Statement: Embrace the gift I've given you: the gift of life, hope, and healing.

Bible Verse: *"Now if a boy can be circumcised on the Sabbath so that the law of Moses may not be broken, why are you angry with me for healing a man's whole body on the Sabbath?"* (John 7:23 NIV)

Devotional: Healing is My gift to you—unique and tailored just for you. You don't need to understand every pattern or timing; that's not for you to figure out. Each healing I do is as special as the child I formed you to be. My love is infinite, and every touch of healing I give is shaped by that love, exactly what you need in this moment.

When you see others experience healing and wonder why your pain still lingers, remember this: My love for you has never changed. I am working in ways that are bigger and better than what you can see right now. I am not limited by time, space, or your doubts. I am working in grace—always for your good, even if it doesn't feel like it at the moment.

So, let go of your questions, your frustration, your anger. Rest in Me. Pray, trust, and believe that I am at work—quietly, powerfully, lovingly. My love holds you close, and I am always working for your ultimate good.

Closing Encouragement. Hold on to hope—your healing is coming, in the way and time that's best for you.

December 29

Topic: You Are Called to Bring Love, Healing, and Hope

Opening Statement: Hey, My Precious One, I want you to know something incredible—I've chosen you to carry My power and love into the world. Just as My Spirit flowed through Jesus to heal, restore, and bring hope, it also flows through you. You're not just here by chance; you're called to walk in His footsteps and be a light to those around you.

Bible Verse: *"How God anointed Jesus of Nazareth with the Holy Spirit and power, and how He went around doing good and healing all who were under the power of the devil, because God was with Him."* (Acts 10:38 NIV)

Devotional: You carry something powerful—My love and My Spirit—designed to heal wounds and bring renewal. The world is starving for love—true, unconditional love—those mend broken hearts and bridges divides. Many people are weary, lost, and disconnected because they've never truly experienced the love I want to pour out through you.

Your role isn't just to see problems; it's to be part of the solution. Share My love freely. Let it be the remedy that restores faith, lifts the weary, and heals the broken. My love is the most potent force on earth—it can heal nations, unite families, and soften even the hardest hearts.

And don't worry—I'm with you every step of the way. Speak boldly, but also gently, with the tone of My divine love. Love is the universal language of healing. When you love like I love, everything can be made new.

Closing Encouragement: Remember, you are anointed by My Spirit to do good, to heal, and to bring hope. You don't have to do it alone—My power is in you.

December 30

Topic: Embracing Your Divine Gifts

Opening Statement: If you feel like you lack certain gifts or talents, don't worry. I've already equipped you with exactly what you need. I didn't make a mistake when I called you; I created you in My image with a unique purpose just for you. Your life is special, and your gifts are part of that divine design.

Bible Verse: *"To one there is given through the Spirit a message of wisdom, to another a message of knowledge by means of the same Spirit, to another faith by the same Spirit, to another gifts of healing by that one Spirit,"* (1 Corinthians 12:8-9 NIV)

Devotional: Sometimes, you might look around and think others have better gifts or more impressive talents. But I want you to understand this: all spiritual gifts come from the same Source—Me. They're like different tools in a divine toolbox, each designed to work together for My purpose and glory. They aren't tools for competition or comparison; they're instruments of love meant to serve and uplift others.

Your calling is unique. I've placed specific gifts inside you so you can shine in the way only you can—whether it's through kindness, faith, healing, or wisdom. Your role isn't to envy others' gifts but to learn how to work with what I've given you, partnering with others in My Spirit to bring love and hope to the world.

When you recognize your divine calling, you'll see how beautifully everything works together. Share your blessings freely, not to compete but to serve—because true greatness is found in using what I've given to love others well.

Closing Encouragement: Remember, your gifts aren't tools for rivalry—they're instruments of My love. Embrace your divine calling and trust that I've equipped you perfectly.

December 31

Topic: The Tree of Life Within You

Opening Statement: Pay attention to the Tree of Life that grows within you.

Bible Verse: *"Down the middle of the great street of the city. On each side of the river stood the tree of life, bearing twelve crops of fruit, yielding its fruit every month. And the leaves of the tree are for the healing of the nations."* (Revelation 22:2 NIV)

Devotional: Imagine a lush, vibrant tree—its branches spreading wide, its blossoms singing a symphony of hope, and its fruit offering grace to everyone who tastes it. That tree is My love, alive in the hearts of My children, including you. When you open your heart to My love, it begins to grow tall and strong, reaching out in kindness, patience, and compassion.

You might feel the seed of this tree—My Spirit—whispering inside you, urging you to nurture it. That seed is alive, ready to flourish if you give it space to grow. As it does, it will create a canopy of love that shelters others and offers them peace. Its fruit nourishes nations—feeding souls with joy, patience, and kindness.

You hold the seed of the tree of life. Your job is to tend it— by choosing love, kindness, and faith—and watch how it blossoms into a beautiful, life-giving tree. This isn't just for you; it's for the world. The more you nurture My love within, the more it spreads, healing and transforming everything it touches.

Closing Encouragement: You are loved more than you know, and I am with you every step to help your tree of life blossom brightly.

www.ingramcontent.com/pod-product-compliance
Lightning Source LLC
Chambersburg PA
CBHW030906120626
46554CB00001B/34